WALT DISNEY WORLD
WITH KIDS

WALT DISNEY WORLD WITH KIDS

1997

Kim Wright Wiley

PRIMA PUBLISHING

PRIMA PUBLISHING and its colophon are trademarks of Prima Communications, Inc.

ISBN 0-7615-0407-9
ISSN1083-2424

96 97 98 99 HH 10 9 8 7 6 5 4 3 2 1
Printed in the United States of America

All products mentioned in this book are trademarks of their respective companies.

How to Order
Single copies may be ordered from Prima Publishing, P.O. Box 1260, Rocklin, CA 95677; telephone (916) 632-4400. Quantity discounts are also available. On your letterhead, include information concerning the intended use of the books and the number of books you wish to purchase.

Contents

SECTION 5: EPCOT CENTER 129

SECTION 6: DISNEY–MGM STUDIOS THEME PARK 161

SECTION 10: LIFE BEYOND DISNEY: UNIVERSAL STUDIOS, SEA WORLD, AND OTHER ORLANDO ATTRACTIONS   275

List of Maps

What Makes This Guide Different?

Once upon a time, people with kids didn't travel. Parents lucky enough to have supportive relatives or nannies may have taken off and left the children behind, but more often people with children stayed home, figuring geographic paralysis was the price of parenthood. Tour buses all over the world are filled with people who deferred their dreams of Maui or Moscow or even Miami until their kids were grown and married.

Things have changed. No one is surprised anymore by the sight of an infant snoozing away in a four-star restaurant, and a recent letter to *Travel and Leisure* magazine inquired about the difficulty of locating Pampers in Nepal. Today people take their kids everywhere, and they especially take them to Orlando, Florida.

Walt Disney World is the most frequently visited man-made tourist attraction on the planet, and at first glance it seems designed to cater specifically to families with young children. But it's not a small world after all, and actually circumnavigating the three major theme parks, five minor parks, 17 on-site hotels, and a shopping plaza requires as much organization and fortitude as a safari.

Guidebooks abound, but they rarely address the questions the parents of young children ask: Which restaurants are suitable for evening dining with a pooped 5-year-old? Where can we get a sitter? a Band-Aid? Will Epcot bore the kids? Is it worth the extra cost to stay at a hotel on the grounds? Is it OK to take the kids out of school for the trip? Where can I breast-feed? Do the men's restrooms have changing tables? Is the Haunted Mansion really all that scary?

This guidebook will take into account the pace and pocketbook of a couple traveling with young kids and feature those attractions, such as the character breakfasts with Mickey and the gang, that first-timers can easily miss, but which can make all the difference to a star-struck toddler. Preplanning is essential since, as you well know, a two-hour wait which would be merely annoying to a lone business traveler can be downright disastrous to a single parent with hungry kids in tow. Nonetheless, some families try to wing it. You know the ones—you see them every morning standing flat-footed in the middle of Main Street, kids bouncing in the strollers and parents huddled over their maps, debating how to get to Splash Mountain. This approach is akin to attempting to learn Lamaze after the contractions have begun.

To minimize problems and maximize fun, you must be oriented before you arrive. By following this guide, you'll learn how to get tickets, maps, and reservations in advance and plot your family path. Over the past seven years, I have passed out hundreds of questionnaires and interviewed dozens of families—their helpful comments and tips are incorporated throughout this book.

With just a little bit of forethought, you'll be able to go against the crowds—moving clockwise while the thundering hordes are moving counterclockwise, touring Epcot while most people are in the Magic Kingdom, and even the ultimate crowd-busting move: planning your trip during the off-season. If you manage to zig while everyone else zags, you can cut waits to a minimum and see twice as much as you would mindlessly drifting from queue to queue.

The basic rule when traveling with young children is to prepare without overplanning. You want to be familiar enough with the layout of Disney World that you can find a restroom fast, but not so driven by a timetable that you don't allow plenty of time for resting and savoring spontaneous pleasures. Fun stuff pops up all around the parks, and if you're grimly trying to make it from Fantasyland to Liberty Square on schedule, you'll miss the key pleasures of this amazing attraction.

And pleasures are what this guide is all about. The three bugaboos of the World—the crowds, the heat exhaustion, and the expense—are especially tough on young families, and no amount of preparation will totally eliminate these problems. Walt Disney World, after all, is a 43-square-mile complex in the middle of Florida, visited by as many as 150,000 people a day. It can cost a family of four up to $144 just to get through the gate. You're going to get hot and tired and you'll spend a lot of money. That's a given.

So why go at all? There's only one reason—it truly is the most fun place on earth.

What Makes Walt Disney World So Special?

The answer to this question is, in a word, *detail*. The entire Disney World fantasy is sustained through painstaking attention to detail.

In an attraction such as Pirates of the Caribbean, the atmospheric mischief begins in the queue, where you wind down into the bowels of a stucco fortress which grows danker and darker with every turn. The ride combines Audio-Animatronics, a catchy theme song, and an attention to detail so relentless that even the hair on the pirates' legs is real. You emerge seven minutes later, blinking into the sunlight which spills through the market stalls of the Caribbean Plaza, fully understanding why Disney insists its "rides" be referred to as "attractions." (The illusion holds up just as well at Epcot, where the Disney people have presented themselves a bigger challenge; this time they're out to snooker adults into believing they're in Norway . . . or the land of the dinosaurs . . . or the human bloodstream.)

The theme parks were designed with the same precision that Disney animators brought to the classic films. Walt was such a perfectionist that he never let four frames per second suffice if eight were possible. Now his successors are successful because of the same sumptuousness. Why not fly in some monkey-puzzle trees for the Japan pavilion? Hire George Lucas as creative consultant for the ride based on his *Star Wars* film series? Who says 11,000 dolls are too many for It's a Small World?

The authors of some guidebooks seem immune to the Disney magic, which is why they can describe Dumbo as a "sporadically loading 10-unit cycle ride of the sort common to most midways," and advise you to skip the ride. But it isn't a sporadically loading cycle ride at all—it's Dumbo, and no 4-year-old worth his salt is going to let you pass it up. The special charm of Walt Disney World is that once we pass through those gates, we're all 4-year-olds—impulsive, impatient, curious, easily duped, essentially cheerful, and ready to believe in magic.

Abbreviations and Terms Used in This Book

MK	the Magic Kingdom
Epcot	Epcot Center
MGM	the Disney–MGM Studios Theme Park
the major parks	the Magic Kingdom, Epcot Center, and Disney–MGM Studios
the minor parks	Typhoon Lagoon, River Country, Pleasure Island, Blizzard Beach, and Discovery Island
TTC	Ticket and Transportation Center: the monorail version of a train station, where riders can transfer to monorails bound for Epcot, the MK, or monorail-line hotels. You can also catch buses at the TTC bound for the parks, the on-site hotels, and the Disney Village Marketplace.
on-site	the Disney-owned hotels that are on the WDW property (the

	Contemporary, the Polynesian, the Grand Floridian, Disney's Old Key West, the Disney Institute Villas, the Caribbean Beach Resort, Fort Wilderness campground, the Yacht and Beach Clubs, Port Orleans, Dixie Landings, Wilderness Lodge, the All-Star Resorts, the BoardWalk, the Disney Swan, and the Disney Dolphin)
off-site	hotels that are not located on WDW grounds or owned by the Walt Disney Company
on-season	the busiest touring times, including summer and the weeks surrounding major holidays
off-season	less busy times of the year, most notably spring and fall
the MK resorts	the Grand Floridian, the Polynesian, the Contemporary, and Wilderness Lodge
the Epcot resorts	the Yacht and Beach Clubs, Caribbean Beach Resort, the BoardWalk, Disney Swan, and Disney Dolphin
Village resorts	Port Orleans, Dixie Landings, Disney Institute Villas, and Old Key West

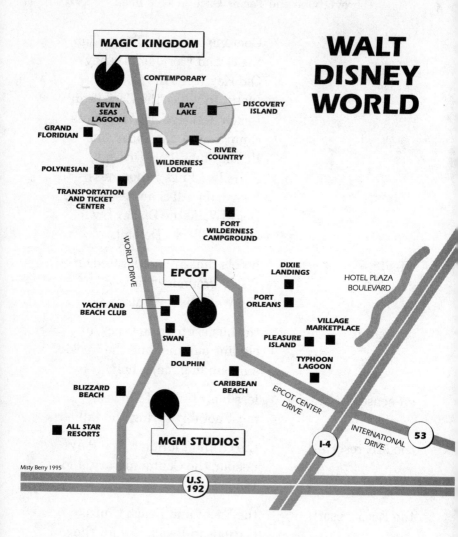

1

★★★★★★★★★★★★★★★★★

*Before You
Leave Home*

WHAT TIME OF YEAR SHOULD WE VISIT?

September through mid-December is the best time of year for families with young children to visit. Crowds are light—around 30,000 visitors a day, as compared to 70,000 in the summer months—and many area hotels offer discounted rates. Even the weather cooperates, with highs in the 80s and lows in the 60s.

There are disadvantages to a fall visit. You may not want to take your children out of school, and the theme parks do close earlier at this time of year. The Magic Kingdom and MGM often close as early as 6 P.M., although Epcot generally remains open later. These earlier closings mean that some of the special evening presentations, such as SpectroMagic in the MK, are suspended during the off-season.

Fall is also hurricane season in Florida, so there is some risk you'll schedule your trip for the exact week Hurricane Laluna pounds the coast. But Orlando is an hour inland, meaning that even the worst coastal storms usually yield only rain. Furthermore, rainy days reach their peak during the summer months, not the fall, so in general the advantages of autumn touring far outweigh the disadvantages.

If fall isn't possible, spring is nearly as nice. With the exceptions of the holiday weeks around Presidents' Day, Spring Break, and Easter, springtime crowds average around 40,000—not as low as fall but still far better than summer. And the weather is sublime, with highs in the 70s, lows in the 60s, and less rainfall in spring than in any other season of the year.

Disney runs longer park hours in spring than in fall, but schedules vary widely in the weeks between January and May. To check projected hours of operation, call (407) 824-4321 before you leave home.

If you must visit in summer, the first two weeks of June and the last two weeks of August are your best bet. Temperatures and attendance peak in July.

The absolute worst times are holidays. Christmas, New Year's, the Fourth of July, and other major holidays can pull in 100,000 visitors per day, which is six times as many people as you'll find on a typical day in October. Extended hours can't compensate for crowds of this size. Although special parades and shows are always planned, you're better off at home watching them on TV.

Note: WDW is fetchingly decorated at Christmas, no doubt about it. But the decorations go up just after Thanksgiving, so if you can work in an early-December visit, you'll have all the trees and wreaths and carolers you could wish for—as well as a nearly deserted theme park. Special holiday packages, which include price breaks on lodgings, a party with the characters, and access to the Christmas parades and shows run from the end of November to mid-December.

Somewhat surprisingly, Fridays and Sundays are the least crowded days of the week. Mondays, Tuesdays, and Wednesdays draw the heaviest traffic.

HOW LONG SHOULD WE STAY?

- It will take at least four days for a family with young kids to tour the MK, Epcot, and MGM. Four- and five-day passes are offered and, since the five-day pass also admits holders to Pleasure Island, Typhoon Lagoon, Blizzard Beach, Discovery Island, and River Country, it is the best buy.

Note: Your admission into the minor parks is unlimited and free only within seven days of the first day the pass is used. In other words, buying a five-day pass does not allow you unlimited entrance into Typhoon Lagoon for life.

• If you plan to take in any of the minor theme parks, schedule five days. Five days are also necessary for families who enjoy boating, tennis, swimming, or golf—or those who'd like to tour at a more leisurely pace.

• If you wish to visit other area attractions such as Sea World or Universal Studios, allow a week.

SHOULD WE TAKE THE KIDS OUT OF SCHOOL?

Even if you're sold on the advantages of fall and spring touring, you may be reluctant to take your children out of school for a week. Here are some ways to temper your guilt.

• Kids remember what they see, so a single day at Epcot can be just as educational as a week of science and geography classes. "That's a Viking ship," my 4-year-old casually observed while we were watching a movie one evening. "You know, like at Epcot." Another mother reports that her son's award-winning science fair project on drip irrigation was inspired by touring the Land pavilion.

• Since you'll have weeks of advance warning before a trip to Orlando, ask your children's teachers if they can do at least some of the lessons they'll miss before you leave. Coming back to piles of makeup work after a vacation can be profoundly depressing.

• Perhaps your children can work out a deal with their teachers whereby they'll do special reports or projects relating to subjects they'll encounter at Epcot or MGM. Some suggestions:

- Into dinosaurs? Check out the Universe of Energy pavilion.

- Students of the natural sciences will find much of interest in the Land pavilion. The 45-minute greenhouse tour is full of information on space-age farming.

- Marine biology is the theme of The Living Seas pavilion.

- Missing health class? The Wonders of Life pavilion is devoted to that greatest of all machines—the human body. It even has hands-on exhibits inside.

- Interested in geography? Some students have done reports on the cultures of countries repre-sented in the World Showcase.

- Art students are bound to pick up pointers during the Animation Tour at MGM.

- Drama students or even budding engineers will learn a lot "behind the scenes" at MGM's Back-stage Studio Tour.

- "Kidventure," a four-hour guided tour of Discovery Island, Disney's zoological park, is open to kids 8 to 14. Park admission, transportation, lunch, and sup-plies to make a nature-themed craft are included in the $32 cost. Kids learn a bit about animal tracking and bird watching, and it's a nice alternative for the 8- and 9-year-olds too young to be admitted to the "Wonders of Walt Disney World" program. For more details or to make reservations, call (407) 824-3784.

- Innoventions at Epcot, although often described as the world's hippest arcade, is also an amazing preview of future technology.

• Along with formal reports on the subjects listed on the previous page, your child might also want to make a scrapbook or collection display. The mother of one preschooler helped him create an "ABC" book before he left home, and he then spent his WDW week collecting souvenirs for each page—Goofy's autograph on the "G" page, a postcard of a Japanese pagoda on the "P" page, and so on. An older child might gather leaves from the various trees and bushes imported from the countries represented in the World Showcase. Or a young photographer could illustrate his proficiency with various lighting techniques by photographing Cinderella Castle in early morning, at noon, at sunset, and after dark.

• If your child is between 10 and 15 and you think he or she might benefit from a more formal type of instruction, try one of WDW's four seminars, collectively titled "The Wonders of Walt Disney World." Some schools will accept these one-day seminars for class credit.

At the day's start, students receive a book on the subject they'll be studying, as well as any needed classroom materials. Then the group boards a special van with their instructor and begins a six-hour tour. At the end of the day, participants receive a "Wonders" certificate of completion and a book with follow-up activities designed to help them expand the knowledge they gained during their seminar. The seminars are altered occasionally to keep them fresh, but the descriptions following should give you some idea of what to expect.

▪ *Wildlife Adventure:* During this tour, young people visit Discovery Island, Disney's 7,500-acre zoological park, study the ways animals and birds become endangered, and learn what they can do to protect their own environment. Seeing wildlife in a natural setting brings home the importance of ecology and the preservation of wilderness areas. Students have use of binoculars, but also have many chances to see birds, apes, and alligators up close. Exploring Nature is offered on Tuesdays and Thursdays.

- *Art Magic:* Students get a firsthand look at the artistic process at work in WDW productions, examine the basic shapes in character animation, and study a Disney attraction to see how sets, costumes, and color combine to create atmosphere. Some tours include a meeting with a Disney animator, who demonstrates how to draw a character and then helps the students learn how to sketch the Disney gang. Students leave with their own hand-painted cel and a sketchbook to encourage them to keep practicing their new skills. Art Magic is offered Monday through Friday.

- *Show Biz Magic:* Described as a "behind-the-scenes look at the hard work, dedication, and pixie dust it takes to put on a great show every time," Show Biz allows students to meet Disney musicians, dancers, and singers. After watching an audition or rehearsal at MGM, students will meet with performers and technicians, watch a show, then go underground into the famous but rarely seen tunnel area, where costumes and props are stored and the huge Disney cast rehearses. Show Biz is offered Monday through Thursday.

- *Passport:* Designed for geography buffs, Passport takes students around Epcot's World Showcase, offering information on the cultures, languages, and cuisines re-created there. Passport is a good chance to go behind the scenes at Epcot to meet some of the international cast of young people Disney imports to represent their home countries. It is offered on Wednesdays and Fridays.

General Information About the "Wonders of Walt Disney World" Program

• Reservations are accepted at (407) 354-1855 and should be made weeks in advance, preferably at the same time you book your hotel room. Class size is limited to 14 students per session. Be sure to verify times, prices, meeting places, and course content when you call.

• You can get brochures completely outlining the seminars either by calling the number above or by writing:

WDW Seminar Productions
P.O. Box 10100
Lake Buena Vista, FL 32830-1000

If you want your child to apply for classroom credit for participating in the program, request an extra brochure for your school principal.

• Cost for one seminar is $79. Some packages include seminar fees, so be sure to check.

• Students are considered to be on a supervised field trip and will not need a park admission ticket during the program.

• Parents need to drop kids off in the morning and pick them up in the afternoon but are otherwise free to do what they please while the seminars are in session. At present, the seminars all meet at MGM at 9:30 A.M. and last six hours.

• Lunch is provided.

• Students 16 and older are welcome on the adult tours, which are also outlined in the "Wonders of Walt Disney World" brochure.

Note: In the interest of offering guests even more varied and unique educational options, Disney has created a new program: the Disney Institute. Housed in a self-contained resort near the Disney Village Marketplace, the Institute combines a campuslike atmosphere with educational and cultural opportunities—as well as one of the most complete spa and fitness facilities in central Florida. Guests can work out their bodies with a personal trainer, and then work out their minds by taking courses in animation, cooking, TV and radio production, and landscape design. Classes are available for adults and kids 11 and older. For more information, see Section 7.

Other Orlando Educational Programs

Sea World *(407) 363-2380.* Sea World offers daily tours and classes, as well as week-long and overnight programs for kids of all ages. You'll find details in Section 10.

Orlando Science Center *(407) 896-7151.* This impressive facility has oodles of hands-on exhibits, many of them designed to be interesting to kids as young as 4, as well as evening planetarium shows. The highly innovative one-day programs range from "Dirt Safaris" geared toward the kindergarten set to "Gator Watches" for kids 11 and older. The Center even sponsors "Camp-In" sleep-overs at the museum, with subjects ranging from Lego Mania to Silly Science—a set of pleasingly messy physics experiments using Silly Putty and slime. Not every class is offered every week, but if you request the brochure, you'll find that something is happening all the time and that the prices are reasonable. All programs must be booked in advance.

Spaceport USA *(407) 452-2121.* Orlando is only about an hour from Kennedy Space Center, so it's an easy daytrip. Kids will enjoy a ride through the Rocket Garden, which holds eight rockets from the Mercury through Apollo programs, as well as the films, projected on the five-story-high screen in the IMAX theater. Call the Center before you leave home to see if a launch is scheduled during the time you'll be in Florida. If so, plan your trip for that day. The crowds will be heavier, but your kids will experience a rare thrill.

IS IT WORTH THE EXPENSE TO STAY ON-SITE?

Staying at one of the Disney-owned hotels is very convenient—and with rates as low as $69 a night at the new All-Star Resorts, staying on-site is becoming more affordable each year.

Off-site hotels are fighting back with special price promotions and perks of their own—such as free child care—arguing that the Disney hotels still cost more and bring you only slightly closer to the action. On-site or off-site? The questions following should help you decide.

• *What time of year are you going and how long are you staying?*

If you're going in summer or during a major holiday, you'll need every extra minute, so it's worth the cost to stay on-site. (Another reason to book on-site in summer: In the Florida heat, it's nearly a medical necessity to keep young kids out of the sun in midafternoon. A nearby hotel room makes that easier.) Likewise, if your visit will be for less than three days, you can't afford to waste much time commuting, so staying on-site is worth considering.

• *What are the ages of your kids?*
If your kids are still young enough to take naps, staying on-site makes it much easier to return to your room after lunch for a snooze. If they're preteens who are up to a full day in the parks, commuting is less of a factor.

• *Are you flying or driving?*
If you're flying and doing only Disney, it may make more economic sense to stay on-site. The WDW transportation system is so efficient that you can manage without a rental car. But if you're driving to Orlando, consider an off-site location. You'll be able to drive into the parks at the hours that suit you, without being dependent on those sometimes-less-than-prompt off-site buses.

• *How strapped are you for cash?*
If money isn't a major issue, stay on-site. If money is a primary consideration, you'll find your best deals at the budget hotels along I-4. Exits 25 and 27, which flank the Disney exit, are chock-full of chain hotels and restaurants. Exit 27 alone has three Days Inns within two blocks of each other.

• *How much do your kids eat?*
Food is expensive at WDW, in both the parks and the on-site hotels. If you're staying off-site, you can always eat at the numerous fast-food and family-style restaurants along I-4, Route 192, and International

Drive. If you book a suite, fixing simple meals in your room is even cheaper, and kids can really load up at those complimentary buffet breakfasts so frequently offered at the off-site hotels.

*   *Do you plan to visit other attractions?*

If you'll be spending half your time at Sea World, Universal Studios, or the other non-WDW attractions, stay off-site, at least during those days. There's no need to pay top dollar for proximity to Disney if you're headed for the Kennedy Space Center.

*   *Will there be times when your party will be splitting up?*

Does Dad want to play golf in the afternoon? Do you have teenagers who can head for Blizzard Beach on their own? Will there be times when it would make sense for Dad to take the younger kids back to the hotel while Mom stays in the park with the older ones? Is your 5-year-old raring to go at dawn while your 15-year-old sleeps until noon? If so, stay on-site, where the use of the WDW transportation system makes it easy for you to each go your own way.

*   *What's your hassle quotient?*

If you simply don't want to be bothered with interstate commutes, parking lots, carrying cash, and maps . . . stay on-site.

THE ADVANTAGES OF STAYING ON-SITE

Surprise Mornings

Under the "Surprise Mornings" program, Disney allows on-site guests into one designated theme park a day an hour earlier than off-site guests. When you check in to your hotel, you're given a brochure which reads something like "Epcot—Tuesday and Friday, MGM—Sunday and Wednesday, Magic Kingdom—Monday, Thursday, and Saturday."

Since visitors are almost always admitted to the theme parks 30 minutes before the stated opening time, this program means that on-site guests may find themselves inside the Magic Kingdom as early as 7:30 on mornings when the official opening time is 9 A.M. Generally, only one part of the park is open during the first hour. For example, in the Magic Kingdom it might be Fantasyland and Tomorrowland, which means you can ride Space Mountain and the other attractions within these sections with minimal waits. Then when the ropes drop at the official opening time, allowing you into the other sections, you're already deep within the park. You can dash straight for Splash Mountain or any other attractions that will be crowded later in the day, beating the surge of people who are still coming down Main Street.

At MGM the shows don't begin until the stated opening time, but many of the continuous-loading attractions are operative during the surprise-morning hour—including the Great Movie Ride, the Twilight Zone Tower of Terror, and Star Tours. So you can ride them and still be in line for the first showing of Voyage of the Little Mermaid far ahead of the day guests. At Epcot generally Innoventions, Spaceship Earth, and selected Future World pavilions open early.

Note: Since Disney has so many hotels, and thus so many on-site guests, some families responding to our surveys indicated that they use reverse psychology and visit one of the parks *not* featured as that day's "Surprise Mornings" park. "If the sheet says 'MGM,' everyone runs to MGM like lemmings," wrote one father. "Let's face it: If 20,000 people are in on the surprise, it ain't much of a surprise."

There's little doubt that the park featured each day gets more people than it ordinarily would . . . and remains more crowded all day. The answer may be to visit the featured "Surprise Mornings" park as early as possible, stay for a couple of hours, during which time you visit the biggie attractions that are opened early, then go to one of the other parks about midmorning.

Length of Stay Passes

These passes, which can be tailored to fit the length of your stay, offer you unlimited access to the major and minor parks and are slightly cheaper than comparable multiday passes.

Restaurant Reservations

On-site guests can call for reservations at the sit-down restaurants both within the theme parks and at the other on-site hotels up to three days in advance. You should make all desired reservations for the first three days of your trip on the night you check in, thus ensuring that you can eat where you want, when you want, and eliminating standing in line. Since there are so many on-site guests, this perk has the effect of freezing off-site visitors out of the most popular restaurants at the most popular times.

Note: Disney is presently trying out a system—which may or may not be permanent—that allows on-site guests to make restaurant and dinner-show reservations a full 60 days in advance. Be sure to ask when you book your room if you can make dining reservations before you leave home.

Transportation

On-site guests have unlimited use of the monorails, buses, and boats of the WDW transportation system, which is your best bet for getting to the major parks. The buses for the on-site hotels, for example, can deliver riders right to the MK gates, eliminating the need to take a ferryboat or monorail from the Ticket and Transportation Center (TTC) and cutting at least 15 minutes off the commute.

If you're headed toward one of the minor parks or another on-site hotel, you'll have to switch buses at the TTC, which takes a little more time. You may save a few minutes by taking your car, but many on-site guests still report that they prefer to leave the driving to Disney.

Use of Other On-site Hotel Facilities

If you want to use the child-care or sporting facilities of other Disney hotels or dine at their restaurants, you'll receive preferential treatment over off-site visitors (although each hotel, reasonably enough, allows its own guests first shot at its services). This means that even if you're staying at the budget Dixie Landings, you can leave your kids at the Neverland Club at the Polynesian or take a tennis lesson at the Grand Floridian.

Access to Parks

The parks are never closed to on-site guests, although when they fill to capacity they may close their gates to day guests. This is a factor only if you're visiting on holidays or during the summer, when the Magic Kingdom and the water parks sometimes reach capacity as early as 10 A.M.

Charging Privileges

If you're staying on-site everyone in your party will be issued a resort ID the day you arrive. The ID entitles you to full use of the WDW transportation system and also allows you to charge food and purchases—either at the hotels or within the parks—to your hotel room. It's certainly better not to have to carry huge amounts of cash all the time, especially at the pools, water parks, and marinas.

It's up to you whether or not your older kids have charging privileges. It makes it easier to send Johnny to the snack bar for a round of Cokes, but if you do opt to give the minors charging privileges, be sure to impress upon them that these IDs work like credit cards—and are *not* an open invitation for the kids to ingratiate themselves with the gang in the arcade by ordering pizza for everyone, purchasing all seven dwarfs from the hotel gift shop, or, heaven forbid, obtaining cash advances. If an ID with charging privileges is lost, it should be reported to the front desk immediately to avoid unauthorized charges.

Family Atmosphere

All the on-site hotels are designed with families in mind, meaning that the ambience is casual, security is very tight, and there are always other kids around to play with. The on-site hotels have Laundromats, generally located near the pools and arcades so you can run a load while the youngsters play; late-night pizza delivery to your room; fast-food courts; and, if there is not a child-care facility at your particular hotel, Guest

Services can help you arrange for an in-room sitter. The emphasis at the Disney hotels is on making life more convenient for parents.

Cool Themes

All the on-site hotels have a theme that is carried out in mega-detail: At the Polynesian, your wake-up call begins "Aloha," jazz music plays all day at Port Orleans, and the bureaus in All-Star Sports look like gym lockers. This makes staying at an on-site hotel almost as exciting for kids as being inside the parks.

In fact, because the on-site hotels are so unspeakably cool, a fun afternoon break from touring can be just visiting the other hotels. Many families mentioned that they ate meals at several different on-site hotels during their visit; the restaurants carry out the themes, too, so if three days at the Polynesian have left you burned out on pineapple juice, try the barbecue at Wilderness Lodge.

THINGS TO ASK WHEN BOOKING AN OFF-SITE HOTEL

If you decide to stay off-site, you should be aware that among the hundreds of hotels in the Orlando area there is a wide range of amenities and perks. To make sure you're getting top value for your dollar, take nothing for granted. Some $250 a night hotels charge you for shuttle service to the parks; some $75 ones do not. Some hotels count 11-year-olds as adults, and others consider 19-year-olds to be children. Some relatively inexpensive resorts have full-fledged kids' clubs; some larger and far more costly ones are geared to convention and business travel and don't even have an arcade. The moral is: Always ask.

There are three main off-site areas that tourists frequent: exits 25 and 27 off I-4, and International Drive. Both exit 27 and exit 25 are within a 10-minute drive of the theme parks. Exit 27 backs up to the hotels of the Disney Village Hotel Plaza, and any number of upscale eateries and hotels are nearby, mixed in with the Days Inns and fast-food places. (The Hyatt Regency Grand Cypress, Embassy Suites Lake Buena Vista, and Holiday Inn Sunspree are all on exit 27.) Exit 25 is older and boasts outlets and gift shops instead of fancy restaurants and resorts, but hotels there run about $30 a night less than at a comparable hotel on exit 27.

International Drive is farther out, about 20 minutes from the theme parks, but it is modern and well kept, the sort of place where you'll find the most beautifully landscaped Pizza Hut in existence. International Drive boasts every chain restaurant you've ever heard of, as well as Fun 'n Wheels, Wet 'n Wild, and a funky Ripley's Believe It or Not, which appears to be sinking into the ground. You'll find ice-skating, miniature golf, and a three-story McDonald's—as well as the Peabody and the Omni.

One note of caution: An extremely cheap hotel rate, say $50 or less, generally means that the hotel is located in a less-desirable part of town, both in regard to proximity to the theme parks and general security. Unless you are personally familiar with the location and quality of the hotel, proceed with caution.

The questions following should help you ferret out the best deal.

• *Does the hotel provide in-room baby-sitters? What are their qualifications? What's the cost? How far in ad-*

vance should I reserve a sitter? Do you have on-site child care? Several of the larger hotels have their own version of a kids' club, a drop-off child-care center with planned activities for the youngsters—see "Great Off-site Resorts for Families" in Section 2 for details.

• *Do you provide bus service to the Magic Kingdom, Epcot, and MGM? The minor parks? How often? How early—and how late—do the buses run? Is there any charge? Are the buses express or do they stop and pick up riders at other hotels?*

• *Do kids stay free? Up to what age?* This can be vitally important. On-site Disney hotels allow kids under 18 to lodge free with parents. The policy at off-site hotels varies.

• *Does the hotel provide a free buffet breakfast?*

• *What fast-food or family-style restaurants are nearby?*

• *Do you have any suites with kitchens?* No one would suggest you should spend a vacation cooking. But many Orlando hotels have villa-style lodgings, and, obviously, if you can eat cereal and sandwiches in your room you'll save significant bucks. Some hotels, such as the Holiday Inn Sunspree, have minikitchens with small refrigerators and a microwave—all you need for simple meals. And the cost is no more than that of a regular room.

• *Does the hotel provide airport pickup?*

• *Is there a Laundromat on the premises?*

• *Can I buy tickets to area attractions through the hotel's Guest Services desk? Are the tickets discounted?* Many Orlando hotels offer discounts to Universal

Studios, Sea World, and area dinner shows. Not only do you save dollars, but you save the time you'd otherwise spend waiting in line.

• *Do you offer any sort of package?* Several of the larger hotels put together their own simple packages that include discounted theme park tickets. It never hurts to ask.

SHOULD WE BUY A PACKAGE?

This is a toughie. There are advantages to package trips, most notable is that it is possible to save a good deal of money. It's also helpful to know up front what your vacation will cost. Often packages require hefty prepayments, which are painful at the time but at least you don't return home utterly maxed out on your MasterCard.

Package trips can have drawbacks, however. Like buying a fully loaded car off a dealer's lot, you may find yourself paying for options you don't want and don't need. Packages are often padded with perks such as reduced greens fees, which are of interest to only a few families, or rental cars, which you may not need if staying on-site. Be doubly wary of the very cheap packages offered in Sunday papers. If a deal sounds too good to be true, it probably is.

Common Types of Packages

Disney's Resort Package Vacations

Several families responding to the survey were sold on Disney's own packages, such as the Grand Plan, which houses guests in the swank Grand Floridian or the almost-as-swank Yacht and Beach Clubs, and includes all food, all tickets, unlimited golf, boating, and other sporting activities as well as such extras as baby-sitting, stroller rental, a personalized itinerary, tuition in one of the "Wonders of Walt Disney World" seminars—and a Fantasia alarm clock. If you want the top of the line, trust me, this is the top of the line.

Such luxury, needless to say, doesn't come cheap. A family of four staying five days at the Grand Floridian on the Grand Plan can expect to pay $3,700. Another drawback is that since all meals are included in the plan, you may find yourself gorging as a cruise ship mentality takes over: "We gotta eat it—it's free." But families who want to sample a wide variety of Epcot cuisine, who have kids who'd love to rent those $13-per-half-hour sailboats for a whole afternoon, or who want child care every night, may decide that it's worth it.

If all this sounds a bit too much, Disney also offers a variety of less expensive packages that lodge families at one of the on-site budget hotels (Dixie Landings, Port Orleans, or Caribbean Beach Resort) and include tickets. Five days for a family of four would be about $1,100. Call (407) W-DISNEY for details on the Disney packages and all on-site hotel reservations.

Magic Kingdom Gold Card Packages
Those who hold a Magic Kingdom Club Gold Card have packages developed solely for them, ranging once again from the all-inclusive to the more affordably priced. The difference is that the Magic Kingdom Club Gold Card packages are 10% to 20% cheaper than comparable Disney packages, so if you're seriously considering booking a package, get thee posthaste to a telephone and call 1-800-56-DISNEY. Paying the $65 for the two-year club membership would be smart, especially if you're traveling during the off-season when

the deepest discounts are in effect. Note: Once you purchase your Gold Card, you're in the Magic Kingdom Club automatically; Disney uses the terms *cardholder* and *club member* interchangeably, so it's a bit confusing. See "The Ultimate Cost-Saving Tip: Order a Magic Kingdom Club Gold Card" later in this section.

Airline Packages

If you're flying, check out the Delta Dream Vacations or USAir packages, which include airfare, theme park tickets for Disney and other Orlando attractions, car rental, and lodging at either on-site or off-site hotels. Again, there's a huge range of amenities—you can have valet parking, character breakfasts, and use of a camcorder if you're willing to pay for them. And again, the packages can be fine-tuned to meet your needs. If you'll be flying Delta, call 1-800-872-7786 and request a brochure. The number for USAir is 1-800-455-0123. Package prices don't fluctuate as rapidly as airfare prices, and if you're traveling during a time when airfare rates are climbing, you may get a good deal.

Cruise Packages

The Walt Disney Company is making changes in its family cruise program, but under the new system there will still be some variation of the very popular cruise and Disney week. Families may opt to spend three or four nights at sea, and the remainder of the week is spent in Orlando. Park admissions are included in the package, as are airfare, a rental car, and your meals while onboard ship. Once onboard you'll find a staggeringly full program for children, including dawn-to-dusk kids' clubs, toddler pools, special menus, parties and mixers geared toward teens and preteens, and the Disney characters. Youth counselors squire the kids around, giving worn-out parents the chance to collapse on deck chairs or wander into the casinos and dance clubs if they find the strength.

You can book the cruises through your travel agent or by calling 1-800-334-4017.

Travel Agents

Once upon a time, Disney paid no commission to travel agents for booking guests into Disney-owned hotels. Ergo, travel agents would try to talk clients out of staying on-site. With the opening of 10 new hotels in five years, however, Disney suddenly has a lot more rooms and more vacancies, so policy has changed; Disney now pays agents commission, and agents are now much more likely to recommend packages that include on-site lodging.

Agents are also aware of other Orlando hotels that offer packages, and are a good source of comparative rate-shopping for families who want to stay off-site. Large travel agencies sometimes put together their own packages, including airfare, lodging at an off-site hotel, and a rental car. If you need all three of these components, you'll probably come out cheaper buying a package through a local agent than trying to book all three separately.

Cheapie Deals

These are frequently seen in the travel sections of major newspapers and offer extremely low rates. Proceed with caution, however. The hotels are sometimes as far as 30 miles away from the Disney gates. (With a rental car and an alarm clock, even this obstacle can be overcome—but you should know what you're up against.) Other pitfalls include tickets that can be used only at certain times of the year or extremely inflexible touring arrangements that require you to ride from attraction to attraction in overloaded, slow-moving buses.

Another consideration is that the hotels featured may not be in a very desirable area of town. Orlando has not suffered the degree of tourist-targeted crime that we've read about in other Florida cities, but unless either you or your travel agent are familiar with the area where the hotel is located, be wary. A family interested in saving money would be far better off driving and camping at Fort Wilderness or trying the All-Star Resorts than signing up for one of these packages.

THE ULTIMATE COST-SAVING TIP: ORDER A MAGIC KINGDOM CLUB GOLD CARD

If your family is really dizzy for Disney, it makes economic sense to order a Magic Kingdom Club Gold Card. Cardholders receive a variety of benefits, most notably discounts on Disney merchandise, theme park tickets, and up to 30% off on Disney-owned hotels. You can order a Magic Kingdom Club Gold Card by calling 1-800-56-DISNEY. The cost of a two-year membership is $65.

The biggest perk, of course, is the substantial discounts on rooms in Disney-owned hotels. The deepest discounts coincide with the least crowded times of the year, so membership in the club is doubly attractive to families with young kids. Although the weeks in which the discounts apply vary somewhat from year to year, the following schedule is typical.

• From mid-July to mid-December and January to mid-February, expect a 30% discount off the regular rates at the following resorts:

- Disney's Yacht and Beach Clubs
- The Contemporary
- The Polynesian
- The Disney Institute Villas
- Wilderness Lodge
- Fort Wilderness Trailer Homes and Campground
- Disney's Old Key West
- The BoardWalk

• From late August to mid-December and from January to mid-February, expect a 20% price break at the following moderately priced resorts:

- Port Orleans
- Dixie Landings
- Caribbean Beach Resort

• If your touring plans call for a spring, summer, or Christmas trip to WDW, you still get a flat 10% discount on the listed resorts.

• Club members get a 10% discount year-round at the Disney Swan, Disney Dolphin, and the hotels of the Disney Village Hotel Plaza.

• Club members get a 10% discount from January to mid-February and mid-August through mid-December at the All-Star Resorts.

• Club members also get a 15% discount on the Disneyland Hotel in California.

• Club members get slight price breaks on tickets and 10% discounts on dining in certain theme park restaurants, including the following:

In the Magic Kingdom:
- Plaza Restaurant
- Crystal Palace
- Liberty Tree Tavern
- Tony's Town Square Cafe

At MGM:
- Hollywood Brown Derby
- Mama Melrose's Ristorante Italiano
- 50's Prime Time Café (dinner only)
- Soundstage Restaurant Character Breakfast

At Epcot:
- Garden Grille Room (character lunch only)
- Akershus
- The Biergarten (lunch only)
- The Coral Reef Restaurant (lunch only)

Given the high price of WDW lodging and dining, it's easy to see how club membership could pay for itself very quickly. But like the Fairy Godmother told Cinderella, "There's one catch": If you are planning to visit either WDW or Disneyland next year, you should order your card as soon as possible, since you must have it in hand when you make your hotel reservation.

Magic Kingdom Club members receive other benefits: discounts of 30% on National car rentals, 10% discounts on Delta airfares to Orlando or Los Angeles, 10% discounts on the Polynesian Luau and varied savings on golf (during some seasons the discounts go as high as 60%). There is a 15% discount on the Disney cruise line. Also expect 10% discounts on merchandise at Disney stores nationwide and on items ordered through the Disney Catalog. Cardholders have their own travel

agency, which offers special packages to WDW, Disneyland, and Disneyland Paris and discounts on a wide variety of Caribbean cruises.

Other perks include membership in Travel America
at Half-Price, which entitles you to 50% savings at
hundreds of hotels. Hotels in the Anaheim and Orlando area are "blacked out" to cardholders, but Travel
America can really come in handy when you're off to
see Grandma in Omaha.

Club members make their hotel reservations and get
information on special packages by calling (407) 824-
2600. Benefits vary slightly from year to year, but are
always substantial enough to guarantee big savings to
any family doing a week at Disney. You'll get a brochure
outlining all the perks when you order your card.

Note: If you're really lucky, you can receive many of
the goodies listed here without having to pay for the
card. Many corporations hold Magic Kingdom Club
Gold Cards, which qualify their employees for the discounts. Check with your personnel or employee benefits department to see if your company is a member.

WHAT KIND OF TICKET
DO WE NEED?

This decision, believe it or not, needs to be made long
before you get to the theme park gates. First of all,
prepare yourself for the news that, at least in the eyes
of the Disney accountants, your 10-year-old is an
adult. Then consider how many days you'll need the
tickets, whether or not you'd like to visit the minor
parks, and if you plan to visit more than one park in a
single day. (Most of the tips and touring plans in this
book assume that you will.)

There are several options, and the prices listed *do not* include tax. Children under three are admitted free.

Length of Stay Pass
Admitting holder to the three major parks as well as the five minor ones, with the option of visiting more than one park a day; for guests of on-site hotels only

Obviously, the cost is tied to how many nights you stay, but, to give you an idea, three-day pass prices are as follows:

- Adult: $128
- Child (3–9): $101

Five-Day World-Hopper Pass
Admitting holder to the three major parks, as well as the five minor ones, with the option of visiting more than one park a day

- Adult: $198
- Child (3–9): $157

Four-Day Park-Hopper Pass
Admitting holder to the three major parks, with the option of visiting more than one park a day

- Adult: $146
- Child (3–9): $117

Four-Day Value Pass
Admitting holder to the three major parks, without the option of moving from park to park in the course of the day

- Adult: $131
- Child (3–9): $103

One-Day Ticket
Admitting holder to one park only

- Adult: $40 plus tax
- Child (3–9): $32

Holders of the five-day pass have unlimited access to Typhoon Lagoon, Blizzard Beach, Discovery Island, Pleasure Island, and River Country for seven straight days after the first date they use the ticket. Considering that a one-day ticket to Typhoon Lagoon is $24 for adults and $18 for kids, the five-day World-Hopper pass is clearly your best buy if you're visiting in the summer and want to hit the water parks several times during the week. Not interested in swishing around the water parks or dancing at Pleasure Island? The four-day pass will suffice, but choose the park-hopper option.

It's also worth noting that the four- and five-day passes do not have to be used on consecutive days and, in fact, never expire. If you come back in two years, the unused days on your multiday pass are still valid, although your access to the minor parks will have expired.

Guests at the on-site hotels should consider the Length of Stay pass, which is good for a stay of any length from one to 10 days. The pass offers unlimited access to both the major and minor parks during the time you're staying at a Disney hotel and is slightly cheaper than the Park-Hopper pass. More significant, the Length of Stay pass means that a guest staying at a Disney hotel has park-hopping benefits even if he's going to be around only for a long weekend.

True Disneyophiles might want to opt for the annual passports which, at a price of $250 for adults and $217 for kids, cost scarcely more than the five-day pass. The minor parks also offer annual passports: The $82 Typhoon Lagoon or Blizzard Beach pass is popular with locals.

One final word of caution about buying tickets: The Guest Services desk at off-site hotels may not be run by your hotel at all, but by a separate company that exists solely to sell tickets and bus fares to tourists. These companies offer their own version of the multiday pass, which they hawk aggressively, usually by telling you that it is much cheaper than the Disney ticket. It isn't. If you are offered a four-day pass with access to River Country, Discovery Island, and Pleasure Island, this is a good buy *only* if you're sure you'll never use that extra day provided on the five-day pass and you don't plan to visit Typhoon Lagoon or Blizzard Beach.

Also, Disney tickets are never discounted, so if you're offered cut-rate tickets you should immediately smell a rat. Sometimes companies offer free or discounted tickets in order to lure you into time-sharing or other "vacation club" promotions. You'll waste a whole day trying to save 20 bucks.

Be wary of buying bus rides into the parks. For starters, many hotels offer free shuttle service, so if you've chosen your hotel carefully there's no reason you should have to pay for transportation. But even if you need a ride, these independent shuttles may not be your best bet. The agents at the desk may tell you that you'll save the "horrendous" cost of Disney parking by taking their shuttle, but the truth is that it costs $5 to park, and the bus tickets run anywhere from $3 to $7 per person. Also, the shuttles offered by these independent services generally stop at several hotels, making your commute time much longer than if you drove your own car or stayed at a hotel offering a direct shuttle. Don't pay for this abuse.

ADVANCE RESERVATIONS AND TICKET PURCHASES: CALL NOW, AVOID LINES LATER

• Get maps of the theme parks and general touring information by calling (407) 821-4321. If you're traveling with someone elderly or in a wheelchair, request the *Guidebook for Disabled Guests*.

• Tickets to the theme parks can be purchased by calling (407) 821-4321. MasterCard, Visa, and American Express are all accepted, and the tickets will be mailed to you. If you'd prefer to pay by check, call first to confirm prices then mail payment to:

WDW Tickets
P.O. Box 10030
Lake Buena Vista, FL 32830-0030

Many area hotels, including all Disney hotels, allow guests to purchase theme park tickets through Guest Services. Inquire when you make reservations.

Theme park ticket prices have spiraled in the past few years, changing about every six months. *Always* call to confirm prices. Once you purchase tickets, however, the price is fixed, so buy in advance when you can. If you live near one of the Disney stores, you can buy theme park tickets there.

• Room reservations for on-site hotels should be made at least two months in advance. Call (407) W-DISNEY for information on all Disney-owned hotels. The line is open seven days a week from 8 A.M. to 10 P.M., and you'll have better luck getting through on evenings and weekends.

Room reservations for off-site hotels can usually be made later, perhaps a few weeks before you plan to arrive. Only the wildly optimistic should arrive in Orlando with no reservations at all.

Booking mistakes are rare, but it never hurts to call and confirm room reservations before you leave home.

• Disney dinner-show reservations should also be made from home, and reservations are accepted up to 30 days in advance—or upon receipt of confirmed reservations for those staying at on-site hotels. Because on-site guests get first crack at reservations, off-site guests may find themselves shut out of the most popular shows and restaurants. If you're going during a busy time of year and want to see the Hoop-Dee-Doo Musical Revue, be sure to call (407) W-DISNEY 30 days in advance.

• To make reservations for Breakfast à la Disney at the Disney Village Marketplace, call (407) 939-3463 up to 60 days in advance. The other character breakfasts are buffet and in general accept no reservations, with two exceptions: During the very busiest times, such as the peak weeks of summer and the week between Christmas and New Year's, policy may change and breakfast buffet reservations will be accepted. Special limited-run character breakfasts may also take advance reservations. Check with Guest Services of your hotel or call (407) 939-3463 before you leave home.

• If you're staying at one of the Disney hotels, dinner reservations for restaurants within the theme parks can be made up to 60 days in advance either by phone from home or through Guest Services in your hotel once you arrive. If you're not staying on-site, you'll need to make reservations in person on the day you plan to visit—by dropping by the actual restaurant in the MK, at the reservations booth at MGM, or at the WorldKey Information System inside the Earth Station under Spaceship Earth at Epcot.

• Members of the Entertainment Club may be surprised to learn that some spiffy area hotels, such as the Hotel Royal Plaza, Marriott Orlando, and Delta Orlando, offer 50% discounts to cardholders, making an upscale resort as inexpensive as an interstate cheapie. But since only a certain number of rooms are set aside for club members, reservations must be made well in advance to get the discounts. (Becoming a member of the Entertainment Club is as simple as buying one of the discount coupon books in your hometown. The books generally cost between $35 and $50 and are best known for their restaurant coupons. Few people seem to realize that a nationwide directory of hotels offering 50% discounts can be found in the back of the coupon books.)

• Another great source of discounts is available by calling the Orlando Visitor's Bureau at 1-800-255-5786 and requesting their Vacation Planner and Magic Card. It takes about three to four weeks to get the package, but inside is lots of discount coupons for hotels, off-site dinner shows, and area attractions.

• Decide in advance if you need a rental car. If you're staying off-site or plan to visit non-Disney attractions, the answer may well be yes. Some rental car companies—Hertz, Avis, and National—have desks at the Orlando airport, with the cars in an adjacent lot. Others, such as the huge and popular Alamo, are located miles from the airport and require a separate shuttle ride. The shuttle adds 20 to 30 minutes to your commute, both going to and arriving from the airport, but Alamo offers slightly lower rental fees to compensate.

To reserve a car, call:

Hertz:	1-800-654-3131
Avis:	1-800-331-1212
National:	1-800-227-7368
Alamo:	1-800-327-9633

If you're staying on-site and doing only Disney, you may not need a rental car. When booking your room, ask about the best way to get from the airport to the hotel. Some hotels run their own shuttles, and others use independent services such as Mears.

THINGS TO DISCUSS WITH YOUR KIDS BEFORE YOU LEAVE HOME

• *The trip itself:* There are two schools of thought on just how far in advance of the trip you should let the kids in on the plan. Since many families make reservations six or more months in advance, it's easy to fall into a "waiting for Christmas" syndrome, with the kids nearly in a lather of anticipation weeks before you leave. In order to avoid the agony of a long countdown, one couple packed in secret, then woke the children up at 5 A.M. one morning and announced, "Get in the car, we're going to Disney World." Probably the best method is somewhere in between the two extremes. Tell the kids at the time you make your reservations, but don't begin pouring over the brochures in earnest until about two weeks before the trip.

• *Height requirements:* Get out your yardstick, because if your kids fall under the height required for riding the Twilight Zone Tower of Terror, Space Mountain, and Splash Mountain (44 inches), or Big Thunder

Mountain Railroad (40 inches), you should break it to them now. Disney vigilantly enforces these requirements, and there is nothing worse than waiting in line for an hour only to have little Nathan ejected unceremoniously just as you approach the ride.

- *The layout of the parks:* Kids 7 or over should have some idea of the layout of the parks; and if you're letting preteens and teens roam about on their own, they definitely should be briefed on the location of major attractions.

Among the more than 200 families surveyed or interviewed for this book, there was a direct correlation between the amount of advance research they had done and how much they enjoyed the trip. Visitors who show up at WDW without any preparation can still have fun, but their comment sheets were sprinkled with, "Next time I'll know . . ." and, "If only we had . . ."

The pleasures of being prepared extend to preschoolers. If you purchase a few WDW coloring books to enjoy on the trip down to Orlando, or watch one of the Disney Channel specials featuring the park, even the youngest child will arrive able to identify the Swiss Family Robinson Treehouse and the Living Seas pavilion. A little knowledge prior to entering the gates helps you decide how to best spend your time and eliminates those "Whadda-we-do-now?" debates.

- *The classic stories of Disney:* If your children are under 7, another good pre-trip purchase is a set of Disney paperbacks with audiotapes. Even though parental eyes may glaze over when *Dumbo* rewinds for its 34th straight hearing, these tapes and books help to pass the trip and familiarize kids with the characters and rides they'll be seeing once they arrive. (If you find kiddie tapes too annoying, you can always bring along a Walkman for the children to use.)

Some families rent Disney movies just before the trip as well: The videotape *Disneyland Fun* is especially good for getting the whole family revved up and in the mood. The park featured is Disneyland in California and not the Magic Kingdom in Florida, but the attractions are similar enough to make the tape an exciting preview. Renting *Honey, I Shrunk the Kids* before you leave will vastly improve your kids' appreciation of the Epcot *Honey, I Shrunk the Audience* show, as well as the Honey, I Shrunk the Kids Adventure Zone at MGM.

The Disneyland Game, which is available through major toy store chains such as Toys R Us, is also a fun way to orient kids ages 2 to 10 to the general layout of the theme parks. Players are required to move about the board, gathering cards from different attractions; the goal of the game—to visit as many rides as possible before the park closes—is considerably like that of the real-life game you'll play when you hit Orlando.

• *Special academic projects:* See "Should We Take the Kids Out of School?" earlier in this section for ideas on special projects and seminars.

• *Souvenirs and money:* Will you save all souvenir purchases for the last day? Buy one small souvenir every day? Are the children expected to spend their own money, or will Mom and Dad spring for the T-shirts? Whatever you decide will depend on your pocketbook and your particular interpretation of fiscal responsibility, but do set your rules before you're in the park. Otherwise, the selection of goodies will lure you into spending far more than you anticipated.

One excellent technique for limiting impulse buys is to request Disney Dollars at the time you order your theme park tickets. Disney Dollars come in denominations of $1 (Mickey), $5 (Goofy), and $10 (Minnie) and are accepted throughout the theme parks, shops, restaurants, and resorts of WDW. Some wily parents have managed to convince their tots that these bills are the only currency the parks accept, and have given them a certain number of Disney Dollars before leaving home, explaining that this money and this money alone is for souvenirs.

Purchase Disney Dollars by writing to:

Walt Disney World Ticket Mail Order
P.O. Box 10030
Lake Buena Vista, Florida 32830-0030

DON'T LEAVE HOME WITHOUT...

• *Comfortable shoes.* This is no time to be breaking in new Reeboks.

• *Minimal clothing.* Many hotels have Laundromats, and you can always use Woolite to wash out underwear in the sink. Most families make the mistake of overpacking, not figuring in all the souvenirs they'll be bringing back. (Guest Services at area hotels report that many families buy so much stuff they end up shipping their dirty clothes home via UPS.) Disney T-shirts are not only great for touring, but can serve as swimsuit cover-ups and pajamas. And unless you're planning a special evening out on the *Empress Lilly* riverboat or at Victoria and Albert's, casual clothing is accepted everywhere.

• *Lightweight jackets,* preferably water-resistant.

• *Disposable diapers, film, blank camcorder tapes, and baby formula.* All of these are available within WDW, but at premium prices.

• *Sunscreen.* Keep a tube with you and reapply it often. Sunburn is the number one complaint at the first-aid clinics in the MK. *Note:* You need sunburn protection all through the year in Orlando, not just during the summer.

• *Juiceboxes.* Not only are they handy in the car for the trip down, but you might want to keep a couple in your diaper bag while touring. There are few places in the parks where you can grab a healthy drink fast, and kids can become dehydrated rapidly.

• *A waist pouch or fanny pack.* This is a good alternative to dragging along a purse while touring and frees up your hands for boarding rides, pushing strollers, and holding on to your kids.

• *Sunglasses.* The Florida sun is so blindingly bright that more than once I've reached into my purse for my sunglasses only to realize that I already had them on. Kids too young for sunglasses need wide-billed caps to cut down on the glare.

• *Strollers.* Earlier versions of this guide suggested renting strollers at the theme parks, because they're rather a hassle on the monorails and boats. But since Disney has raised its stroller rental fee to an unconscionable $6 a day, you're better off bringing a stroller from home. If you're staying at one of the more sprawling resorts, such as the Caribbean Beach Resort, the All-Star Resorts, Dixie Landings, or the Fort Wilderness Campground, you'll need your own stroller just to get around your hotel.

• *A credit card.* It's no joke. The Sun Bank, with locations throughout WDW, gives cash advances on most major cards, which can be a lifesaver.

HELPFUL PHONE NUMBERS

All Orlando numbers have a (407) area code.

General WDW information	824-4321
General accommodations information	W-DISNEY
All Star Music Resort	939-6000
All-Star Sports Resort	939-5000
Beach Club	934-8000
BoardWalk Resort	939-5100
Caribbean Beach Resort	934-3400
Contemporary Resort	824-1000
Dinner-show and character breakfast reservations	W-DISNEY or 939-3463
Discovery Island	824-3784
Disney Institute Villas	827-1100
Disney Institute	1-800-496-6337
Disney Village Marketplace	828-3800
Disney's Old Key West	827-7700
Dixie Landings	934-6000
Dolphin	934-4000
Fort Wilderness Campground	824-2900

Grand Floridian Resort	824-3000
Pleasure Island	934-6374
Polynesian Resort	824-2000
Port Orleans	934-5000
River Country	824-2760
Swan	934-3000
Typhoon Lagoon	560-4141
Wilderness Lodge	824-3200
Yacht Club	934-7000

2

★★★★★★★★★★★★★★★★★★★★

*Choosing
a Hotel*

RATING THE ON-SITE DISNEY HOTELS

Not content with merely dominating the entertainment market, the Walt Disney Company has begun turning its attention to lodging the 10 million visitors who stream into Orlando each year. Orlando has more than 100,000 hotel rooms, more than any other U.S. city, and an increasing percentage of these rooms are Disney-owned, that is, on-site.

The majority of the new hotels added by Disney fall into the budget category. In the past five years, Port Orleans and Dixie Landings have joined the mammoth Caribbean Beach Resort to bring the total rooms in the $99 to $129 price category to well over 5,000. The All-Star Sports and All-Star Music Resorts, opened in 1995, have added another 4,000, these in the $69 to $79 category. Up until now, cost has been the primary reason for visitors to opt to stay off-site; with the advent of the on-site budget resorts, Disney is working to eliminate even that objection. Each time Disney opens a new resort, your options increase.

So do your decisions. All this expansion means that even if a family has decided to stay on-site, they still face a bewildering number of choices. Does the convenience of being on the monorail line justify the increase in price? Do you want to stay amid turn-of-the-century Victorian splendor or is a fort more your style? Is it important to be near the swimming, golf courses, stables, and other sporting activities, or do you plan to spend most of your time in the parks? As in all of WDW, making the best choice hinges upon your awareness of what your particular family really needs.

Magic Kingdom Hotels

The Grand Floridian

Modeled after the famed Florida beach resorts of the 1800s and possibly the prettiest of all Disney hotels, the Grand Floridian has 900 rooms encased amongst its gabled roofs, soaring ceilings, and broad white verandahs.

Proximity to the MK: Excellent, via direct monorail or launch.

Proximity to Epcot: Good, via monorail with a change at the TTC.

Proximity to MGM: Fair, via bus.

Pluses:

- Convenient location on the monorail line.
- A private beach on the Seven Seas Lagoon and numerous water sports.
- Excellent dining choices, including 1900 Park Fare, which serves a buffet with the characters.
- On-site child-care center.
- On-site health club.
- Exceptionally lovely rooms. The Grand Floridian is a favorite with honeymooners and others seeking a romantic ambience. (It's within sight of Disney's wedding chapel.)

Minuses:

- Extremely pricey, with rooms about $255 to $485 a night; discounts rarely apply, and only the most expensive packages include the Grand Floridian.
- The elegance puts off some families, who feel funny trooping past a grand piano in dripping bathing suits.

Overall grade: B. Expensive but luxurious.

The Contemporary Resort

You'll either love or hate the Contemporary, which has 1,050 rooms surrounding a mammoth high-tech lobby full of shops and restaurants. This place is always hopping.

Proximity to the MK: Excellent, via direct monorail.

Proximity to Epcot: Good, via monorail with a change at the TTC.

Proximity to MGM: Fair, via bus.

Pluses:
- Located on the monorail line.

- Fairly easy to book, and discounts are available.

- Disney movies are shown nightly, and the Contemporary is also home to the Fiesta Fun Center, a giant arcade.

- The standard water sports are available, along with tennis and a spa.

- The Contemporary Cafe is one of the best restaurants in all of WDW for families, offering a chance to visit with the characters while enjoying an all-you-can-eat buffet.

Minuses:
- It's loud, with a big-city feel, which is exactly what many families come to Florida to escape. "Like sleeping in the middle of Space Mountain," wrote one mother. *Note:* The Garden Wings are both quieter and cheaper than the main building.

- Like the other hotels on the monorail line, the Contemporary is expensive. Expect around $195 to $320 a night, unless discounts apply.

Overall grade: B–. Convenient and lively. Perhaps a little too lively.

The Polynesian Resort

Designed to emulate an island village, the Polynesian is relaxed and casual. The main desk as well as most of the restaurants and shops are in the Great Ceremonial House, along with orchids, parrots, and fountains. Guests stay in one of the 863 rooms in the sprawling "long houses." The Polynesian enjoys a loyal repeat business, with many of the families surveyed raving about the laid-back ambience and pretty lagoon views.

Proximity to the MK: Excellent, via direct monorail, launch, or ferryboat.

Proximity to Epcot: Good, via monorail with one change at the TTC.

Proximity to MGM: Fair, via bus.

Pluses:
- The Polynesian offers the most options for transport to the MK. You're on the monorail line but are also within walking distance of the ferryboats. Launches leave from the docks regularly, as do buses from the Great Ceremonial House. Your best route to the MK depends on the location of your room. Near the lagoon? Take the launch. Near the Great Ceremonial House? The monorail is faster. On the beach? Walk to the ferryboat.
- Private beach with an especially attractive pool and numerous water sports available. Like the beach at the Grand Floridian, the Polynesian has canvas shells, which provide shade for napping babies and toddlers digging in the sand.
- On-site child care.
- Numerous discounts apply in the off-season.

Minuses:
- Without a discount, expect to pay $210 to $360 a night.

Overall grade: A. An outstanding resort, and your best choice if you're willing to pay the bucks required to be on the monorail line.

The Wilderness Lodge

Disney opened the Wilderness Lodge near the campgrounds of Fort Wilderness in 1994. At about $150 a night, the rustic-looking, western-spirited resort is aimed at filling the gap between the budget and luxury hotels.

As is typical with the newer resorts, the theme of the Wilderness Lodge is extended into every aspect of the hotel's design—the pool begins indoors as a hot spring, then flows into a meandering creek, culminating in a waterfall into the rocky caverns of the outdoor pool. The awe-inspiring lobby, which looks like a Lincoln log project run amok, centers around an 82-foot fireplace, which blazes all year-round. The quilted bedspreads and Native American–motif wallpaper of the guest rooms, the staff dressed like park rangers, and even the stick ponies children ride to their tables in the Whispering Canyon Cafe—all combine to evoke the feel of a National Park Service lodge built a hundred years ago.

When you check in, you're given a brochure on Wilderness Lodge lore, which will help you find the 100 animals hidden in the lobby, many of them carved into totems or branded into chandeliers. And you'll learn that "it took over 2 billion years to build the fireplace," since the rock represents strata from all the layers of the Grand Canyon.

For those who just like to appear to be roughing it, the Wilderness Lodge is perfect—you can jump into the spa right after your trail ride.

Proximity to the MK: Good, via launch.
Proximity to Epcot: Fair, via bus.
Proximity to MGM: Fair, via bus.

Pluses:
- The lodge is brand-new, and looks it. The pool area is especially dramatic.
- You have close access to River Country and all the down-home fun of Fort Wilderness without having to camp.
- On-site child care, in the Club's Den.
- Wilderness Lodge is small for a Disney resort—760 rooms in contrast to the budget hotels that have as many as 2,000—which gives it a more intimate feel and makes it easier to get around.

Minuses:
- At $155 to $205 a night, it's still not cheap.
- This is the only Magic Kingdom resort without monorail access to the MK. The boat takes slightly longer.
- The rooms sleep four people, whereas the other full-priced resorts sleep five.
- The Wilderness Lodge has received many complaints about its bus service. Part of the problem is due to the out-of-the-way location—you have to ride through the woods to get anywhere—but part seems to be due to uncharacteristic Disney inefficiency. The sheer number of disgruntled guests has resulted in some changes in the bus schedule, but the commute to the theme parks is still longer than it should be.

Overall grade: B+

On-site Budget Hotels

Budget is somewhat of a misnomer, because both the price and the quality are higher than a typical chain hotel in Orlando. For paying about $30 more a night than a comparable off-site hotel, you get a mood that's pure Disney. As you sip a drink and watch your kids zoom down the tongue of the beloved sea serpent slide at the Port Orleans pool, you certainly won't feel like you're slumming. The hotels are well maintained and landscaped, with gobs of atmosphere thrown in to carry their motifs to the nth degree.

The budget hotels don't run with quite the legendary efficiency of the more expensive resorts—I recently endured a 40-minute check-in procedure at the All-Star Music Resort, something that would be unheard of at the Grand Floridian. A woman behind me was grousing about the fact that there was no freebie Mickey Mouse lotion in her room like they had at the Yacht Club. But these minor inconveniences pale when you consider that most of the on-site benefits—easy transportation to the parks, a plugged-in Guest Services system to help you with tickets and reservations, and the surprise-mornings perk—are just as available to those paying $69 a night at the All-Star Resorts as those paying $369 at the Grand Floridian.

Port Orleans and Dixie Landings

These hotels are both based on an Old South theme and offer unbeatable amenities and ambience for the price. Port Orleans transports guests to the heart of the French Quarter with manicured gardens, wrought-iron railings, and street names such as Rue d'Baga. The Mardi Gras mood extends to the pool area, dubbed the Doubloon Lagoon, where alligators play jazz while King Triton sits atop the water slide regally surveying his domain.

Dixie Landings is a bit more down-home, with a steamboat-shaped lobby, general stores run by gingham-clad girls in braids, and Ol' Man Island—a swimming area based on the Disney film *Song of the South.* A bit schizophrenic in architecture, with white-column buildings encircling fishin' holes and cotton mills, Dixie Landings manages to mix in a variety of southern clichés without losing its ditzy charm. If Huck Finn ever married Scarlett O'Hara, this is where they'd come on their honeymoon.

Comparatively speaking, Port Orleans is only half the size of Dixie Landings, the major reason why it gets our nod as the best. At Port Orleans the odds are you'll be close to the pool, lobby, food court, and shuttle bus station; at Dixie Landings getting around is more of a headache. Both resorts have a fast-food court, a sit-down restaurant, and a bar that offers live entertainment. The food court at Dixie Landings is more complete, but the sit-down restaurant at Port Orleans is quieter and more relaxing. If you're in a rush, the Creole munchies in the Port Orleans bar and the Cajun ones at the Dixie Landings bar make an adequate meal.

Proximity to the MK, Epcot, and MGM: Fair, via bus.

Pluses:

- Great water areas, which can easily keep the kids entertained for a full afternoon.

- So cleverly designed and beautifully maintained that you won't believe you're paying as little as $99 a night.

- Both hotels have marinas with the standard selection of watercraft.

- The *Sassagoula* steamboat offers both resorts easy water access to the Disney Village Marketplace and Pleasure Island.

- More dining options than Disney's first budget hotel, the Caribbean Beach Resort.

Minuses:
- Unless you drive your own car, you are dependent upon buses for transport to the major and minor parks, and this means a slightly longer commuting time.

- No on-site child care.

Overall grade: A+. You get a good deal here in more ways than one.

Fort Wilderness Trailer Homes and Campground

A resort unto itself, Fort Wilderness offers campsites for tents and RVs as well as air-conditioned trailers for rent. The wide-open spaces, perfect for volleyball, biking, and hiking, are a relief for families with children old enough to explore on their own.

Proximity to the MK: Good, via bus or launch.

Proximity to Epcot: Fair, via bus or bus to the monorail line.

Proximity to MGM: Fair, via bus.

Pluses:
- Fort Wilderness offers a huge variety of activities for kids, such as hay rides, horseback riding, bike trails, and a petting zoo with ponies, pigs, goats, and geese.

- Proximity to River Country and Discovery Island.

- You have access to the MK via a private launch. Shuttle buses run to Epcot, MGM, and the minor theme parks.

- Proximity to the Hoop-Dee-Doo Musical Revue.

- This is your least expensive on-site option with hookups and tent sites as low as $35 a night. The trailers rent for about $185 a night but sleep six people and offer full kitchens.

- Groceries are available at the on-site trading posts.

- Daily maid service is free in the rental trailers.

- The *Fort Wilderness Gazette* keeps you up-to-date on campground amenities, special happenings, and your somewhat confusing transportation options.

Minuses:
- Camping may not seem like a vacation to you.

- A large number of people are sharing relatively few facilities, and the beach, marina, and pools can get crowded.

- The place is so spread out that it requires its own in-resort bus system just to get campers from area to area. You can also rent golf carts or bikes, but make no mistake: Fort Wilderness is large and hard to navigate.

Overall grade: B. If you like to camp and are willing to put up with a little inconvenience for great savings, this is a good option.

Caribbean Beach Resort

This family-priced 2,112-room resort is located on 200 acres with a private lake and white-sand beaches.

Each section of this mammoth hotel is painted a different tropical color and named after a different Caribbean island. Each "island" has its own shuttle-bus stop, private beach, and pool. The rooms, although small, are attractively decorated.

Proximity to the MK, Epcot, and MGM: Fair, via bus.

Pluses:

- The price is right, at $95 to $124 a night.

- Parrot Cay, a man-made island with a playground, climbing fort, and small aviary, is fun for young kids.

- Water sports abound, and the Toobies—small, motorized bumper boats which can be rented at the marina for $10 per half hour—are especially popular.

- This is one of the best places in all of WDW to explore by bike. Bikes can be rented at the marina for $3 an hour or $7 a day, with specialty bikes like tandems costing a bit more. (If you're driving to Orlando and plan to bike a lot, it's definitely cost-effective to bring your own wheels.)

- Inexpensive food can be found in the Old Port Royale fast-food plaza.

Minuses:

- The fast-food plaza is the only restaurant on the grounds, and it's always swamped. For more-elaborate fare or faster fast food, you'll have to leave the hotel. Why on earth didn't the hotel planners put at least a burger-and-fries stand in each section?

- Although the buses are regular, they're not as swift as the water-taxis or monorail. Expect a longer commute time.

- The place is huge. It may be a major hike from your hotel room to the food plaza or marina. If you have young kids, bring your own stroller.
- No on-site child care.

Overall grade: B. Solid value for the money.

All-Star Sports and All-Star Music Resorts

This nearly 4,000-room complex opened in stages throughout 1994 and 1995, providing Disney's cheapest rooms to date. All-Star Sports contains five sections—tennis, football, surfing, basketball, and baseball, with the decor themed appropriately. At the All-Star Music Resort, you can choose between jazz, rock 'n roll, country, calypso, and Broadway tunes.

The pow graphics of the brightly colored buildings and the general zaniness appeal to kids. There are giant tennis ball cans and cowboy boots, a walk-through jukebox, and footballs the size of houses. At the calypso pool in All-Star Music, the buildings are lime green and punctuated with maracas; pitcher Goofy throws water in the baseball diamond–shaped pool at All-Star Sports. Palm trees are set to tip off before a gargantuan backboard in the basketball section, and show tunes play all day under the marquee on the streets of the Broadway section. It's budget, but it ain't boring.

Proximity to the MK, Epcot, and MGM: Fair, via bus.

- In a word: *cost*. Rooms start at $69.
- All-Star Resorts offer an affordable option for families with a handicapped member. For $79 a night, you can have a slightly larger ground-floor suite with roll-in showers.
- The shuttle buses are a good transportation option considering the price. When you get into this

price range at the off-site hotels, you often have to pay for a shuttle. These run every 15 minutes, and guests report that service is prompt.

- Proximity to Blizzard Beach.
- There's a food court which, although crowded, provides a fair selection. The arcade is huge.

Minuses:
- Food options are limited. Fast-food courts only, with no restaurants or indoor bars.
- Sporting options are limited; swimming is about it.
- The rooms are very small. They sleep four, but you'll be bunched.
- By breaking each resort into five separate sections, Disney is striving to eliminate that sleeping-in-the-middle-of-Penn-Station feel. But there's no way around the fact that it takes more effort to get around a huge hotel than a small one.
- Longer check-in than is typical for Disney resorts.

Overall grade: A–. Lots of bang for the buck here.

Epcot Center Resorts

The Disney Swan and Disney Dolphin
This convention/resort complex is connected to Epcot and MGM by water-taxi and bridges. The Swan and Dolphin are "twin" hotels (like the nearby Yacht and Beach Clubs), meaning that although they have separate check-ins (and are in fact owned by separate companies), the resorts are alike in architecture and mood and share some facilities. Both the Swan and the Dolphin have an emphatically sophisticated feel, but since their openings both have also made great strides to

become more family-oriented and offer amenities directed toward the parents of young children.

Proximity to the MK: Fair, via bus.

Proximity to Epcot: Excellent, via tram, or a moderate walk.

Proximity to MGM: Excellent, via water-taxi.

Pluses:

- Disney is aggressively going after the convention trade with the Swan and Dolphin. If a working parent is lucky, she can score a free family vacation here.

- Transportation to MGM by water-taxi and Epcot by shuttle tram takes less than 10 minutes from lobby to theme park gate, with a slightly longer shuttle ride to the MK. These hotels offer extremely easy access to Epcot, with a private entrance into the back of the World Showcase, allowing Dolphin and Swan guests to completely avoid arriving and departing crowds. You even have your own stroller-rental booth at the World Traveler Shop, and breakfast at the Boulangerie Patisserie in the nearby France pavilion is sublime. (During the off-season, when the World Showcase section of Epcot often doesn't open until 11 A.M., guests are transported directly to Future World in double-decker buses.) If you like MGM and Epcot, it's hard to beat the location of these two.

- Camp Swan and Camp Dolphin offer excellent on-site child care. Planned activities range from tennis programs to craft classes, are geared for kids as young as 3, and are reasonably priced.

- The new, expanded beach area offers a playground, kiddie pools, water slides, and a small marina with paddleboats.

- Bike rentals, tennis courts, and health clubs are also available. *Note:* The Body by Jake health club at the Dolphin is by far the most inclusive gym in the whole Walt Disney World complex.

Minuses:
- Expensive, at $185 to $375 a night.
- Because of the proximity to Epcot and MGM and the fact that they're gunning for the convention trade, these are adult-oriented resorts, with a citi-fied atmosphere.

Overall grade: B. A great place to go if the company is picking up the tab. Otherwise, try the Yacht and Beach Clubs first.

The Disney Yacht and Beach Clubs

Designed to resemble a turn-of-the-century Nantucket seaside resort, the Yacht and Beach Clubs are situated on a 25-acre freshwater lake. The Yacht Club, with 635 rooms, is the more elegant of the two, but the sunny gingham-and-wicker-filled Beach Club, with 580 rooms, is equally charming. The Yacht and Beach Clubs hit the perfect balance for families with young kids in tow—homey, lovely, and not one bit fancy.

Proximity to the MK: Fair, via bus.

Proximity to Epcot: Excellent, via a short stroll over a bridge.

Proximity to MGM: Excellent, via water-taxi.

Pluses:
- Stormalong Bay, the water recreation area which separates the two resorts, is almost like being next door to a private water park. The sand-bottomed "bay" contains pools of varying depths, water slides,

and a wrecked ship for atmosphere. It's especially fun to climb the shipwreck nearly to the top of its rigging, then zoom through a long tube into the middle of the pool. In fact, the water areas at the Yacht and Beach Clubs are so nice you'll have no trouble convincing the kids to return "home" for a dip in lieu of a more time-consuming trek to Typhoon Lagoon or Blizzard Beach.

- Like the Dolphin and Swan, the Yacht and Beach Clubs are on the doorstep of the Epcot World Showcase and an easy boat commute to MGM as well.
- The Sandcastle Club offers on-site child care for children 3 to 12. Disney characters are on hand for breakfast at the Cape May Cafe in the Beach Club.
- The two resorts share an on-site health club.
- Bayside Marina offers paddleboats, pontoons, and Toobies.

Minuses:
- Rates run about $215 to $335 a night, but discounts do apply in the off-season.

Overall grade: A+. These hotels enjoy a large repeat business from satisfied families. If your kids like water sports, and you all like Epcot, try the Yacht or Beach Club on your next trip down.

Villa-Style Accommodations

The BoardWalk

This huge complex is set to open as we go to press, and is thus unavailable for review. The centerpiece will be the ESPN sports club and production facility, but there will also be a large convention center, restaurants, miniature golf, shops, and the BoardWalk Resort. The

mood? Turn-of-the-century Atlantic City. The resort offers rental rooms, suites, and villas—located far closer
to MGM and Epcot than the existing Disney Institute
Villas or Disney's Old Key West. Sounds like a good option for big families who like to be in the thick of
things—but who still need plenty of room to stretch
out after a hard day of touring. Prices will range from
$200 to $355 a night.

Proximity to the MK: Fair, via bus.

Proximity to Epcot: Excellent, via a short stroll.

Proximity to MGM: Excellent, via water-taxi.

Disney's Old Key West

Designed to be sold as time-shares, the villas of Old Key
West (formerly known as the Vacation Club Resort) are
available for nightly rentals. You'll get all the standard
amenities of a Disney resort, plus a lot more room.

Proximity to the MK, Epcot, and MGM: Fair, via bus.

Pluses:

- If you have more than two children and need to
  spread out, or if you'd like a kitchen where you
  can prepare your own meals, Old Key West is a
  good on-site option. The villas are bright, cheery,
  and beautifully decorated.

- Tennis, pools, a cute sand play area with a permanent castle, and a marina are on-site. There's also
  an arcade and fitness room, and free Disney movies
  are shown nightly.

- You can pick up groceries at the Conch Flats General Store, and a full service restaurant and snack
  bar are also available.

- Prices run from $215 for a studio with a kitchenette
  to $725 for a three-bedroom Grand Villa, which
  could easily accommodate 12 people. A roomy two-

bedroom villa with full kitchen is about $385, which compares with a room at the Grand Floridian or Yacht Club. If you're willing to swap proximity to the parks for more space and the chance to cook your own meals, Old Key West may be just what you need.

Minuses:
- Still much pricier than off-site villas such as Embassy Suites.

- Quieter, with less going on than the resorts.

- No child-care options.

The Disney Institute Villas

Designed for families—and for large families—these villas are far from the maddening crowd, tucked behind the Disney Village Marketplace. Formerly known as the Disney Village Resort Villas, the resort offers one-, two-, and three-room villas. Many of the guests are taking classes at the Disney Institute or are golfers looking for action on the nearby courses.

Proximity to the MK, Epcot, and MGM: Fair, via bus.

Pluses:
- Proximity to the Disney Village Marketplace and Pleasure Island.

- Proximity to golf.

- Best choice for those traveling with a huge brood, such as a family reunion; several villas easily sleep up to 12 people.

- Some of the villas are designed like treehouses, others have lofts and skylights.

- Each villa has a complete kitchen with coffee maker, microwave, and wet bar.

- As well as great access to golf, you'll find tennis, boating, biking, six small swimming pools, and a health club nearby.

Minuses:
- You're a fairly long way from the theme parks, even by bus.
- There's only one restaurant, although if you're cooking in your villa a lot this may not be a problem. You also have access to plenty of eating places at the nearby Disney Village Marketplace and Pleasure Island.
- The villas, although recently refurbished, are much older than those at Old Key West or the BoardWalk.
- It's quite expensive, with villas ranging from $185 to $775 a night. Average villas run about $300, and far cheaper suites can be found off-site.
- This place is very quiet. You may have trouble keeping older kids entertained.
- Guests of the Disney Institute get first crack at the villas. If the Institute isn't full, other people are welcome to rent the villas—but you may feel like a stranger at someone else's party.

Overall grade: C. Lots of space, but you have to rely on buses or your own car to get to where the action is.

Disney Village Hotels

The Disney Village Hotels include the Buena Vista Palace, the Grosvenor Resort, the Guest Quarters Suite Resort, the Hilton, the Royal Plaza, the Howard Johnson Resort Hotel, and the Travelodge Hotel.

Since they're neither owned by Disney nor built on Disney property, the Disney Village Hotels are somewhat of a hybrid between the on-site and off-site lodgings. Located just across the road from the Disney Village Marketplace and Pleasure Island, these seven hotels are also considered to be "official" WDW hotels, meaning they run very frequent shuttles to all Disney theme parks and offer access to the restaurant reservation system and price breaks on admission tickets.

Proximity to the MK, Epcot, and MGM: Fair, via bus.

BEST ON-SITE CHOICES
AT A GLANCE

Best Magic Kingdom Resort: The Polynesian
People who come here always seem to come back, and that says something.

Best Epcot Resort: The Beach Club
You like Epcot? It's a stroll away.

Best Budget Hotel: Port Orleans
The best of both worlds—all the charm and intimacy of a full-priced hotel at budget prices.

Best Super-Budget: All-Star Sports and Music Resorts
The All-Star Resorts have the distinction of being both the winner and the only entry in the category . . . but it's still worth mentioning because of strong reader support.

Best Villa: Disney's Old Key West
Bright and airy villas—this is like staying in the Key West condo you always wished you owned. Fans of the Old Key West like the fact that it's off the beaten bath and quieter than most on-site hotels. Although the BoardWalk is better located, we'll reserve judgment until the reviews are in.

Best Disney Village Hotel: The Hilton
Great child-care program, great restaurants, and lots of extra activities and freebies for youngsters.

GENERAL INFORMATION ABOUT THE ON-SITE DISNEY HOTELS

- A deposit equal to the price of one night's lodging is required within 21 days of making your reservation. You may pay by check or with MasterCard, Visa, or American Express. If you cancel at least 48 hours in advance, your deposit will be fully refunded.

- All Disney hotels operate under the family plan, meaning kids 18 and under stay free with parents. The rooms at the budget hotels, the Swan, the Dolphin, and the Wilderness Lodge are designed for four people; the other on-site hotels can easily sleep five in a room. If your family is larger, consider either a villa or a trailer home.

- Check-in time is 3 P.M. at most Disney resorts, but 4 P.M. at the villas. You can drop off your bags and pick up your tickets and resort IDs in the morning and tour until midafternoon. Then return to your hotel to check in.

- Check-out time is 11 A.M., but once again, you needn't let this interfere with your touring. Check out early in the morning and store your bags with the concierge or Guest Services. Then enjoy your last day in the parks. If you pay with a credit card, you can arrange for automatic check-out; an itemized charge statement is slipped under your door early on the morning you'll be leaving, a definite timesaver.

- You'll be issued a resort ID when you check in that allows you to charge meals, drinks, tickets, and souvenirs to your room, and also gives you access to all WDW transportation.

• "Value season" usually runs in January, from mid-April to mid-June, and from mid-August to mid-December. All guests booking rooms during this time will receive a slightly reduced rate—about $20 off per night. The budget hotels do not qualify for value season.

• Room service at the Disney hotels can be painfully slow, with 45-minute waits not uncommon. (Pizza delivery is faster.) Breakfast, which can be ordered the evening before, is more prompt, but even then it is far quicker to get your own food. Every hotel has a fast-food restaurant or snack bar on-site that is open very early; the larger hotels even send around pastry and beverage carts. If you're in a rush to get to the parks, one parent can go out for muffins and cereal and take the food back to the room so you can eat while you dress.

• Now that Disney has so many rooms on-site, it's possible to stay on-site without making reservations. If you get to Orlando and aren't satisfied with your off-site hotel, call W-DISNEY to see what's available.

GREAT OFF-SITE RESORTS FOR FAMILIES

Hilton at Disney Village Hotel Plaza

Conveniently located with shuttle service to nearly all area attractions, the Hilton has the additional boon of a kids' club, called Vacation Station, for kids 4 to 12. It's open from 5 P.M. until midnight with a charge of $4 an hour, with a $3 add-on for siblings. Kids can eat dinner at the Soda Shoppe next door while their parents are out on the town. (The Hilton is a mere stroll away from Pleasure Island.) There's a playroom, large-screen TV with Disney movies, Nintendo games, and even a six-bed dormitory complete with teddy bears, so sleepy preschoolers can be bedded down.

The Hilton concierge has a lending library of games, and kids get a Family Fun Kit with freebies and discount coupons when they check in. Rates are $150 to $250. Call 1-800-782-4414 or (407) 827-4000.

The Hyatt Regency Grand Cypress Resort

The Grand Cypress isn't a hotel, it's an event. With 750 rooms, an enormous pool and grotto area with waterfalls and caves, golf courses, lakes, and riding trails, you could spend a vacation here without ever leaving the hotel. (But should you decide to venture out, WDW is only three miles away.) The Grand Cypress is home to Camp Hyatt, a child-care center that plans daily activities for children 5 to 15, at a cost of $5 an hour or $25 a day. Rock Hyatt, a weekend evening program that gives teenagers the chance to hang out with other kids their age, provides specially trained counselors to oversee volleyball and Ping Pong, video tournaments, and dances. The Grand Cypress also boasts five restaurants—including Hemingway's, a Key West–style getaway perched dramatically atop the resort waterfall—and a stellar Sunday brunch that's widely conceded to be the best in town, even by the staffs at other hotels.

Rates are $200 to $420, and suites begin at $275. Call 1-800-233-1234 for reservations and (407) 239-1234 for information about Camp Hyatt and Rock Hyatt.

The Peabody Orlando

Despite having nearly 900 rooms, the Peabody has the feeling of a small, elegant hotel, and kids adore the daily Royal Duck March, when the famed Peabody ducks are escorted by the tuxedo-clad DuckMaster down a red carpet to their personal wading pool in the hotel lobby. The ducks come into the lobby at 11 A.M. and leave at 5 P.M. (*Note:* As the most special of all special perks, you may be able to arrange for your child to lead a parade as honorary DuckMaster during your stay. Request information when you book your room.) Even if you're not staying at the Peabody, it's worth dropping by for the afternoon tea and 5 P.M. duck march.

The Peabody is home to one of the finest restaurants in Orlando: Dux, which serves, not surprisingly, no duck on its menu. Children will prefer the '50s-style B-Line Diner, which serves such kid-pleasing specialties as peanut-butter-and-jelly milkshakes 24 hours a day.

Rates are $210 to $270. Call 1-800-732-2639 or (407) 352-4000.

Delta Orlando Resort

Located just across from Universal Studios and convenient to both Wet 'n Wild and the Mystery Fun House, the Delta Orlando offers resort-style amenities at budget prices. Wally's Kids' Club, named after resort mascot Wally Gator, provides free daily activities from 11 A.M. to 5 P.M. for children 4 to 12. As well as scavenger hunts, pool games, and crafts, one special activity is highlighted daily: It might be a cooking lesson with the resort chef (the kids return wearing chef hats and clutching sacks of chocolate cookies that they made themselves), a scuba demonstration in the pool, a tennis clinic, or a magic class taught by a professional magician. There's a small fee (usually around $5) for these special activities. Each evening from 6:30 to 9:30, there's a themed Kid's Night

Out featuring dinner, games, and movies for a price of
$10 per child.

The Delta also offers The Oasis, a recreation area in
the center of the resort with an enormous pool, three
hot tubs and saunas, two kiddie pools, a small putt-
putt course, volleyball, and two playgrounds. Fishing,
tennis, and golf lie farther out.

The commitment to pleasing families shows through
in small ways, such as the fact that kids under 6 eat
free in the food court; here they also have a separate
dining section with crayon drawings on the wall and
cartoons on TV. The weekly resort newsletter keeps
you up-to-date on scheduled sandcastle-building contests, Frisbee golf, and water volleyball. Wally Gator is
frequently on hand for the activities and will come to
your room at night for tuck-in service. All in all, the
Delta is a clear winner in its price range.

Rates are $99 to $149. Call 1-800-776-3358 or (407)
351-3340.

The Holiday Inn Sunspree

Located less than two miles from the Disney gates,
the Holiday Inn Sunspree provides a minikitchen
with refrigerator, microwave, and coffee maker in
every room. It's a nice option for families who don't
need a full suite (and who don't want to pay suite
prices) but who'd like to save a few bucks by eating
cereal and sandwiches in their room. The Sunspree
offers a kids-only restaurant with an all-you-can-eat
buffet and big-screen TV, which continuously plays
cartoons and kiddie movies for guests under 12. (Kids
eat for free here when their parents dine at the
adjacent restaurant, Maxine's.) Children also have
their own special check-in, where they receive a bag
full of small gifts and surprises, which is a fun way to

start the vacation and makes the kids feel terribly special.

As you walk through the Sunspree, it's immediately evident that children aren't just tolerated here—they're welcomed guests. Camp Holiday posts daily activities, such as kids' karaoke and the kids' kazoo band, and the works of winners of coloring and essay contests are prominently displayed in the hall. Many of the rooms have VCRs, and a wide selection of movies is available for rent.

Each evening from 5 to 10 P.M., activities are provided for kids 2 to 12 at Max's Magic Castle for a very nominal charge. Hotel mascot Max the Raccoon and his friends supervise bingo games, magic shows, and movies. (Note that the Holiday Inn is licensed to take kids in the 2-to-4 age range—a rarity.) Beepers are available for rental, which adds to parental peace of mind, and daytime child care is available on-site. Max will also come to your room to tuck in tired toddlers after a tough day in the parks.

Rates for the Sunspree are $99 to $129 per night. Call 1-800-HOLIDAY or (407) 239-4500.

Embassy Suites Resort Lake Buena Vista

This relatively new resort, with a beautiful coral stucco exterior and dramatic open-air atrium decorated in Caribbean shades of teal and purple, offers very good deals for families. The 280 suites have pleasant sitting areas, can sleep as many as six people easily, and feature kitchens with microwaves, refrigerators, and coffee makers. A full range of sporting activities is close at hand, including an indoor/outdoor pool, tennis, basketball, volleyball, shuffleboard, and a jogging trail with exercise stations. The resort also offers several significant freebies to guests: shuttle service to the Disney parks, drinks at the manager's daily cocktail party from 5:30 to 7:30 P.M., and a bountiful breakfast buffet. (What many hotels advertise as a free breakfast often turns out to be a paper cup of orange juice and a wrapped roll, but this spread features a fruit bar, sausage, bacon, eggs, pancakes, French toast, and made-to-order omelets.)

Garfield is the resort mascot, and the Crazy Cat Kids' Club cranks up from 4 to 10 P.M. for kids 3 to 12. (You can opt for the $18 Crazy Cat package, which includes dinner, craft supplies, and a snack, or pay an hourly rate.) Beeper service is provided for parents, and the kids' club has plenty of Nintendo games, a video wall with five separate TV sets for high-tech viewing, a crawl castle, and a small ball pit.

Poolside games—such as egg tosses, relay races, and the popular "Daddy Splash" wherein the dad with the most impressive belly flop wins a prize for his kid—keep things hopping all day. The guests at this resort are almost exclusively families, so it is easy for a child in any age group to meet new friends.

At $129 to $249 for a suite, and so many perks included in the price, the Embassy Suites offer decent value and a great location just off exit 27 on I-4, a mere 10-minute ride from the Disney parks. Call 1-800-EMBASSY or (407) 239-1144.

Renaissance Stouffer Resort

Huge and gorgeous, with an indoor atrium so cavernous that indoor fireworks displays are set at New Year's and the Fourth of July, the Renaissance Stouffer is one of very few area hotels to offer drop-off child care for babies and toddlers. Babies as young as 6 months are welcome at Shamu's Playhouse, named for the Sea World star who lives right across the street.

Shamu's Playhouse is bright and cheery with an all-sand playground and small wading pool. Open 8 A.M. to 11 P.M., with reservations required, the cost varies with the age of the child. Ages 6 months to 2 years costs $10 an hour, and kids 2 to 12 are $6 an hour, with a $3 add-on for each additional child. The hours are designed to accommodate the parents who are part of the resort's sizable convention traffic, but daytime baby-sitting is also perfect for vacationers who'd like to visit the spa or sneak in a morning of tennis or golf.

At various times in the past, the Stouffer has run promotions wherein diners at Haifeng or Atlantis, the resort's flagship restaurants, receive three hours of complimentary child care. The Stouffer is also known for its Sunday brunch, during which a 400-foot-long buffet lines the atriums, offering everything from sushi to Rock Cornish game hens for $30. Kids chow down at a separate buffet ($16) geared to younger tastes.

Rates are $179 to $229. Call 1-800-327-6677 or (407) 351-5555.

HOW TO FIND A CHEAP OFF-SITE HOTEL

At least six weeks before you leave home, call 1-900-89MAGIC. There will be a $4 charge for the call, but in return you'll get a visitor's guide and accommodation information from the Orlando Chamber of Commerce and Visitor's Bureau. The guide will give you info on all Orlando hotels, from the interstate truck stops to the full-service resorts, and there will be numerous discount coupons for hotels, restaurants, and attractions included in the package.

Unless you are familiar with the specific hotel, your best bet is to choose a reliable chain such as Days Inn or Quality Inn, and then look for a location off I-4, preferably at either exit 25 or exit 27, the two exits that flank Disney. Exit 27 is the newer and more upscale of the two. The rate at an exit 27 Days Inn or Holiday Inn, for example, will run about $30 more than a hotel of the same chain on exit 25. Beware of an extremely low rate (below $50), which generally indicates you're both far from the theme parks and probably in a run-down side of town.

3

★★★★★★★★★★★★★★★★★★★

Touring Plans

GENERAL WALT DISNEY WORLD TOURING TIPS

The size of Walt Disney World is often a shock to first-time visitors, many of whom arrive with vague notions that they can walk from Epcot to the Magic Kingdom or even that they are separate sections of the same theme park. There is also some confusion over the names; some people use *Walt Disney World and Magic Kingdom* as synonymous terms, when in reality the Magic Kingdom is a relatively small part of the much larger Walt Disney World complex. There's more to this place than Cinderella Castle and Space Mountain.

Hence, an understanding of the WDW transportation system is vital, since you'll be covering many miles in the course of your touring. Despite the distances involved, the following tips encourage you to visit more than one park a day, using the ever-present WDW transportation system to allow you to follow a morning of bodysurfing at Typhoon Lagoon with an afternoon show at MGM. The best way to avoid overstimulation and burnout is to work a variety of experiences—some active, some passive, some educational, some silly—into each day.

Most of the tips in this section assume you'll be visiting WDW for more than one day. If you aren't staying longer, see "A One-Day Touring Plan" later in this section.

• Come early! This is the single most important piece of advice in this entire book. By beating the crowds, not only can you visit attractions in quick succession, but you can also avoid the parking and transport nightmares that occur when the parks fill to peak capacity around 11 A.M.

For families with kids, it is especially important to avoid the exhaustion that comes with just trying to get there. If you're staying off-site, it can take a full two hours from when you leave your hotel to when you board your first ride, which is enough to shatter the equanimity of even the best-behaved kid. They've been waiting for this vacation a long time, and flying and riding a long time: You owe it to them to get into the parks quickly.

• On the evening you arrive, call 824-4321 to confirm the opening time of the theme park you plan to visit the next morning. If you learn, for example, that the Magic Kingdom is scheduled to open at 9 A.M., be at the gate by 8:30. Frequently—for no apparent reason—the gates open a half-hour early. This is a gift from the gods, and you should be prepared to capitalize on it. On the mornings the park is opened ahead of the stated time, you can ride a dozen attractions while the other 50,000 poor saps are still out on I-4.

• Even if the park doesn't open ahead of the stated time, guests are frequently ushered into one section early. This means you can get maps and entertainment schedules before you enter the body of the park, and have breakfast if you order something simple and eat fast.

In the MK, visitors are usually allowed to travel the length of Main Street before the park actually opens. You can window-shop, grab a muffin at the Main Street Bakery, and still be at the ropes blocking the end of Main Street by 9 A.M. Similarly, at MGM visitors are often allowed onto Hollywood Boulevard to browse the shops and nibble a bite at Starring Rolls before the main park opens. If you have young kids and a special morning showing of Voyage of the Little Mermaid is scheduled, you should go there first. Older kids? Try the Twilight Zone Tower of Terror first, then head for Voyage of the Little Mermaid.

At Epcot the advantages of an early arrival are even greater. Spaceship Earth (aka The Big Ball) stands silent and empty at the day's beginning. A family can get strollers, ride Spaceship Earth, make dinner reservations at the WorldKey Information System (inside the Earth Station under Spaceship Earth), and have a quick breakfast at the Electric Umbrella—all before the park officially opens.

• Plan to see the most popular attractions either early in the day, late at night, or during a time when a big event siphons off other potential riders (such as the 3 P.M. parade in the MK).

• Eat at "off" times. Some families eat lightly at breakfast, have an early lunch around 11 A.M., and supper at 5 P.M. Others eat a huge breakfast, have a late lunch around 3 P.M., then a final meal after the parks close. If you tour late and you're really bushed, all on-site hotels and many off-site hotels have in-room pizza delivery service.

• Be aware that that kids usually want to revisit their favorite attractions. (My daughter insisted on riding Dumbo every single day the first time we visited WDW, something I hadn't foreseen and which radically restructured our touring plans.) Parents who overschedule to the point that there is no time to revisit favorites risk a mutiny.

One way to handle this is to leave the entire last day of your trip free as a "greatest hits" day so you can go back to all your favorites at least one more time. If you feel like lugging the camcorder around only once, make this the day.

• Use the touring plan to cut down on arguments and debates. It's a hapless parent indeed who sits down at breakfast and asks, "What do you want to do today?" Three kids will have three different answers, and the indecision and bickering waste valuable time.

• When making plans, keep the size of the parks in mind. MGM is small and can be easily crisscrossed to take in various shows. The MK is larger and though some cutting back and forth is possible, you'll probably want to tour one "land" thoroughly before heading to another. Epcot is so enormous you're almost forced to visit attractions in geographic sequence or you will spend all your time and energy in transit.

• If you're going to be in the MK for two days or more, plan to visit the most popular attractions on different days. Many families arrive in the MK determined to take in Space Mountain, Splash Mountain, Big Thunder Mountain Railroad, Alien Encounter, and Pirates of the Caribbean their first day . . . then wind up spending hours in line. Better to try to see a couple of the biggies during the first hour after the park opens. After that, move on to less popular attractions, saving the other biggies for subsequent mornings.

• If you leave a park and plan to return to either that park or another, save your stroller receipt and have your hand stamped. You won't have to pay a new stroller deposit at the new park if you can show a receipt, and you can reenter the new park swiftly by showing your hand stamp and ticket. (Don't worry if you're leaving to swim—the hand stamps are waterproof, although sunscreen can smear them.)

Likewise, if you're staying off-site and using your own car to visit more than one park in a day, save your parking receipt so you won't have to pay the fee more than once.

• Park-hop. Many families with a five-day pass figure: We'll spend Monday in the MK, Tuesday at MGM, Wednesday at Blizzard Beach, and Thursday at Epcot." Sounds logical, but a day in the MK is too much riding, 12 hours at Epcot is too much walking, a whole day at MGM is too much sitting, and anyone who stays at Blizzard Beach from dawn to dusk will wind up waterlogged. It's especially essential to take Epcot in small doses; if you do all the Future World attractions at once, the Audio-Animatronics will run together in the kids' heads. They'll likely get antsy from too much sitting, and all educational potential will be lost.

• If you're trying to predict how crowded a ride or show will be, four factors come into effect:

  ▪ *The newness of the attraction.* In general, the newer the hotter, particularly if it's a thrill ride like Splash Mountain or the Twilight Zone Tower of Terror.

  ▪ *The quality of the attraction.* Space Mountain, the Beauty and the Beast stage show, IllumiNations, and other Disney "classics" will be mobbed five years from now.

  ▪ *Speed of loading.* Continuous-loading attractions such as Pirates of the Caribbean, It's a Small World, Spaceship Earth, and the Great Movie Ride can move thousands of riders through in an hour. The lines at the start-and-stop rides such as Dumbo, Astro Orbiter, and the Mad Tea Party move much more slowly.

- *Capacity.* Movies like *O Canada!* at Epcot, shows like *MuppetVision 3-D* at MGM, and the Country Bear Vacation Hoedown in the MK can seat large crowds at once. Lines form then disappear rapidly as hundreds of people enter the theater. For this reason theater-style attractions are good choices in the afternoon when the park is crowded.

- At some rides you might opt to do a "baby swap" (which does not mean you can trade your shrieking 2-year-old for that angelically napping infant behind you!). It enables the family that has some coaster-warriors and some uneasy-riders to enter the line together, rather than split up or go through the lines twice.
  As you approach the ride, inform the attendant that you'll need to swap off the baby or younger kid. One parent rides, then the waiting parent passes the baby through and rides himself. (Older kids are often allowed to ride back-to-back with Mom and Dad if the lines aren't too bad.)
  If you're unsure if a ride is too intense for your kids, you can use the baby swap as a test: Let one parent ride, then return with the verdict. If the first parent thinks it's OK, the second parent can then immediately board the ride with the child.

- When planning your touring days, take time to familiarize yourself with the Ticket and Transportation Center (TTC). Located near the MK, the TTC is the main station for the monorails and buses and where you'll make all your transfers.
  If you're staying on-site, you'll be able to take a direct bus, boat, or monorail to any of the three major theme parks, but if you're trying to get to a minor park, you'll have to go through the TTC.

Off-site visitors can drive directly to Epcot, MGM, or any of the minor parks, all of which have their own parking lots and shuttle trams. But the parking lot for the MK is so far from the actual park that off-site visitors will have to park, catch the shuttle tram, and then go through the TTC in order to catch a monorail or ferryboat to get to the Magic Kingdom. (This is why we recommend that off-site visitors allow 45 minutes to get to the MK, even if their hotel is close to the park.) Likewise, if you're park hopping, you'll need to go through the TTC to get, say, from Epcot to the MK, or from the MK to Typhoon Lagoon.

It may sound like a big bowl of alphabet soup, but everything is very well marked, and there are always plenty of Disney employees on hand to answer questions. Once you get the hang of the system, you'll find using the WDW transportation services easier than trying to get around on your own.

• If you'll be at WDW for more than four days, consider planning a "day off" in the middle of your vacation. Families sometimes feel so compelled to do it all that they come back from their trip exhausted and irritable. But a day in the middle of the trip devoted to sleeping in, hanging around the hotel pool, taking in a character breakfast, visiting the other hotels, or shopping can make all the difference. You'll start the next day refreshed and energized.

• Tickets are expensive, so use them wisely. Each time you enter the gates of a major park, you get a day marked off your multiday pass—even if you visit for only a couple of hours. So on the days when you'll be in a major park, make sure that the hours spent warrant losing a day of your multiday pass.

One way to stretch your ticket is to spend one day solely in the minor parks. If you visit Blizzard Beach in the morning and Pleasure Island at night, for example, you won't have a day marked off your World-Hopper pass.

TOURING TIPS FOR VISITORS STAYING ON-SITE

• By far the greatest advantage of staying at one of the hotels within WDW is the easy commute to the theme parks. Visitors with small kids can return to their hotel in midafternoon, then reenter the parks about 5 or 6 P.M. Remember the mantra: Come early, stay late, and take a break in the middle of the day.

If you arrive early, you'll have been touring for five or six hours by 1 P.M. and will be more than ready for a rest. Have a late lunch either at one of the Main Street restaurants, which are reasonably empty at midday, or back at your hotel. (Neither the shuttle buses nor the monorail is crowded in midafternoon, but if you're staying at the Polynesian or Grand Floridian, taking the launch or the ferryboat is even faster.) Once "home," nap or take a dip in the pool.

At least one day you'll want to remain in the Magic Kingdom until 3 P.M. for the Main Street parade. Be sure to watch near the Railroad Station, at the Main Street hub, so you'll be close to the main gates and can make a clean getaway once the parade has passed.

• Think twice before ordering a meal through room service at a Disney hotel—it can take forever. Service at the sit-down restaurants in Disney hotels can also be maddeningly slow, so either try the snack bar or food court at your hotel, or get through the gates early and eat breakfast in the parks.

• In the off-season, the MK and MGM sometimes close at 6 P.M., but Epcot stays open later, even during the least crowded weeks of the year. The solution? Spend mornings in the MK or MGM, return to your hotel for a break, and then spend late afternoons and evenings at Epcot. Not only does this buy you more hours per day in the theme parks, but the best places for dinner are all at Epcot anyway.

• It's hard to overemphasize the importance of the "Surprise Mornings" program. If Epcot is the featured park on Tuesday, go to Epcot on Tuesday. By getting in the park an hour and a half ahead of the stated time, you can easily ride the most popular attractions before the crowds arrive; during Christmas week my family was able to ride nine rides in the Fantasyland and Tomorrowland sections of the MK during our first hour. Later in the day, we noticed that some of those same rides were posting 90-minute waits.

Since the program has been in effect, however, many families have pointed out that the designated park for that day draws a disproportionate number of visitors, who come early and stay all day. The solution is to park-hop. If the park of the day is the MK and it's mobbed by 10 A.M., take the monorail over to Epcot.

TOURING TIPS FOR VISITORS STAYING OFF-SITE

• Time your commute. If you can make it from your hotel to the theme park gates within 30 minutes, it may still be worth your while to return to your hotel for a midday break. This is a distinct possibility for guests of the hotels at the Disney Village Hotel Plaza and some I-4 establishments. If your hotel is farther out, it's doubtful you'll want to make the drive four times a day.

• If it isn't feasible to return to your hotel, find afternoon resting places within the parks. (See the "Afternoon Resting Places" sections in the discussions of each theme park.) Sometimes kids aren't so much tired as full of pent-up energy. If you suspect that's the case, take preschoolers to the playground in Mickey's Starland in the MK or let older kids run free among the forts and backwoods paths of Tom Sawyer Island. The Honey, I Shrunk the Kids Adventure Zone at MGM is also perfect for burning off excess energy.

• If you're willing to leave the parks in the middle of the afternoon, you have even more options. Cool off at a water park or in the 10-screen movie theater beside Pleasure Island. *Note:* River Country is an easy commute from the MK, since it runs its own launch. If you stash your bathing suits in one of the lockers under the Railroad Station in the MK, you can retrieve them around lunchtime and go straight to River Country without having to return to your car.

The hotel restaurants in the MK resorts are never crowded at lunch, and the dining is much more leisurely than in the parks. An early dinner (around 5 P.M.) can also effectively break up a summer day, when you may be staying at the park until midnight. The buffets at 1900 Park Fare in the Grand Floridian and the Contemporary Cafe in the Contemporary are especially good bets. *Note:* If you take the monorail, be sure to line up for the train marked "Monorail to the MK Resorts." Most of the monorails are expresses back to the TTC.

• If you'll be touring all day, get strollers for all preschool-age kids. Few 5-year-olds can walk through a 14-hour day.

•. Visit one of the parks *not* featured as the "Surprise Mornings" park for the on-site guests. (You can find out which is the featured park by calling 824-4321.)

• Staying for a late-evening show such as Illumi-Nations at Epcot or SpectroMagic in the MK? Either choose a location near the main exit so you can get a jump on the rest of the departing crowd, or stop for shopping and a snack after the show and exit the park about 20 minutes behind the main surge of people. Not staying for the late show? Leave the park while it's in progress, and you'll miss the departing crowds altogether.

HOW TO CUSTOMIZE A TOURING PLAN

There's no substitute for a good touring plan, especially if it's geared toward the ages, interests, and risk tolerance of your family.

In creating a personalized touring plan, the first step is to request maps at the time you make your hotel reservations. Familiarize yourself with the overall layout of WDW and the maps of the three major theme parks so you can arrive in Orlando with some sense of proximity and the location of major attractions. Getting to Big Thunder Mountain Railroad early is considerably easier if you know where Big Thunder Mountain Railroad is. Next, poll your family on which attractions they most want to see and build these priorities into the plan.

Third, divide each day of your visit into three components: morning, afternoon, and evening. It isn't necessary that you specify where you'll be every hour—that's too confining—but you need some sense of how you'll break up each day. Check out the following plan, which is an adaptation of the perfect four-day touring plan described later in this section. This plan is custom-designed for a family with a 4-year-old girl and 7-year-old boy who will be at WDW for five days in October, staying at the on-site Caribbean Beach Resort. The younger child is sold on the characters and most yearns to meet Minnie Mouse up close and personal. She still naps in the afternoon. The older child likes action rides, is pretty fearless when it comes to special effects, and especially wants to see the Indiana Jones stunt show at MGM. The dad asks only that one afternoon be left open for golf. The mom would like some time in the parks without the kids to get an early jump on Christmas shopping and wants to get a sitter one evening for a parents' night out.

A touring plan for this family might look something like this:

Wednesday A.M.:	The Magic Kingdom—tour Fantasyland, Mickey's Starland, and Tomorrowland.
Wednesday P.M.:	Return to hotel for lunch and naps around 2 P.M.
Wednesday night:	Epcot—tour a couple of Future World pavilions.
Thursday A.M.:	MGM Studio Theme Park.
Thursday P.M.:	Return to hotel after the parade. Mom supervises swimming and naps while Dad golfs.

Thursday night:	Hoop-Dee-Doo Musical Revue at Fort Wilderness; afterward watch Electrical Water Pageant.
Friday A.M.:	The Magic Kingdom—Ride Big Thunder Mountain Railroad and Splash Mountain first, then tour Adventureland, Liberty Square, and Frontierland. Lunch late at King Stefan's in Cinderella Castle, then take in 3 P.M. parade.
Friday P.M.:	While Dad takes kids to River Country via the launch, Mom stays behind to shop.
Friday night:	Sitter comes to hotel room for kids while Mom and Dad visit Pleasure Island.
Saturday A.M.:	Return to Magic Kingdom and reride all favorites.
Saturday P.M.:	Lunch at Mexico pavilion at Epcot. Tour World Showcase, encouraging kids to rest during films, since they won't be returning to the room for an afternoon nap.
Saturday night:	Dinner at Coral Reef restaurant. Then tour the rest of Future World and see IllumiNations.
Sunday A.M.:	Take in character breakfast. Return to room to check out, then leave bags with the concierge or go ahead and load the car. Return to MGM to see anything missed on the first morning.

This touring plan has much to recommend:

- You can get an early start every day.

- A nap, or at least down-time, is built into the afternoon.

- You see the characters every day.

- Minimal time is spent waiting in lines. Certain reservations, such as for the Hoop-Dee-Doo Musical Revue and character breakfasts, can be made before you leave home. Other reservations, such as for the final dinner meal at the Coral Reef, can be made from your hotel room.

If your kids are older, the plan can be easily adapted. Substitute the wilder rides for the tamer, Typhoon Lagoon or Blizzard Beach for River Country, cut out the naps and character breakfasts and you still have the prototype of a workable plan.

THE PERFECT TOURING PLAN FOR FOUR- OR FIVE-DAY VISITS

This touring plan assumes that you have a multiday pass and you're visiting at a time when all three parks are open past 8 P.M.

Day 1

Be at the end of Main Street in the MK by the stated opening time. When the ropes drop (assuming your kids are 7 or older and up to it) head directly for Space Mountain.

After you ride Space Mountain, go to Fantasyland. (If your children are younger or frightened by roller coasters, go to Fantasyland first.) If you want to eat lunch inside Cinderella Castle, make your reservation at King Stefan's Banquet Hall. Visit these Fantasyland rides in rapid succession:

- Dumbo
- Cinderella's Golden Carousel
- Snow White's Scary Adventures
- Peter Pan's Flight
- It's a Small World
- Legend of the Lion King
- Mr. Toad's Wild Ride
- The Mad Tea Party

After you exit the Mad Tea Party, teeter on to Mickey's Starland. The kids can enjoy the petting zoo and playground while you wait for the next show.

When the show is concluded and you've met Mickey, stop for a snack before you head toward Adventureland. It's a fairly long walk.

In Adventureland, visit Pirates of the Caribbean, the Jungle Cruise, and the Swiss Family Robinson Treehouse. By now it should be midmorning and some of the lines may be prohibitive. If you face a wait of more than 20 minutes at an attraction, skip it. You'll need to be back out on Main Street by 2 P.M., and you'll be returning to the MK on other days.

As you exit Adventureland and head toward Main Street, stop at either the Crystal Palace, the Plaza Restaurant, or Tony's Town Square Cafe to eat lunch.

(If you've made lunch reservations for King Stefan's in Cinderella Castle, go there now.)

Watch the 3 P.M. parade from the Main Street hub.

After the parade, exit the theme park. It is now time for your well-deserved midday break. Be sure to have your hand stamped as you exit the park.

About 6 P.M., go to MGM. Pick up an entertainment schedule at Guest Services as you enter. You should easily be able to catch the Indiana Jones Epic Stunt Spectacular, SuperStar Television, one of the stage shows, and *MuppetVision 3-D*. Eat last of all; the restaurants stay open after the attractions close down.

Enjoy the fireworks presentation. (Times for this finale show vary, so consult your entertainment schedule.)

Day 2

Spend most of the day at either Typhoon Lagoon or Blizzard Beach. Exit the park in the afternoon, take a break in your hotel room if needed, then head for Epcot.

Enter Epcot in early evening. If you haven't made advance reservations and you want a sit-down meal, stop by the WorldKey Information System and see which restaurants still have seating times left. Avoid booking a time just before IllumiNations—you don't want to miss the show.

Tour the Living Seas and the Land pavilions and Journey Into Imagination. See *Honey, I Shrunk the Audience*.

Eat dinner, then watch the closing presentation of IllumiNations.

Day 3

Be through the MK gates early. This time when the ropes drop, hoof it to Big Thunder Mountain Railroad and Splash Mountain.

Tour the Haunted Mansion in Liberty Square.

See the Country Bear Vacation Hoedown.

If you missed any Adventureland or Fantasyland attractions on the previous day, tour them now. If the kids are restless, you might opt to visit Tom Sawyer Island and have a snack at Aunt Polly's Landing while they explore. If they're tired, take in the Hall of Presidents.

Visit the Tomorrowland Grand Prix Raceway, Alien Encounter (for older kids), and any other Tomorrowland attractions that appeal to your family. Eat a fast-food lunch.

Exit the park and take an early midday break.

Either take in a family-style dinner show such as the Hoop-Dee-Doo Musical Revue, go shopping at the Disney Village Marketplace, or try out the water sprites or some other sort of boating fun. If your kids are older, consider visiting the other major water park. The crowds taper off in the evenings.

Day 4

Start your day at MGM. If you dare, ride the Twilight Zone Tower of Terror immediately upon entering. If an early showing of Voyage of the Little Mermaid is scheduled, go there next. Make lunch reservations for either the 50's Prime Time Café or the SciFi Drive-In at the reservation booth on Hollywood Boulevard.

See Star Tours and the Great Movie Ride.

Visit the Honey, I Shrunk the Kids Adventure Zone.

See the earliest Beauty and the Beast stage show.

Take the Animation Tour.

See the parade.

Have lunch, then take the Backstage Studio Tour.

Visit the Monster Sound Show and the Hunchback stage show.

Exit the park around 4 P.M. for swimming and resting.

This is parents' night out. If your hotel does not have a kids' club or if you plan to be out past 10 or 11 P.M., you should have arranged a sitter in advance. Orlando has many elegant restaurants (some of them inside Epcot), or you may prefer a rowdier evening at Pleasure Island.

Day 5

Start your day early at Epcot. With any luck, you should be able to make lunch reservations and tour Spaceship Earth before the ropes drop.

Head straight for the Wonders of Life pavilion. Ride Body Wars first, then proceed to Cranium Command.

Tour Horizons and World of Motion.

Head toward the World Showcase Lagoon.

Ride El Rio del Tiempo in Mexico and Maelstrom in Norway, then have lunch in either pavilion.

Continue circling the World Showcase Lagoon. The presentations at the China, America, France, and Canada pavilions are all compelling and extremely well done, as are the comedy street shows in Italy and the United Kingdom. Take in as many of these as time and your children's stamina permit. Finish with the Universe of Energy pavilion on your way out of the park.

Exit Epcot and enjoy an afternoon rest.

Enter the MK in early evening. Revisit a couple of favorite rides—Splash Mountain and Big Thunder Mountain Railroad are especially neat at night. See SpectroMagic, Tinkerbell's Flight, and the fireworks at closing.

A ONE-DAY TOURING PLAN

If you're going to be in WDW only one day, your task is challenging indeed. A one-day ticket entitles you to the use of a single Disney park, so select carefully. Time will be at a premium, so you'll probably want to forgo your midday break, opting instead for finding afternoon resting places inside the theme park.

1. If you have only one day, it is imperative you be at the park and through the gates a half hour before the stated opening time. (In the MK with its convoluted transportation system, this will mean leaving your hotel 60 to 75 minutes before the stated park opening time.)

2. Turn to the section of this book that refers to your theme park of choice and read the section on your first hour in the park.

3. See as many attractions as possible in the morning, moving swiftly from one to the next. If any attraction has a line requiring more than a half hour wait, skip it for now. You can try it again just before park closing, when lines are usually shorter.

4. Have lunch, then move on to theater-style attractions that allow you to sit, or consult the "Afternoon Resting Places" list for your theme park.

5. The parades and character shows are quite worthwhile, even on a packed schedule. They're what make Disney, Disney.

6. Around 6 P.M. crowds thin out a bit. Eat a snack supper then return to any sections of the park you missed or which had long lines earlier. Save the most popular attraction for last.

7. At park closing, one parent should stake out a spot as near as possible to the main exit, where

you can watch the closing festivities, while the other parent takes the kids to pick out a souvenir. Turn in your strollers and make a final potty run. This may also be a good time to grab a dessert or ice cream while waiting for the parade/fireworks/laser show to begin.

8. As soon as the closing festivities conclude, head directly out of the park. Don't look back—the crowds behind you will be the scariest thing you've seen all day.

A ONE-DAY TOURING PLAN FOR THE HIGHLY ENERGETIC

The following is an eclectic but efficient touring plan for families with a Park-Hopper pass who are driving their own car.

This plan works well as a wrap-up on your final day, because it allows you to visit two major parks, revisit favorite attractions, eat in an Epcot restaurant, and see as many as three major presentations. Admittedly, this plan requires a lot of energy and probably shouldn't be attempted with preschoolers. But for families determined to see as much as possible in the smallest amount of time, it can't be beat!

1. Epcot is much easier to access by car than the Magic Kingdom is. Early-arriving visitors can park very close to the main entrance and simply walk in, often circumventing even the need for a tram.

2. Drive to Epcot at least 30 minutes before the stated opening time, get strollers and maps, and make your evening dinner reservations at the WorldKey Information System inside the Earth Station under Spaceship Earth. Have breakfast if you haven't eaten, and ride Spaceship Earth.

3. Tour Future World until about 11 A.M., then exit Epcot, turning in your stroller and keeping the receipt. Take the monorail to the TTC and transfer to the MK monorail. You'll be running just behind the surge of visitors who usually glut the MK main gates between 10 and 11 A.M. Use your receipt to get a new stroller in the MK and have lunch on Main Street.

4. Tour the MK until 2:45 P.M. Return to the Main Street hub and watch the 3 P.M. parade.

5. Exit the MK immediately after the parade. Again, monorail traffic should be light since most MK visitors are still watching the parade snake its way through the rest of the route. Go back to the TTC and take the monorail to Epcot. Eat at the Epcot restaurant for which you made your reservations that morning, and tour the World Showcase until the closing presentation of IllumiNations.

6. After IllumiNations, you'll feel mighty smug as you bypass the horrendous crowds in line for the monorails and parking trams. Walk to your car and exit the park.

Note: An alternative to this plan is to exit Epcot around lunchtime via the "back door" located between the France and United Kingdom pavilions in the World Showcase. Walk to the Yacht and Beach Club's marina and catch the water-taxi to MGM. Tour MGM until 5 P.M., then return to Epcot via the same water-taxi for your evening activities.

4

★★★★★★★★★★★★★★★★★

The Magic Kingdom

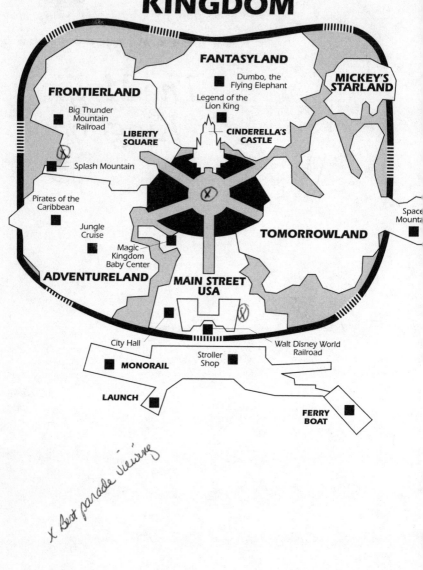

MAGIC KINGDOM

FANTASYLAND

■ Dumbo, the Flying Elephant

Legend of the Lion King

FRONTIERLAND

■ Big Thunder Mountain Railroad

LIBERTY SQUARE

CINDERELLA'S CASTLE

MICKEY'S STARLAND

■ Splash Mountain

Pirates of the Caribbean ■

■ Jungle Cruise

Magic Kingdom Baby Center

ADVENTURELAND

TOMORROWLAND

Space Mountain ■

MAIN STREET USA

City Hall

■ **MONORAIL**

Stroller Shop

Walt Disney World Railroad

LAUNCH ■

FERRY BOAT ■

X Best parade viewing

GETTING TO THE MAGIC KINGDOM

If you're staying off-site, prepare for a complicated journey. Either drive or take a shuttle bus to the Ticket and Transportation Center (TTC). From the TTC, you can cross the Seven Seas Lagoon by ferryboat or monorail. (*Note:* Make it a habit each time you board the monorail to ask if the driver's cab is vacant; people who'd like to ride up front wait in a special holding area. Since monorails run every three minutes during the peak times, you shouldn't have to wait long and the view is spectacular.) As you enter the front gates, the turnstiles to the right are usually less crowded than those to the left.

• If you're staying at the Contemporary, you can bypass the TTC and take the monorail directly to the MK.

• Likewise, if you're staying at the Grand Floridian, the monorail will have you in the MK within minutes. Or you can take the launch from the marina dock.

• Guests at the Polynesian have the most choices of all: the launch, the monorail, or the ferryboat. If your room is on the lagoon, walk to the ferryboat. If you're in one of the buildings near the Great Ceremonial House, the monorail is a better bet. If your room is close to the pool, take the launch.

• From Fort Wilderness campground or the Wilderness Lodge, take the launch.

• Guests at Disney hotels that are not on the monorail line can take direct shuttle buses directly to the MK, bypassing the TTC. This saves you at least 10 minutes of commuting time, more during the morning rush hour.

LEAVING THE MAGIC KINGDOM

- When leaving at the end of the day, visitors staying off-site should pause for a second as they exit the gates. If a ferryboat is in the dock to your far left, that's the fastest route back to the TTC. If there's no boat in sight, you're probably better off queuing up for the monorail, which runs directly back to the TTC.

- Guests at the Contemporary should always exit via the monorail, making sure they take the one designated for the resorts.

- Guests staying at the Polynesian or the Grand Floridian should glance down at the launch dock, which is straight ahead as you exit the MK gates. If a launch is in the dock, take it back to your hotel; otherwise, head for the resort monorail.

- Guests staying at the other Disney hotels should return to the shuttle-bus station.

Note: The launches, which are not to be confused with the gargantuan ferryboats, are a pleasant alternative to the monorails, especially in the afternoon. As well as transporting guests directly to the Grand Floridian, the Polynesian, Fort Wilderness, and the Wilderness Lodge, launches also run to Discovery Island and River Country.

GETTING AROUND THE MAGIC KINGDOM

Walking is by far the fastest means of transport in the MK. The trolleys, vintage cars, and horse-drawn carriages are fun, but think of them as pleasant rides that offer charming views, not as a serious means of getting around the park.

The WDW Railroad, which leaves from the main gate with stops near Splash Mountain in Frontierland and Mickey's Starland, can save you a bit of time and effort if you happen to hit it right. Don't think, however, that catching the train to Splash Mountain in the morning is your fastest way there. The Railroad Station is busy in midmorning, and you may have to wait for a second or third train; by that time, you could have walked. If you're entering in the afternoon or some other time when the station is less crowded, odds are you can catch the next train. This may save you a few steps, especially if you're headed toward Mickey's Starland.

Be prepared to make frequent rest stops while touring the MK. You won't walk as much as you do at Epcot, but you're likely to spend more time waiting in lines. Standing still is ultimately harder on the feet—and the nerves—than walking.

YOUR FIRST HOUR IN
THE MAGIC KINGDOM

Be through the gates 20 minutes earlier than the stated opening time, 40 minutes if you plan to have breakfast on Main Street. Get strollers and pick up a map and entertainment schedule at City Hall.

• Be at the end of Main Street by the stated opening time. When the ropes drop, if your kids are 6 or older, head for Splash Mountain, then Big Thunder Mountain Railroad, then across to Space Mountain.

• If your kids are under 6, head straight through Cinderella Castle to Fantasyland. When most people reach the end of Main Street, they tend to either veer left toward Adventureland or right toward Tomorrowland, and thus begin touring in a clockwise or counterclockwise fashion. If you go straight to Fantasyland, you'll not only be able to tour five or six attractions before 10 A.M., you'll also spend the rest of the day moving against the crowds.

• If there's a gap in the ages of your children and the 9-year-old is ready for roller coasters but the 4-year-old isn't, split up. Mom can take one child, Dad the other, and you can meet up again in an hour.

MAIN STREET TOURING TIPS

• Although you might want to spend a few minutes mingling with the characters who greet you as you enter, don't stop to check out the shops or minor attractions of Main Street in the morning—you need to hurry on to the big rides.

• Return to Main Street to shop in midafternoon. Especially worthwhile are Disney Clothiers, Uptown Jewelers, and the Emporium. Main Street is also a good place for lunch.

• If you're looking for souvenirs, be aware that there's no point in comparison shopping within the confines of WDW. A $22.50 stuffed Simba at the Emporium will also be $22.50 at a gift shop at the Polynesian Resort or the Disney Village Marketplace.

• After shopping, stow your purchases in the lockers underneath the Railroad Station. If you're not planning to see the parade, be sure to be off Main Street by 2:30 P.M. After that, it's a mob scene.

• A fun diversion for kids is having their bangs trimmed amid the old-fashioned splendor of the Harmony Barber Shop beside the flower market on Main Street. The barbers are jovial, even by Disney employee standards, and happy to explain the history of the mustache cups, shaving mugs, and other tonsorial paraphernalia.

• If you're touring the MK late and your party splits up, make sure you choose a spot on Main Street as your meeting place. Disney employees clear people out of the other sections of the park promptly at closing time, remaining firm even if you explain you were supposed to meet Lauren by Dumbo at 10:00 P.M. But Main Street stays open up to an hour after the rides shut down and is the best place to reassemble the family before heading for the parking lot.

• A blackboard posted at the end of Main Street provides up-to-date information about the approximate waiting times for MK rides, as well as all showtimes and where to meet the characters. Consult it whenever you're unsure about what to do next.

FANTASYLAND

The aptly named Fantasyland, located directly behind Cinderella Castle, is a cross between a Bavarian village and a medieval fair. Most of the kiddie rides are here, and it is the most congested section of the Magic Kingdom.

Fantasyland Attractions

It's a Small World
During this 11-minute boat ride, dolls representing children of all nations greet you with a song so infectious

you'll be humming it at bedtime. The ride loads steadily, so the lines move fast, making this a good choice for afternoon. And it's one of the best of all attractions to film with a camcorder.

Note: Although beloved by preschoolers, this ride can be torturous for older siblings. One family's 10-year-old wrote that Disney should offer an "I survived It's a Small World" T-shirt similar to those they sell outside of Alien Encounter or the Twilight Zone Tower of Terror.

Peter Pan's Flight

Tinkerbell flutters overhead as you board miniature pirate ships and sail above Nana's doghouse, the sparkling night streets of London, the Indian camp, and Captain Hook's cove. Of all the MK attractions, this one is most true to the movie that inspired it.

Legend of the Lion King

This show is a huge hit with kids, combining complex human-controlled puppets, live action, special effects, and music to retell Simba's familiar story. Like Voyage of the Little Mermaid at MGM, the presentation is sophisticated enough to charm even the most cynical of parents.

The show runs every 30 minutes, and 480 people are seated at once, meaning that even if the line looks discouraging, you should still queue up. Afternoons are mobbed, sometimes requiring you to wait through two shows before being seated, so visit midmorning after you've ridden several rides and the kids could use a rest.

Mr. Toad's Wild Ride

Cars careen through a funhouse, narrowly missing a chicken coop, an oncoming train, and being crushed by a teetering grandfather clock. Although the special

effects are nowhere near up to the standard of Peter
Pan's Flight, younger kids enjoy "driving" the cars.

Cinderella's Golden Carousel

Seventy-two white horses prance while a pipe organ
toots out "Chim-Chim-Cheree" and other Disney classics.
   Note: This is absolutely gorgeous at night, and
benches nearby let Mom and Dad take a breather.

Snow White's Scary Adventures

This ride was updated two years ago, devoting more
time to Snow White herself and cutting down a bit on
the scary elements. You still ride mining cars through
the dark, however, and the Wicked Witch appears several times quite suddenly, giving a few toddlers the
willies. The acid test: How well did your kids handle
the scene in the movie when Snow White flees through
the forest? My 4-year-old liked the ride while she was
on it but, perhaps significantly, didn't want to try it
again the next day.

Skyway to Tomorrowland

This overhead cable car offers great views, especially
at night.

Dumbo, the Flying Elephant

This happy little elephant has become the center of
some controversy: Is he worth the wait or not? Although
the lines do indeed move slowly, making a one-hour wait
possible for a 90-second ride, there's something special
about this attraction. It's frequently featured in the ads,
so it has become an integral part of our collective Disney
consciousness. A 4-year-old behind me in line once
earnestly assured me: "I've wanted to do this my whole
life," and she speaks for many.

Recognizing that Dumbo lines can bottleneck, Disney recently added eight more elephants to the herd and created a second holding area, which does cut down somewhat on the wait. Obviously, if you visit this ride first thing in the morning, you can cut down the wait even more, perhaps to only a few minutes. The height of your Dumbo flight can be controlled by a joystick, making the ride appropriate for any age.

The Mad Tea Party

Spinning pastel cups, propelled by their riders, swirl around the Soused Mouse, who periodically pops out of the teapot. Since you largely control how fast your teacup spins, this ride can be enjoyed by people of all ages.

Note: Rider volume ebbs and flows at this attraction. If the line looks too daunting, grab a drink or make a bathroom stop. By the time you emerge, the crowd may have dispersed.

FANTASYLAND TOURING TIPS

• Visit Fantasyland either before 11 A.M., after 5 P.M., or during the 3 P.M. parade.

• Don't eat or shop in Fantasyland. Similar food and toys can be found elsewhere in far less crowded areas of the MK.

• Park your strollers in one spot and walk from ride to ride. Fantasyland is geographically small, so this is easier than constantly loading and reloading the kids only to push them a few steps.

• Stay alert. Because the kiddie rides tempt them to wander off, this is the most likely spot in all of WDW to become separated from your child.

MICKEY'S STARLAND

More like a single, unified attraction than a "land," Mickey's Starland was opened in 1989. Mickey's house dominates the miniature town of Duckburg, which also contains an unassuming petting zoo and a playground with slides, "treehouses," and a maze. The unchallenged star of the petting zoo is a cow dubbed Minnie Moo, whose spots form a perfect outline of Mickey Mouse. After cooing over the animals and playing awhile on the slides, the kids will undoubtedly want to meet some of the characters, who regularly wander the streets of Starland signing autographs and posing for pictures.

The main attraction of Starland is the musical stage show featuring the stars of the Disney afternoon TV shows. File through Mickey's house and take a rest while watching the cartoon clips, which are shown in the Starland tent. Within 20 minutes you'll be ushered into the theater and treated to a lively show. As the characters are hitting their last note, prepare to exit via the doors to your left and head for Mickey's Hollywood Theater, which is next door to the show tent. Many people leave the show without realizing they can visit Mickey in his personal dressing room; if you exit promptly now, you'll be the first in line. (You can always return to the interactive games and "Walk of Fame" in the tent later—after you've visited Mickey.)

Guests are taken in groups of 10 to meet Mickey. This is by far your best chance in all of WDW to meet the main mouse without getting mobbed. Families who have toured several days without yet snagging that obligatory picture of the kids posing with Mickey are almost in tears of gratitude as they enter the dressing room.

Mickey's Starland is a must if your kids are under 10, probably skippable for others. Also, be advised that you can meet Mickey without taking in the show; just go straight to the Hollywood Theater and get in line.

Note: Mickey's Starland is undergoing an expansion, which will include more play areas and ultimately a miniature roller coaster designed for preschoolers. The expanded section, which will be similar to the popular Toontown in Disneyland, will undoubtedly be mobbed from midmorning on. As with all new attractions, visit it early in the morning or late at night.

TOMORROWLAND

After years of trying to constantly update Tomorrowland to keep it fresh, the Disney imagineers have decided to go with a '50s sci-fi look that reflects "the future that never was." In this new, completely redesigned Tomorrowland, the mood is decidedly camp—as evidenced by the robot paperboy hawking tomorrow's news and the street sweepers on rollerblades.

Tomorrowland Attractions

Space Mountain
This three-minute roller-coaster ride through inky darkness is one of the few scream-rippers in the MK. The cars move at 28 mph, a fairly tame pace compared to that of the monster roller coasters at some theme parks, but the entire ride takes place inside Space

Mountain, and it's impossible to anticipate the turns and dips in the blackness, which adds considerably to the thrill. Space Mountain is the most popular MK attraction with visitors between 11 and 21 years of age.

Children under 7 must be 44 inches tall and be accompanied by an adult. Children under 3 and pregnant women are prohibited. Some kids 3 to 7 loved the ride, but many surveyed found it too scary. Only you know whether your children are up to this.

Grand Prix Raceway

These tiny sports cars circle a nifty-looking racetrack, and although the ride isn't anything unusual, kids under 11 rated it very highly, perhaps due to the fact that even young drivers can steer the cars themselves. (If Jennifer's legs are too short to reach the gas pedal, Mom or Dad can handle the pedals while she steers.) Kids 52 inches and taller can drive solo.

Note: Try to convince your child not to rush through the ride; loading and unloading the race cars takes time, and you may as well drive slowly, savoring the loops of the track, rather than sit for five minutes in the pit, waiting to be unloaded.

Galaxy Palace

This large outdoor theater hosts a variety of shows, including a character show in midafternoon. Check your entertainment schedule or the blackboard at the end of Main Street for details.

The shows are fun and fast-paced and, since the theater is so huge, you can almost always be seated by showing up 10 to 15 minutes before showtime.

Skyway to Fantasyland

Pretty views, especially at night, but by the time you wait in line to board, you could have walked.

Delta Dreamflight

A happy, upbeat ride tracing the history of flight. Nothing terribly special, at least not in comparison to similar Epcot attractions, but it loads quickly and preschoolers like it.

Astro Orbiter

The Tomorrowland makeover has turned this ride into one of the jazziest-looking ones in the park.

A circular thrill ride, sort of a Dumbo on steroids, Astro Orbiter is a bit too much for preschoolers and a bit too little for teens. It's a good alternative for those kids 5 to 9 who aren't quite up to Space Mountain. Like Dumbo, it loads slowly; if you wait to ride at night, the crowds are lighter and the astro-ambience is even more convincing.

Transportarium

This CircleVision 360 film has replaced *American Journeys*. Now Jules Verne and H. G. Wells, along with the audience, travel from 19th-century Paris into the future. The voices of Robin Williams and Rhea Perlman, your time-travel pilot and navigator, add to the fun.

The show is well done, but guests stand throughout the presentation, and strollers are not allowed inside the theater, which means babies and toddlers have to be held during the show, a condition that eliminates it for many families.

Note: Lines disappear every 20 minutes, making Transportarium a good choice for the most crowded times of the afternoon.

Tomorrowland Transit Authority

This little tram circles Tomorrowland and provides fun views, including a glimpse inside Space Mountain.

Carousel of Progress
Another fairly long show (22 minutes), another high-capacity attraction, and thus another good choice for the crowded afternoon. Kids under 10, however, may be bored by this salute to the uses of electricity, especially once they've seen the more high-tech presentations at Epcot.

Alien Encounter
Alien Encounter opened last year amid considerable controversy. After the original version was dubbed too tame, the second manifestation was too terrifying; people were literally screaming so loudly they couldn't hear the story. Worse, the preshow had misled parents into believing this was a fun, *Star Wars*–type presentation, and several children had been thoroughly traumatized by the show that followed.

The present version of Alien Encounter is about a time-travel experiment that runs amok, "releasing" an alien into your theater. Although you never totally see the beast, you see flashes of parts of his body and hear him rattling around above your head and behind you. Like *Honey, I Shrunk the Audience*, some of the special effects are tactile; the shoulder harness gives the sensation that the monster is just behind you, slipping around your shoulders and down your back. The danger is mostly implied, since the imagineers working on the attraction theorized that the mind can conjure up far worse things than they can create. At one point in the presentation, when the tactile and aural effects are at their peak, you sit in total darkness for more than a minute.

Teens and preteens love Alien Encounter, but most parents conclude it is too much for younger kids. One mother pointed out that the shoulder harness not only gave her 8-year-old the sense he was strapped down, but also prevented her from putting her arm around him or comforting him when he panicked. I'd send a parent through first to preview the experience before going in with kids under 10.

MICKEY'S STARLAND AND TOMORROWLAND TOURING TIPS

• If you plan to ride Space Mountain, make a beeline for it immediately upon entering the park gates. After 9:30 A.M. there are substantial lines. By midmorning, Alien Encounter also has lines.

• If you don't plan to ride Space Mountain or see Alien Encounter, save Tomorrowland for afternoon, when the park is at its most crowded. Several Tomorrowland attractions, such as Transportarium and Carousel of Progress, are high capacity and relatively easy to get into, even during the most packed part of the day. Others such as the Tomorrowland Transit Authority and Delta Dreamflight board quickly and offer the added bonus of letting you rest for a while.

• Looking for fast food during peak dining hours? Tomorrowland food stands are rarely as busy as those in other areas of the MK.

• The characters appear throughout the day in Mickey's Starland; your entertainment schedule gives specific times.

• When the expanded Starland opens, it will undoubtedly be crowded from midmorning to early evening. If you can't visit before 10 A.M., wait till evening.

ADVENTURELAND

Thematically the most bizarre of all the lands, sort of a "Bourbon Street meets Trinidad by way of the Congo," Adventureland still manages to convey an exotic mood.

Adventureland Attractions

Jungle Cruise

You'll meet up with headhunters, hyenas, water-spewing elephants, and other varieties of frankly fake wildlife on this 10-minute boat ride. What distinguishes this attraction is the amusing patter of the tour guides—these young adventurers in pith helmets are unsung heroes of Disney casting genius.

The cruise is not at all scary and is fine for any age, but the lines move with agonizing slowness. It's skippable, but if you decide to take the cruise, go in the morning or during the 3 P.M. parade.

The Swiss Family Robinson Treehouse

There's a real split of opinion here—some visitors love this replica of the ultimate treehouse, others rate it as dull. One word of warning: This is a tough attraction to tour with toddlers. The steps are numerous and at times the climbing is a bit too precarious for unsteady little legs. Lugging a 2-year-old through the exhibit is tiring, but the real problem is that the bamboo and rigging look so enticing that kids want to climb on their own—and at their own pace. This may not sit well with the 800 people in line behind you.

The Enchanted Tiki Birds, a.k.a. Tropical Serenade

Interestingly, these singing/talking birds, and the singing/talking flowers and statues around them, represent Disney's first attempt at the Audio-Animatronics that are now such an integral part of Epcot magic. The attraction is dated and boring, however, in comparison to the newer robotics and is quite skippable unless you're just looking for a cool, quiet place to sit down in midafternoon.

Pirates of the Caribbean

The Pirates inspire great loyalty, and a significant number of guests of all ages name this ride as their favorite in all the MK. Your boat goes over a small waterfall and there is a bit of menace on the faces of some buccaneers, but very few kids leave the Pirates frightened. Most would agree with the 5-year-old who voted the ride the "best reason to leave Fantasyland."

FRONTIERLAND

Kids love the rough-and-tumble, Wild West feel of Frontierland, which is home to several of the MK's most popular attractions.

Frontierland Attractions

Big Thunder Mountain Railroad

A roller coaster disguised as a runaway mine train, Big Thunder is considerably less scary than Space Mountain, but almost as popular. The glory of the ride is in the setting. You zoom through a deserted mining town populated with bats, rainmakers, and saloon denizens—all crafted Disney-style.

If you're wondering if the coaster may be too much for your kids, be advised that Big Thunder Mountain Railroad is more in the rattle-back-and-forth school than the lose-your-stomach-as-you-plunge genre. Almost any child over 7 should be able to handle the dips and twists, and many preschoolers adore the ride. If you have doubts, see how your 5-year-old reacts to Pirates of the Caribbean or the Maelstrom in Epcot's Norway pavilion first.

Note: Children under 7 must ride with an adult, and no one under 40 inches tall is allowed to board.

Splash Mountain

Based on *Song of the South* and inhabited by Brer Rabbit, Brer Bear, Brer Fox, and the other characters from that film, Splash Mountain takes riders on a watery, winding journey through swamps and bayous, culminating in a 40-mph drop over a five-story waterfall. "Zip-A-Dee-Doo-Dah," perhaps the most hummable of all Disney theme songs, fills the air, making the ride both charming and exhilarating—truly the best of both worlds.

Note: Splash Mountain can get very crowded; ride early in the morning or in the last hour before closing. The intensity of that last drop, along with the 44-inch height requirement, will eliminate some preschoolers as riders. If your kids are unsure whether they're up to it, watch a few cars make the final drop before you decide.

Also, you can get really soaked on this ride, which is great fun at noon in June, but less of a thrill at midnight in January. During the chilly season, some people bring big black Hefty bags to use as ponchos, then discard them after the ride.

The Diamond Horseshoe Jamboree

Snacks and drinks are served during this 30-minute saloon show, which is full of hokey humor and lively dance. Some of the puns will go over the heads of younger children, but the material is delivered in the same broad style as the Hoop-Dee-Doo Musical Revue, so kids find themselves laughing even when they're not quite sure why.

During the busy season, you can make reservations for the Jamboree at Guest Services as you enter in the morning. During the off-season, continuous shows are run, and no reservations are necessary. Between standing in line, eating, and the show, you'll end up devoting nearly an hour to the Jamboree. That may be an advantage if you have young kids who nap, if you're pregnant, or if you just want a midday place to rest. But it's a disadvantage if you're on a tight touring schedule. See the Jamboree only if: (1) you'll be in the MK for more than one day and (2) you aren't planning to see the similar Hoop-Dee-Doo Musical Revue at the Fort Wilderness campground.

Note: If you just want to see the show, you don't have to order food.

Frontierland Shootin' Arcade

Bring your quarters. This is a pretty standard shooting gallery, but a good place for the kids to kill a few minutes while adults wait in line at the Country Bear Vacation Hoedown.

Country Bear Vacation Hoedown

Younger kids fall for the funny, furry Audio-Animatronic critters featured in this 15-minute show. From the coy Teddi Barra to the incomparable Big Al, from Bubbles, Bunny, and Beulah (a sort of combination of the Andrews Sisters and the Beach Boys) to Melvin the Moosehead, each face is distinctive and lovable.

The Hoedown is popular, but you can slip in easily in the evening or during the 3 P.M. parade. (But don't, for heaven's sake, try to get in just after the parade, when thousands of tourists suddenly find themselves on the streets of Frontierland with nothing to do.) Kids 11 and up rate the bears as hokey; if there's a split in your children's ages, one parent can take the little kids to the Hoedown while the other rides nearby Splash Mountain with the older ones.

Note: A different but equally charming show runs at Christmastime.

Tom Sawyer Island

A getaway playground replete with caves, bridges, forts, and windmills, Tom Sawyer Island is a good destination when the kids become too rambunctious to handle. Adults can sip a lemonade at Aunt Polly's Landing, the island fast-food restaurant, while the kids run free.

The big drawback is that the island is accessible only by raft, which means you often have to wait to get there and back. If your kids are under 5, don't bother making the trip. The terrain is too rough and widespread for preschoolers to play without supervision, and young kids can better blow off steam at the playground in Mickey's Starland. Likewise, there is little on the island for adults and teenagers to do. But if your kids are 5 to 9 and getting squirrelly, stop off at Tom Sawyer Island, where such behavior is not only acceptable, it's de rigeur.

Davy Crockett Explorer Canoes

Like the riverboat and keelboats of Liberty Square, these craft circle the Rivers of America around Tom Sawyer Island, affording you unusual views of Big Thunder Mountain Railroad and the other sights of Frontierland. Unlike the riverboat and keelboats, however, the canoes are human powered, which makes them appealing to some tourists, appalling to others. Don't board unless you're prepared to row.

Note: The canoes are in dock only during the summer and major holidays. Kids need to be able to pull their own weight—literally—to board, so if you have preschoolers, choose another type of boat instead.

LIBERTY SQUARE

Walk on a few feet from Frontierland and you'll find yourself transported back another hundred years, to Colonial America, strolling the cobblestone streets of Liberty Square.

Liberty Square Attractions

Liberty Square Riverboat

The second tier of this paddle-wheel riverboat offers outstanding views of Liberty Square and Frontierland but, as with the other Rivers of America craft, board only if you have time to kill and the boat is in the dock.

Note: There are some seats but most riders stand.

The Hall of Presidents

This attraction may remind you that one of the villains in the movie *The Stepford Wives* was a Disney engineer. The Hall of Presidents is indeed a Stepford version of the presidency, with eerily lifelike and quietly dignified chief executives, each responding to his name in the roll call with a nod or tilt of the head. In the background other presidents fidget and whisper. Bill Clinton made his debut in 1994, and Maya Angelou narrates the show.

The presidential roll call and the film that precedes it will probably bore most kids under 10. Older children will find the 20-minute presentation educational. Babies and toddlers consider the Hall a fine place to nap. A good choice for afternoon.

Note: The theater holds up to 700 people, which means that lines disappear every 25 minutes. Ask one of the attendants at the lobby doors how long before the next show, and amble in about 10 minutes before showtime.

Mike Fink Keelboats

These small boats follow the same route as the canoes and riverboat. But the riverboat holds more people at a time, so if you're in a rush, take the riverboat.

The Haunted Mansion

More apt to elicit a giggle than a scream, the Mansion is full of clever special effects—at one point a ghost "hitchhikes" a ride in your own "doom buggy"! The cast members, who dress as morticians and never smile, add to the fun with such instructions as, "Drag your wretched bodies to the dead center of the room." A significant number of kids 7 to 11 listed the Haunted Mansion as one of their favorite attractions, but the mothers of several children under 7 reported that their kids were frightened. The spooks are played for laughs, but the entire ride does take place in darkness.

The Mansion is best viewed before noon or, if you have the courage, in the last two hours before closing.

ADVENTURELAND, FRONTIERLAND, AND LIBERTY SQUARE TOURING TIPS

• If you have two days to spend touring the MK, begin your second in Frontierland at Splash Mountain.

Move on to Big Thunder Mountain Railroad, then the Haunted Mansion in Liberty Square. All three attractions are relatively easy to board before 10 A.M., and you can return to ride less-crowded Liberty Square and Frontierland attractions later in the day.

• Because most visitors tour the lands in a clockwise or counterclockwise fashion, these three lands reach peak capacity around noon and stay crowded until around 4:30 P.M., when the people lined up to watch the 3 P.M. parade finally disperse. So if you miss Splash Mountain, the Jungle Cruise, the Haunted Mansion, or Big Thunder Mountain Railroad in the morning, wait until evening to revisit them.

• Should you, despite your best intentions, wind up in one of these three sections in midafternoon, you'll find a bit of breathing space on Tom Sawyer Island, with the Enchanted Tiki Birds, in the Hall of Presidents, or among the shops in the shady Adventureland Pavilion. Surprisingly, Pirates of the Caribbean isn't that difficult to board in midafternoon. The lines look terrible, but at least you wait inside, and it is one of the fastest-loading attractions in WDW.

• As of this writing, Splash Mountain stays mobbed almost all day long, so anytime you find a wait of less than 20 minutes, you should queue up immediately and thank your lucky stars.

Everyone dashes to Splash Mountain the minute the ropes drop in the morning, and on very busy days this means the line may be massive within minutes after the park opens. If you hustle straight to Frontierland and arrive only to find yourself facing a wait longer than 30 minutes, move on to Big Thunder Mountain Railroad; check Splash Mountain again immediately afterward and you may find that the initial surge of people has moved through and the line is a bit shorter.

The lines also shorten in the last hour before closing, especially on the nights when SpectroMagic is scheduled. Even if you've already ridden once, you'll find that Splash Mountain is a whole new experience after dark.

FULL-SERVICE RESTAURANTS IN THE MAGIC KINGDOM

Tony's Town Square Cafe
Located in the Main Street hub

This thoroughly enjoyable restaurant is dedicated to *Lady and the Tramp,* with scenes from the popular film dotting the walls, and a statue of the canine romantics in the center. The cuisine, like that of the cafe where Tramp wooed Lady, is classic Italian, and the portions are generous.

Tony's is a good choice for breakfast because, along with the other Main Street eateries, it begins serving before the park officially opens. The Lady and the Tramp character waffles are a big hit with preschoolers.

The kiddie menus, which feature pictures of Lady and the Tramp to color, are handed out with crayons, and the wait at Tony's is rarely long, making it a good choice for families with toddlers in tow. Tony's is moderately priced and open for breakfast, lunch, and dinner. On-site guests can make reservations in advance; for off-site guests, reservations are accepted at the door.

The Plaza Restaurant
Located on Main Street

The sandwiches, burgers, and salads served at the Plaza are very filling. Try the chicken pot pie, which is encased in a huge puff pastry, or the milkshakes, which are trotted over from the Sealtest Ice Cream Parlor next door. The Plaza is moderately priced and open for lunch and dinner. No reservations are accepted.

Crystal Palace
Located between Main Street and Adventureland

The MK's only cafeteria offers something for everyone and allows picky eaters a chance to pick. You can find a classic eggs-and-bacon breakfast here, salads and sandwiches at lunch, and nearly anything you please at dinner—even that most elusive of all MK foods: vegetables. And the setting is absolutely lovely.

One warning: Because of its central location and distinctive architecture, few visitors pass by the Crystal Palace without checking it out. The cafeteria is especially crowded from noon to 2 P.M., so you should aim to go around 11 A.M. or in midafternoon. The Crystal Palace is moderately priced and open for breakfast, lunch, and dinner. No reservations are accepted.

Liberty Tree Tavern
Located in Liberty Square

Crammed with antiques and decorated in a style reminiscent of Colonial Williamsburg, the tavern serves salads, sandwiches, and clam chowder at lunch. The dinner menu offers classic American cuisine, such as turkey and dressing or pot roast, as well as prime rib, seafood, and chicken. A local food critic voted Liberty Tree Tavern as having the best food in the MK—which, admittedly, is an honor a bit like being the tallest building in Bismarck. A character dinner, featuring the characters in Revolutionary War–era garb, has recently been added.

Reservations are recommended, but, unlike King Stefan's Banquet Hall in the Cinderella Castle, there's no one at the door to take them until 11 A.M. Make reservations midmorning as you leave Fantasyland. The Tavern is open for lunch and dinner—and it's expensive.

King Stefan's Banquet Hall
Located in Cinderella Castle, Fantasyland

Nestled high amid the spires of the castle, this restaurant—named, mysteriously enough, for Sleeping Beauty's father—is the most glamorous in the MK. Make reservations at the restaurant door first thing in the morning, but even with reservations you can expect to wait for both your table and your food. Because the service is slow and the menu pricey, King Stefan's is not a place to drop into casually.

Cinderella appears downstairs throughout the day to greet diners and pose for pictures. (Ask what times she is scheduled before you make your reservations.) Kids love the distinctive pumpkin-shaped kiddie menus, and often bring them back downstairs for Cinderella to autograph. The setting of the massive banquet hall with its high ceiling is spectacular, and the leaded-glass windows overlook the rides of Fantasyland, offering a stunning view, especially at night. King Stefan's offers a relatively ambitious menu, including a gorgeous fruit plate, but in general the food is only so-so. Open for lunch and dinner. Reservations are required.

DECENT FAST-FOOD PLACES IN THE MAGIC KINGDOM

• The **Mile Long Bar** in Frontierland is a good place for tame Tex-Mex, and lines move more swiftly than those at the **Pecos Bill Cafe** next door.

- The **Starlight Cafe** in Tomorrowland is by far the fastest of the sandwich-and-fries places.

- **Sleepy Hollow** in Liberty Square is a good place for the health conscious, offering veggie sandwiches and meatless chili. The shady park across the street is a great place to relax while you eat.

- Try a citrus swirl at the **Sunshine Tree Terrace** in Adventureland. Like Sleepy Hollow, this snack shop is tucked out of the way with its own quiet courtyard.

- Families who demand healthy snacks will be pleased by the addition of the **Liberty Square Market**, where fresh fruit and juices are available. **Auntie Gravity's** in Tomorrowland serves fresh fruit and yogurt.

- **Luminere's Kitchen** in Fantasyland provides the Disney version of a Happy Meal, featuring a cartoon-covered box with a burger, fries, and a souvenir pin inside. If you buy one of these meals, carry the food into a less crowded part of the park and look for a bench.

In general, the fast-food places in Fantasyland should be avoided completely; likewise the Adventureland Veranda, where you wait far too long for mediocre Chinese food.

AFTERNOON RESTING PLACES

- The WDW Railroad (you can rest while you ride).
- The small park across from Sleepy Hollow in Liberty Square.
- The Diamond Horseshoe Jamboree.
- The Hall of Presidents.

- Legend of the Lion King.
- Galaxy Palace.
- Tom Sawyer Island.
- Guests with a five-day pass can take the launch marked "Campground and Discovery Island" to either River Country or Discovery Island. If it's hot, bring your swimsuits along or wear them under your clothes—an hour or two in River Country can cool you off and revive your spirits.
- And if you want a leisurely, quiet lunch, take the resort monorail to one of the MK hotels. The coffee shops and restaurants are rarely crowded in the middle of the day.

BEST VANTAGE POINTS FOR WATCHING THE PARADES

• The absolute best location is at the very beginning of Main Street, along the hub in front of the Railroad Station. (The parade begins here, emerging from behind City Hall.) You do lose the vantage point of the floats coming down Main Street, but it's worth it to not have to fight the crowds.

The crowds grow less manageable as you proceed down Main Street and are at their worst in front of Cinderella Castle. In fact, if you find yourself four layers of people back on Main Street, send one of your party toward the main entrance to check out the situation at the hub; you may find there's still curb space there when the rest of the route is mobbed.

• If you find yourself deep in the bowels of the theme park at parade time, don't try to fight your way up Main Street to the hub—you'll never make it.

Instead, go to the end of the route, in front of Pecos Bill Cafe in Frontierland. The crowds here are thinner than in front of Cinderella Castle or in Liberty Square.

- On very busy days, the parade may run more than once—going from Main Street to Frontierland and then back from Frontierland to Main Street. Ask the nearest Disney attendant which direction the parade will be coming from and try to get as close as possible to the beginning of the parade route. Being near the beginning of the route saves the kids a 20-minute wait to see the show and also ensures that you won't be caught among the exiting crowd.

BEST RESTROOM LOCATIONS IN THE MAGIC KINGDOM

By *best* I mean least crowded. You can get in and out of these rather quickly:

- Behind the Enchanted Grove snack bar near the Mad Tea Party.
- In the passageway between Adventureland and Frontierland. This one draws traffic, but is so huge that you never have to wait long.
- Near the Skyway to Fantasyland in Tomorrowland.
- If you're in the Baby Services center for other reasons, make a pit stop.
- The sit-down restaurants have their own restrooms, which are never very crowded.
- And as you leave Pirates of the Caribbean, make a stop at the restroom located at the back of the mar-

ket stalls. This one is so secluded that I found it myself only on my 17th fact-finding trip to WDW.

THE MAGIC KINGDOM DON'T-MISS LIST

If your kids are 7 or older:

- Space Mountain
- Splash Mountain
- Pirates of the Caribbean
- Big Thunder Mountain Railroad
- Haunted Mansion
- Legend of the Lion King
- Alien Encounter—if they're 10 or older
- The parades
- Any of the Fantasyland rides that catch their fancy

If your kids are under 7:

- Dumbo, the Flying Elephant
- Grand Prix Raceway
- Mad Tea Party
- It's a Small World
- Peter Pan's Flight
- Mickey's Starland
- Pirates of the Caribbean
- Country Bear Vacation Hoedown
- Legend of the Lion King
- The parades

- Splash Mountain—if they pass the height requirement
- Big Thunder Mountain Railroad—if they pass the height requirement

YOUR LAST HOUR IN THE MAGIC KINGDOM

• Some rides—most notably Big Thunder Mountain Railroad, Cinderella's Golden Carousel, Dumbo, Splash Mountain, and the Skyway between Tomorrowland and Fantasyland—are particularly beautiful at night.

• If you missed any of the biggie rides earlier in the day, return in the last hour; lines are shorter just before closing, especially in Fantasyland.

• If you're visiting on an evening when Spectro-Magic is scheduled, move as far as possible up Main Street and stake your curb space near the hub. Turn in your strollers and make a final potty run before the parade starts, so you'll be ready to make a fast exit once the final float rolls by.

THE SCARE FACTOR IN THE MAGIC KINGDOM

Few attractions at WDW are truly terrifying. In fact, young visitors raised on a steady diet of roller coasters called "Corkscrew" and "Python" are apt to find Disney offerings pretty tame.

But Disney plays on your emotions in more subtle ways. Children who would seem to be anesthetized by the violence of movies like *Halloween VIII* have been known to sob inconsolably over the demise of Old

Yeller. And the attention to detail, which is so much a Disney trademark, is especially evident in attractions such as Alien Encounter—he's believable.

This makes the scare factor tough to gauge. With the exception of Space Mountain, nothing at WDW will knock off your glasses or shake out your fillings. But remember, Walt was the guy who bumped off Bambi's mother, and preschool children may be shaken in a totally different way.

Snow White's Scary Adventures

Don't expect to leave this attraction humming "Whistle While You Work." Riders take the role of Snow White as she flees through the woods, and the witch does leap out at you several times. But the ride is a short one, and the special effects are fairly simple.

Final verdict: Not too scary, fine for most kids over 4.

Mr. Toad's Wild Ride

Your car careens through a funhouse. At one point you make a wrong turn onto a railroad track with a train approaching. Mr. Toad also—briefly—goes to hell.

Final verdict: Not too scary, fine for most kids over 4.

Big Thunder Mountain Railroad

An exciting three-minute ride, one of the best-loved in the Magic Kingdom. At no time does the train go very high, although it does travel fairly fast. Riders exit giggly but not shaky.

Final verdict: Fine for the 7-and-above crowd. Children must be 40 inches tall to ride, and some kids under

7 who rode with their parents loved Big Thunder. If you're debating which of the three "mountains" (i.e., Splash Mountain, Big Thunder Mountain, and Space Mountain) is most suitable for a preschooler, Big Thunder is your best bet.

The Haunted Mansion

This is more funny than scary. The teenagers who load you into your black "doom buggy" are dressed like morticians and never smile or meet your eyes . . . the ceiling in the portrait hall moves up . . . and the mansion is home to ravens, floating objects, swirling ghosts, glowing crystal balls, and doors that rap when there's no one there.

Final verdict: Fine for any child over 7, and most younger kids. A few parents reported that their preschoolers got nervous.

Alien Encounter

This is risky business. A shoulder harness secures you in your seat, but also holds you hostage to a variety of creepy sensations. The theater is totally darkened for long stretches of time, and the visual and sound effects were overwhelming to some kids.

Final verdict: An intense show, best suited for kids over 10.

Pirates of the Caribbean

My 4-year-old daughter grew a bit apprehensive as we wove our way through the drafty, dungeonlike queue area, but she loved the ride that followed. Although there are gunshots, skeletons, cannons, mangy-looking buccaneers, and even a brief drop over a "waterfall" in the dark, the mood is decidedly up-tempo.

Final verdict: Fine for anyone.

Splash Mountain

The atmosphere inside the mountain is so happy and kid-oriented that it's a shame the final plunge over the waterfall is so steep. This last drop gives you the feeling that you're coming out of your seat and momentarily takes your breath away. The same 44-inch height requirement applies as at Space Mountain, meaning that many children under the age of 7 technically qualify to ride, and the final verdict rests with parents.

Final verdict: The general consensus among the families we surveyed is that the ride is OK for any child 5 and over.

Note: Don't let the fact that Splash Mountain has the same height requirement as Space Mountain fool you—it's nowhere near as wild. The height requirement is partially due to the construction of the log boats, which are built with high walls to limit how much riders are soaked during the final drop. But an unhappy side effect of the log construction is that a child shorter than 44 inches wouldn't be able to see much—and might be tempted to stand.

Astro Orbiter

You can control how high your spaceship flies in this cyclic ride. A good choice for those not quite up to Space Mountain, unless you're prone to motion sickness or vertigo.

Final verdict: Fun for kids 7 to 11.

Space Mountain

It's not just the fact that this is a roller coaster, it's the fact that you plunge through utter darkness, which makes Space Mountain unique. There are lots of sharp dips with very little warning. Kids under 7 must pass the 44-inch height requirement and be accompanied by an adult. Children under 3 cannot ride.

Final verdict: Forget it for preschoolers. Kids in the 7-to-11 age range in general like Space Mountain. Teens adore it.

5

★★★★★★★★★★★★★★★★★★★

Epcot Center

EPCOT CENTER

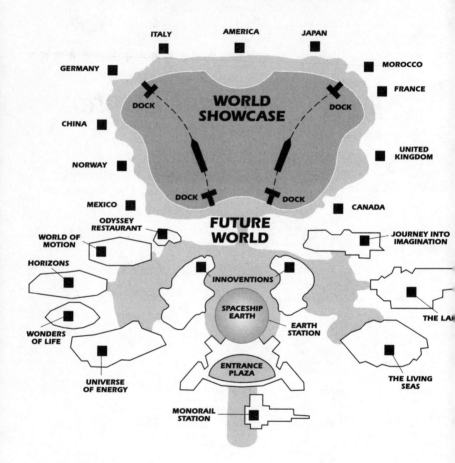

GETTING TO EPCOT CENTER

• Epcot is easy to reach by car. If you arrive early in the morning, you can park very close to the main entrance and forgo the tram ride. If you arrive a bit later, however, the trams do run quickly and efficiently. Just be sure to write down the number of the row where you parked your car.

• Many off-site hotels offer shuttle buses to Epcot. Fort Wilderness, Port Orleans, Dixie Landings, the Disney Institute Villas, Wilderness Lodge, the All-Star Resorts, Disney's Old Key West, and the Caribbean Beach Resort all run direct shuttles as well.

• If you're staying at the Polynesian, Grand Floridian, or Contemporary, it's fastest to take the monorail to the TTC and then transfer to the Epcot monorail.

• The Swan, the Dolphin, the BoardWalk, and the Yacht and Beach Clubs are connected to a special "backdoor" World Showcase entrance by bridge. Either take the shuttle tram or, if you're staying at the Yacht and Beach Clubs, simply walk over the bridge.

GETTING AROUND EPCOT CENTER

As any Disneyophile can tell you, *Epcot* is an acronym for the Experimental Prototype City of Tomorrow. But as one of the players at the Comedy Warehouse on Pleasure Island suggests, maybe Epcot really stands for Every Person Comes Out Tired.

Epcot is indeed sprawling—more than twice the size of the MK—but the FriendShips that crisscross the World Showcase Lagoon and the double-decker buses that encircle the lagoon should be viewed as rides, not transportation. Your fastest means of getting around is walking.

YOUR FIRST HOUR AT EPCOT CENTER

• As soon as you enter the main gate, veer left to rent strollers. Then, assuming it's operative, ride Spaceship Earth.

• One parent should take the kids and the camera and order breakfast at the Electric Umbrella near Innoventions. (The characters, dressed in nifty spacesuit garb, sometimes show up around 8:30 A.M. Appearances are noted on your entertainment schedule, and there's usually a sign outside the door as well.)
The other parent should stop by the WorldKey Information System inside the Earth Station under Spaceship Earth and make dinner reservations, then enter Guest Services and pick up an entertainment schedule.

• If you have time before the rest of the park opens, browse through Innoventions. It's probably a mistake to let the kids at the games—once they start, it'll be hard to get them out—but scope out the exhibits you'd like to return to later.

• After the ropes are dropped and you're allowed to enter the body of the park, veer sharply left to the Wonders of Life pavilion. Ride Body Wars first.

• After Body Wars, leave the Wonders of Life pavilion—knowing you can always return for the films and interactive exhibits later—and head for the first showing of *Honey, I Shrunk the Audience*. If Body Wars is too wild for you, go to *Honey, I Shrunk the Audience* first.

EPCOT CENTER TOURING TIPS

• In the off-season, Epcot hours are often staggered. Future World is generally open from 9 A.M. to 7 P.M., and the World Showcase from 11 A.M. to 9 P.M.

• Visit newer attractions such as *Honey, I Shrunk the Audience* and the revamped World of Motion first thing in the morning.

• Avoid the high-capacity shows such as Universe of Energy or *O Canada!* in the morning. Your time is better spent moving among the continuous-loading attractions such as Body Wars, World of Motion, Horizons, the Land pavilion, the Living Seas pavilion, and Journey Into Imagination. With the exception of *Honey, I Shrunk the Audience,* save the theater-style attractions until afternoon.

• Touring Epcot is easier if you zig when everyone else zags. During the summer and other busy times, Future World stays crowded from midmorning until late afternoon, then empties as people head toward their dinner reservations in the World Showcase. You can avoid crowds by touring Future World until midmorning, then drifting toward the World Showcase in the afternoon, where you can escape to the films and indoor exhibits during the hottest and busiest times. Then, after an early dinner, head back into Future World. Attractions such as Journey Into Imagination, Innoventions, and the Living Seas pavilion are rarely packed in the evening.

• If you are touring in the off-season and plan to spend your mornings in the MK or at MGM and your evenings at Epcot, make Epcot dinner reservations for as early as possible, leaving yourself several hours to tour after dinner.

Another alternative: If your children have had a good afternoon nap and can keep going until 10 P.M., make your dinner reservations for very late. The restaurants accept their final seating just before the park shuts down, and all the transportation stays operative for at least 90 minutes after the official park closing time. Eating late buys you maximum hours in the park, assuming your kids can handle the schedule.

• Upon entering a World Showcase pavilion that has a show or film—France, Canada, America, or China—ask the attendant how long until the show begins. If the wait is 10 minutes or less, queue up. If the wait is longer, browse the shops of the pavilion until about 10 minutes until showtime. The World Showcase theaters are large, and everyone who shows up within 10 minutes of the film's starting time will be seated.

• Most people circle the World Showcase Lagoon in a clockwise fashion, beginning with Mexico. You'll make better time if you move counterclockwise, beginning with Canada.

• Innoventions and the interactive exhibits in the Wonders of Life, Journey Into Imagination, and World of Motion pavilions are very worthwhile—and a nice break from the enforced passivity of all the rides. But do the rides first and save the interactive games for midafternoon or early evening.

• If you're not staying for IllumiNations, begin moving toward the exit while the show is in progress.

If you miss the chance to exit before the Illumi-Nations crowd or you've opted to stay for the show, don't join in the throngs that mob the exit turnstiles and shuttle buses just after the show has ended. Pick up dessert before the show and then, after IllumiNations, find a table, sit down, relax, and let the crowds pass you by. The trams and monorails will still be running long after you finish your snack, and the lines waiting for them will be shorter.

FUTURE WORLD

Future World comprises nine large pavilions, each containing at least one major attraction, and is very much like a permanent World's Fair, mixing educational opportunities with pure entertainment. Most visitors are drawn first to the rides with their spectacular special effects, but don't miss Innoventions and the chance to play with the smaller, interactive exhibits. Many of these encourage young visitors to learn while doing, and stopping to try them out helps kids avoid what one mother termed "Audio-Animatronics overload."

Sensitive to complaints that Epcot "was boring" and "never changed," Disney has made efforts to render Future World more appealing to kids. Three pavilions—Horizons, World of Motion, and Universe of Energy—have undergone substantial alterations to make the preshows and technical presentations shorter and the special effects zippier. And Innoventions is constantly changing, with new exhibits moving in and out on a regular basis.

Future World Attractions

Spaceship Earth
Few travelers, whatever their age, can remain blasé at the sight of Spaceship Earth, the most photographed and readily recognizable symbol of Epcot.

The ride inside, which coils toward the top of the 17-story geosphere, traces developments in communication from cave drawings to computers. The voice of Jeremy Irons croons in your ear as you climb past scenes of Egyptian temples, the Gutenberg press, and a performance of Oedipus Rex. Even preschoolers rated Spaceship Earth highly, probably due to the excitement of actually entering "the Big Ball" and the impressive finale, which flashes a planetarium sky above you as you swirl backward down through the darkness.

Note: If you can't ride Spaceship Earth early in the morning, save it for evening.

Global Neighborhoods is the interactive area as you exit Spaceship Earth.

The Living Seas

The Living Seas pavilion features a saltwater aquarium so enormous that Spaceship Earth could float inside it. You begin with a short film that discusses the critical role of the ocean as a source of energy, then swiftly move on to board a gondola which takes you through an underwater viewing tunnel. More than 200 varieties of marine life, including stingrays, dolphins, barracuda, sharks, and an occasional scuba-clad Mickey, swim above you.

The most enjoyable part of the attraction, however, comes after you disembark at Seabase Alpha. You can remain here as long as you choose, wandering through two levels of observation tanks that allow you to view the fishes and human divers at startlingly close quarters. (A new program allows visitors—for $125—to suit up and enter the tank with a guide.)

Note: It's easy to spend an entire afternoon at the Living Seas pavilion. But if you plan to devote a day to Sea World while in Orlando, you'll find much of the same stuff there, so hold your time at the Living Seas pavilion to a minimum.

The Land

This cheerful pavilion, sponsored by Nestle and devoted to the subject of food and how we get it, is home to three separate attractions as well as a rotating restaurant and fast-food court. Because it is the hub of so much activity, The Land pavilion is crowded from midmorning on.

Living with the Land   Visitors travel by boat past scenes of various farming environments, ending with a peek at fish farming, drip irrigation, and other innovative agricultural technologies. Perhaps because there are few special effects and no cute "tour guide" like Figment, who lives in the Journey Into Imagination pavilion next door, this attraction is less interesting to preschoolers. But, as is the case in all of Future World, the presentation moves swiftly. In short, this won't be your children's favorite attraction, but they won't complain either.

Circle of Life   This film, presented in the Harvest Theatre, graphically illustrates how we interact—both positively and negatively—with our environment. It has been revamped to make it more appealing to kids. Pumbaa and Timon from *The Lion King* are the new hosts, and the lessons on conservation are winningly presented.

Food Rocks   This funny 15-minute show features famous rock 'n' roll stars masquerading as food. The Peach Boys sing about "Good Nutrition," an eggplant is dubbed "Neil Moussaka," and the Refrigerator Police oversee "every bite you take."

Note: Both *Circle of Life* and *Food Rocks* are good choices for the most crowded times of the afternoon.

Journey Into Imagination and
Honey, I Shrunk the Audience

One of the best pavilions in Future World for young kids, the ride inside features Dreamfinder and the charming purple Figment of his imagination. Together they take you through a variety of scenes celebrating art, literature, music, and other products of human creativity. Be forewarned—there's a sudden flash of light near the end of the ride. This pavilion is sponsored by Kodak, and a wide-screen photograph of you in all your glory is waiting around the next turn.

Beside Journey Into Imagination is Epcot's new sleeper hit, the 3-D film *Honey, I Shrunk the Audience.* This show is so fun that several families reported that their kids insisted on seeing it more than once. Based on the popular movie series, the presentation begins as Dr. Wayne Szalinski is about to pick up the award for Inventor of the Year. The scene quickly dissolves into mayhem as the audience is accidentally "shrunk," one son's pet snake gets loose, and the other's pet mouse is reproduced 999 times. Although the 3-D images are dazzling, the effects go far beyond the visual—you actually feel the "mice" running up your legs, and the kid-pleasing, dog-sneezing finale is not to be missed.

After you disembark from Journey Into Imagination a huge digital clock tells you how many minutes until the next presentation of *Honey, I Shrunk the Audience.* While you wait, it's fun to explore the Image Works, a series of hands-on exhibits such as the Magic Palette, with an electronic paintbrush, or Stepping Tones, where kids can create music by jumping into different-colored puddles of light. Or volunteers may get the chance to act as characters in a video short story told by the Dreamfinder himself: Five or six children se- lected from the crowd are "inserted" into the back- ground of a space adventure, and by following such simple commands as "jump" or "run in place," they ap- pear to be interacting with the figures on-screen. Image Works is especially fun from 6 P.M. on, when the crowds disperse and kids don't have to wait in line to try everything out.

As you leave the Journey Into Imagination pavilion, take time to check out Splashtacular, a fountain show full of special effects.

Note: If your kids are freaked out by the special ef- fects in *Honey, I Shrunk the Audience,* tell them to lift their legs off the floor and take off the 3-D glasses. The effects are brief, and they can put the glasses back on and resume sitting normally within a minute or two.

World of Motion

This ride is in the process of being completely re- vamped, moving from an Audio-Animatronic survey of the history of transportation to a race car simulation ride. As with Epcot's other simulation ride, Body Wars, expect realistic effects that may not be appropriate for younger kids or anyone prone to motion sickness. When the ride reopens, it will bring a welcome rush of adrenaline to the rather sedate Future World and is bound to be popular with kids over 7.

Note: New rides get lots of press and draw big crowds. Go early . . . or during IllumiNations.

Horizons

How will the average family live in the future? General Electric takes riders into the next century, where robots clean house, families "visit" via holographic telephone, and cities flourish on the ocean floor. Needless to say, Disney's predictions for the year 2020 are all sunny, and this ride has also been recently revamped to make the effects zippier.

Note: Horizons loads fast and is rarely too crowded. A good choice for when the World of Motion and Wonders of Life pavilions next door are swamped.

Wonders of Life

Devoted to celebrating the human body, the Wonders of Life pavilion resembles a brightly colored street fair full of hands-on exhibits. You can check out your health profile via computer, get advice on your tennis or golf swing, and test your endurance on a motorized bike. Kids enjoy the film *Goofy About Health,* and the Sensory Funhouse. (Despite the provocative name, this exhibit is devoted to only the most wholesome of tactile sensations.) Like The Land pavilion, the Wonders of Life pavilion houses three major attractions and is crowded by 11 A.M.

Body Wars   As close as Epcot comes to a pure thrill ride, Body Wars incorporates the same flight-simulation technology found at MGM's Star Tours to take riders on a turbulent high-speed chase through the human body. After being miniaturized to the size of a pinhead and injected into a patient, the crew is briefed to expect a routine medical mission for the purpose of removing a splinter from the "safe zone just under the skin." But when shapely Dr. Lair is sucked into a capillary, your crew is off on a rescue chase through the heart, lungs, and brain.

No expectant mothers or kids under 3 are allowed to board, and Body Wars does indeed have its queasy moments, due more to the accuracy of flight-simulation technology—and perhaps the subject matter—than the bouncing of the ship. Those prone to motion sickness should skip the trip, but others will enjoy it.

Note: If you have any doubts about whether your child can handle it, ask attendants to help you do a "baby swap."

The Making of Me This 15-minute film provides a fetus-eye view of conception, gestation, and birth. Martin Short travels back in time to show us his own parents as babies, then chronicles how they met and ultimately produced him. (One glaring anachronism: Martin must have been the only kid born in America in the '50s who was delivered through Lamaze.) Although the film is direct and unflinching, it's appropriate for any age.

The line for the film is long, so let one parent queue up while the other takes the kids around to some of the interactive exhibits. Coach's Corner, which gives visitors a chance to have their golf, tennis, or baseball swing videotaped, replayed in slo-mo, and then analyzed by Nancy Lopez, Chris Evert, or Gary Carter, is especially fun.

Cranium Command One of the funniest presentations at Epcot, Cranium Command mixes Audio-Animatronics with film. General Knowledge taps an unfortunate recruit, Fuzzy, to pilot "the most unstable craft in the fleet"—the brain of a 12-year-old boy. If he fails in his mission, Fuzzy will be demoted to flying the brain of a chicken or, worse, a talk-show host. Fuzzy tries to guide his boy through a typical day of junior high school without overloading his system—which isn't easy, especially when the body parts are played by this cast: Charles Grodin as the right brain, Jon Lovitz as the left brain, Hans and Franz from "Saturday Night Live" pumping it up in the role of the heart, Norm from

"Cheers" as the stomach, and, in a particularly convincing performance, Bobcat Goldthwait as adrenaline.

Note: Ride Body Wars early, then return later in the day to see Cranium Command and *The Making of Me.*

Universe of Energy

This technologically complex presentation can be enjoyed by any age on any level. Kids are dazzled by the dinosaurs, and parents leave the pavilion muttering, "How did they do that?"

A digital clock at the entryway keeps you posted on how much longer until the show begins. Don't file in until the wait is 10 minutes or less; this is a nearly 30-minute presentation, and there is no point in wearing the kids out before you begin.

Note: Disney has recently shortened both the pre-show and the postshow, making them "newer, hipper, and with more famous faces."

The Disney twist comes when the 97-seat theater begins to break apart in sections, which align themselves in sequence and move toward a curtain. Your theater has become your train, and the curtain slowly lifts to reveal an Audio-Animatronics version of the film you've just viewed. The air reeks of sulfur, as it presumably did during the prehistoric era, the light is eerily blue, and all around you are those darn dinosaurs, the largest Disney robots ever created—and unnervingly authentic. The ride concludes with a final film, after your train has once again metamorphosed into a theater. Most amazing of all, you learn that your traveling train has been partially fueled by the solar panels on top of the Universe of Energy pavilion; you've been, as they say, "riding on sunshine."

Note: Despite its proximity to the front gate, this is not a good choice for the morning; save it for afternoon or early evening, when you'll welcome the chance to sit for a half hour. Also, the Universe of Energy seats a lot of people at one time, meaning that lines form and dissipate quickly. If the line looks prohibitive, check out nearby pavilions and return in 30 minutes. You may be able to walk right in.

Innoventions

Innoventions is the arcade of the future, where you can try out new Sega Genesis games before they hit the market, fly on a virtual-reality magic carpet, and play with beyond-state-of-the-art technology such as video controller chairs and computers that translate voice dictation directly into the printed word.

Innoventions is a showcase for such corporations as Apple, IBM, Motorola, Sega, and AT&T. The products displayed either have just come on the market or are straight from the inventor and not yet available. Exhibits range from toilets that clean themselves to a stationary bike with a Nintendo attached—the idea is that you'll become so absorbed in the game that you won't notice how hard you're pedaling.

The most popular, by far, are the virtual-reality games; people line up for five minutes on a machine, and many become so hooked that they reenter the line over and over for the chance to be a cue ball in a pool game, a driver in the Indy 500, or to visit the great museums of the world. (Observers can see what the player sees on an overhead screen.) Cast members are quick to point out that these much-maligned games are what pushed the envelope in computer technology, especially in the area of graphics. Preteens and teens will obviously be dazzled, but there are Pico computer games for preschoolers as well.

If you plan to spend much time in Innoventions, pick up a map as you enter. The film *Bill Nye, the Science*

Guy, in Innoventions East, is also a good intro to what's available, and well-informed cast members are on hand to answer questions or help you get the hang of the games and experiments. Exhibits change frequently, keeping things fresh.

If the blinking and beeping become too overwhelming, parents can take a break outside at the nearby Expresso and Pastry Cafe. The Fountain of Nations between Innoventions East and West—so named because it contains water from all the countries of the World Showcase—puts on a lovely evening show.

Note: Innoventions becomes unbearably crowded midmorning, as people enter the Epcot gates and make a dash for the first thing they see. Visit in late afternoon or during IllumiNations.

WORLD SHOWCASE

Pretty by day and gorgeous by night, the World Showcase comprises the pavilions of eleven nations—Mexico, Norway, China, Germany, Italy, America, Japan, Morocco, France, the United Kingdom, and Canada—stretching around a large lagoon. Some of the pavilions have full-scale attractions, listed as follows; others have only shops and restaurants. Demonstrations, music, and shows are scheduled throughout the day, and the characters, dressed in culturally correct garb, frequently appear in the afternoon.

Most important from an educational and cultural perspective, each pavilion is staffed by citizens of the country it represents. Disney goes to great pains to recruit, relocate, and, if necessary, teach English to the shopkeepers and waiters you see in these pavilions, bringing them to Orlando for a year and housing them with the representatives from the other World Showcase nations. It's a cultural exchange program on the highest level. (One Norwegian guide told me her roommates were from China, Mexico, and Canada.)

These young men and women save the World Showcase from being merely touristy, add an air of authenticity to every aspect of the experience, and provide your kids with the chance to rub elbows, however briefly, with other cultures. So even if pavilions such as Morocco or Japan don't have a ride or film, don't rush past them: Stop for a honeyed pastry or an origami demonstration and chat with the young person behind the counter.

World Showcase Attractions

O Canada!

This 20-minute CircleVision 360 film is gorgeous, stirring—and impossible to view with kids under 6. In order to enjoy the effect of the circular screen, guests are required to stand during the presentation, and strollers are not allowed into the theater. This means babies and toddlers must be held, and preschoolers, who can't see anything in a room of standing adults, often clamor to be lifted up as well. So we regretfully suggest that families with young kids pass up this presentation, as well as the equally lovely *Wonders of China: Land of Beauty, Land of Time*. Possible solution: If you're dining at Epcot during your parents' night out, this would be a good time to take in those World Showcase attractions that just aren't oriented toward kids.

Impressions de France

What a difference a seat makes! Like all the Epcot films, *Impressions de France* is exceedingly well done, with lush music and a 200-degree wide-screen feel. It's fairly easy to get in, even in the afternoon, and no one minds if babies take a little nap.

The American Adventure

This multimedia presentation, combining Audio-Animatronic figures with film, is popular with all age groups. The technological highlight of the show comes when the Ben Franklin robot actually walks upstairs to visit Thomas Jefferson, but the entire 30-minute presentation is packed with elaborate sets that rise from the stage, film montages, moving music, and painless history lessons.

Note: The America pavilion becomes quite crowded in the afternoon, but since it's located at the exact midpoint of the World Showcase Lagoon, it's impractical to skip it and work your way back later. If you're faced with a half hour wait, enjoy the excellent Voices of Liberty preshow or have a snack at the Liberty Inn next door.

Wonders of China

See the previous listing for *O Canada!*

Maelstrom

This Norwegian boat ride is a hit with kids. Your Viking ship sails through fjords and storms, over waterfalls, and past a threatening three-headed troll . . . all within four minutes. Riders disembark in a North Sea coastal village, where a short film is presented. The Norway pavilion is the newest of the World Showcase nations and can draw large crowds. Ride Maelstrom before 11 A.M. or just before park closing, when most people have lined up to await IllumiNations.

El Rio del Tiempo: The River of Time
There's rarely a wait at this charming boat ride, located inside the romantic Mexico pavilion. Reminiscent of It's a Small World in the MK, El Rio del Tiempo is especially appealing to younger riders.

GENERAL INFORMATION ON EPCOT CENTER RESTAURANTS

Among the families we surveyed, there was a great difference of opinion as to which Epcot restaurants are best. "We loved Alfredo's," writes one family, "but the Coral Reef was a big disappointment. It was overpriced, and you can get the same view for free upstairs at the Living Seas." "The Coral Reef was our absolute favorite," wrote another family. "Alfredo's, on the other hand, is a waste of time." (Alfredo di Roma and the Coral Reef are the most expensive, most popular—and most controversial—Epcot eateries. Perhaps because reservations are so hard to come by, diners enter with exalted expectations and leave either profoundly disappointed or convinced they've had a mountaintop experience.)

The following are some general tips for the obligatory Epcot dining experience.

• If you are staying on-site, you can make reservations for both dinner and lunch up to three days in advance through Guest Services in your hotel, and such foresight may be necessary if you're aiming to get into the Coral Reef on a Friday night in July. If you're not staying on-site, make your reservations first thing in the morning at the WorldKey Information System inside the Earth Station under Spaceship Earth. Visitors who have no reservations sometimes get seated by simply showing up at the restaurant door, especially if they try a large restaurant, such as the Biergarten, or eat dinner very early.

• If you'd like to try several Epcot restaurants, remember that lunchtime selections are just as impressive as dinner, and the fare is much cheaper.

Many Epcot restaurants also offer an Early Value Meal between 4:30 and 6 P.M. The meal includes an appetizer, entrée, dessert, and beverage for about $15, an excellent deal at a restaurant such as Chefs de France where a three-course dinner would more typically run about $35.

• Kids are welcome at any Epcot eatery, although some are more entertaining for youngsters than others. (See the following section for details.) High chairs, booster seats, and kiddie menus are universally available.

The World Showcase restaurants offer "Mickey's Child Deals" for about $4. The food is a nod to the country whose cuisine is being represented, i.e., skewered chicken in Morocco and fish and chips in the United Kingdom. But the entrées are smaller, less spicy, and look enough like chicken nuggets and fish sticks that the kids will eat them.

• Casual attire is OK anywhere in the park. It may seem strange to eat oysters with champagne sauce while wearing a Goofy sweatshirt, but you'll get used to it.

• The Epcot restaurants take reservations seriously. If you show up at Mitsukoshi at 12:45 for a 12:30 reservation, expect to be told "sayonara."

• Be careful when booking for France, which is home to two sit-down restaurants: Chefs de France, which is streetfront, and Le Bistro de Paris upstairs. Many visitors get these confused and risk losing their reservations by showing up at the wrong place.

• Be bold. Your hometown probably has good Chinese and Italian restaurants, but how often do you get to sample Norwegian or Moroccan food?

• The Epcot dining experience doesn't come cheap. Dinner for a family of four will run about $60 without drinks or wine. But as throughout WDW, portions are large, even on items ordered from the kiddie menu. Two children can easily share an entrée; for that matter, so can two adults.

• If you want to save both time and money, stick to the fast-food places for meals—but make a reservation at a sit-down restaurant for a truly off time, say 4 P.M. or 10 P.M., and just have dessert. You can soak up the ambience for an investment of 30 minutes and 10 bucks.

FULL-SERVICE RESTAURANTS AT EPCOT CENTER

How much is this place going to cost? Is the service so slow we'll miss IllumiNations? Is it hard to get reservations? Is there anything to keep the kids entertained while the adults sip their sake? Read on for an overview of the suitability of the full-service restaurants for kids, and keep in mind that if you have fussy eaters in the family, all the full-service restaurants post menus outside their doors.

If you wish to cut the cost of Epcot dining, either go at lunch or during the Early Value Meal hours, leave off wine or alcohol, and choose a restaurant, such as the Nine Dragons in China, where patrons are encouraged to share entrées.

Note: See Section 8, "Disney World After Dark," for more information on the most romantic and adult-oriented of the Epcot restaurants.

Chefs de France
France

Booking: Difficult. *Suitability for kids:* Moderate. It's fun to watch the crowds go by, but the tables are close and the waiters move at quite a clip, so there is no place for children to stand and stretch their legs. Older kids might be wowed by the atmosphere and the chance to order a *croquette de boeuf en brioche,* surely the classiest hamburger they'll ever wolf down.

Bistro de Paris
France

Booking: Difficult. *Suitability for kids:* Low. This is one of the more romantic (and expensive) Epcot restaurants, with dim lighting and leisurely service. Try it on the night you leave the kids back at the Mouseketeer Club.

Rose and Crown Pub and Dining Room
United Kingdom

Booking: Easy. *Suitability for kids:* High, especially if you eat outside and can watch the FriendShips go by on the lagoon. Pub atmosphere, charming service, mediocre food.

Mitsukoshi
Japan

Booking: Easy. *Suitability for kids:* High. Diners sit at large common tables while chefs slice and dice in a flamboyant fashion. If there's a Benihana in your hometown, you get the idea. The night we visited, ladies were circulating among the tables, making origami souvenirs for the kids.

L'Originale Alfredo's di Roma
Italy

Booking: Difficult. *Suitability for kids:* Moderate. Most children like Italian food, and the kiddie menu is well conceived, but the restaurant is very crowded and service is slow.

Marrakesh
Morocco

Booking: Easy. *Suitability for kids:* Moderate. Exotic surroundings, and kids enjoy the belly dancers. The unfamiliarity of the food may pose a problem, but the children's portions are not as spicy as those served to the adults, so if the kids can be persuaded to give it a try, they'll find that roasted chicken tastes pretty much the same the world over.

Nine Dragons Restaurant
China

Booking: Easy. *Suitability for kids:* Moderate. The service is fast, and the staff is quite happy to accommodate special requests, as in, "Can you hold the sweet-and-sour sauce on the sweet-and-sour chicken?" The ambitious menu here extends far beyond the typical Chinese fare at your favorite take-out place back home. Experimenting with an unknown dish such as red bean ice cream can lead to some very pleasant surprises.

San Angel Inn Restaurante
Mexico

Booking: Fairly difficult at lunch. *Suitability for kids:* High. The service is swift and friendly, and kids can browse among the market stalls of the Mexico pavilion or ride El Rio del Tiempo while waiting for the food. One of the best bets at Epcot.

Biergarten
Germany

Booking: Easy. *Suitability for kids:* High. There's plenty of room to move about, as well as a rousing, noisy atmosphere and entertainment in the form of yodelers and an oom-pah-pah band.

Akershus
Norway

Booking: Moderate. *Suitability for kids:* Moderate. There's a buffet, so you get your food fast and have the chance to see things before you make a selection. But most of the food is apt to be unfamiliar to the kids, and there's a lot of fish, so picky eaters may rebel. This is a fine spot for hearty eaters, because you can load up at the hot-and-cold buffet tables. Also a good chance to sample a variety of unusual dishes.

Le Cellier
Canada

Booking: Doesn't apply—Le Cellier is a cafeteria and takes no reservations. *Suitability for kids:* High. The menu features food hearty enough to please a lumberjack—pork pie, meatball stew, cheddar cheese soup, and, in case your blood sugar is a little low from too much touring, maple-syrup pie. If the kids rebel against anything too exotic, but the parents can't face another burger, head for the neutral territory of the Canada cafeteria.

The Garden Grille Room
Land pavilion

Booking: Easy. *Suitability for kids:* High. Easily recognizable American dishes served family style, with some of the food grown in the greenhouses downstairs.

The booths are large, which lets you stretch out, and the restaurant rotates, allowing diners to observe scenes from the Living with the Land boat ride below. Best of all, the characters, dressed in gingham and dungarees, circulate among the diners, and everyone is given a free straw hat to complete the down-home theme.

The Coral Reef Restaurant
Living Seas pavilion

Booking: **Extremely difficult.** *Suitability for kids:* **High.** One whole wall is glass, giving diners an unparalleled view of the Living Seas tank, and because the restaurant is arranged in tiers, every table has a good view of the fish. The character breakfast here is very popular. Sometimes Mickey, in scuba gear, swims by in the tank, which is guaranteed to bring down the house.

DECENT FAST-FOOD PLACES AT EPCOT CENTER

Fast food is a somewhat relative term at Epcot, where long lines are the norm during peak dining hours. But the choices are far more varied and interesting than those in the Magic Kingdom. And the views are so charming—especially at the places in the Mexico, Japan, and France pavilions—that Epcot blurs the distinction between fast food and fine dining.

• The skewered chicken and beef at the **Yakitori House** in Japan are excellent, and the little courtyard outside gives the feel of a Japanese tea garden.

Note: As is the case in many of the World Showcase eateries, a child's combination plate is more than adequate for an adult, especially if you'll be snacking in a couple of hours.

- The **Cantina de San Angel** in Mexico serves tortillas and tostadas at tables clustered around the lagoon.

- You'll find open-faced salmon or ham sandwiches and unusual pastries at **Kringla Bakeri og Kafe** in Norway.

- If your kids are suffering hamburger withdrawal, there's always the **Liberty Inn** at the America pavilion, the **Odyssey Restaurant** on the bridge connecting Future World to the World Showcase, or the **Electric Umbrella** near Innoventions.

- Pizza is available in the **Pasta Piazza** near Innoventions.

- Simply want a snack? You can't beat the **Boulangerie Patisserie** in France for pastries. The **Odyssey Restaurant** offers at least five choices of homemade pie daily, such as Florida key lime or chocolate French silk. (During the on-season, the characters sometimes appear at the Odyssey in midafternoon.)

- If you find yourself in Future World at lunchtime, or your party can't agree on a restaurant, visit **Sunshine Season** in the Land pavilion. The food court here features plenty of choices, including clam chowder, quiche, barbecue, stuffed potatoes, scooped-out pineapples filled with fruit salad, and killer chocolate-chip cookies.

- If it's raining, you'll probably want to avoid the outdoor tables of many of the fast-food places, so head for Sunshine Season in the Land, the Odyssey Restaurant on the bridge connecting Future World to the World Showcase, or either the Electric Umbrella or Pasta Piazza, both located near Innoventions.

• **La Maison du Vin** offers wine tastings throughout the afternoon and evenings. The fee is minimal, and you get to keep the souvenir glass. If you find something you like, the bottles can be sent to Package PickUp for you to retrieve as you exit the park, or, if you're staying on-site, delivered directly to your room.

EPCOT CENTER EXTRAS

Special Shows

• Singers, dancers, jugglers, and artisans from around the globe perform daily throughout the World Showcase. Most of these presentations (which are detailed in the daily entertainment guide) are not especially oriented toward children—although kids over 7 will catch the humor of the World Showcase Players, who put on wacky farces with lots of audience participation.

• Sometimes very special performers, such as Chinese acrobats or stars of the Moscow Circus, are showcased in Future World. These acts draw high ratings from kids in every age group.

• For the time being, Barbie is cruising Epcot in her Pepto Bismol–pink limo and stopping for photos and autographs. Check your entertainment schedule for times and places, then show up at least 10 minutes early, 15 minutes during the on-season.

IllumiNations

This display of laser technology, fireworks, syncopated fountains, and classical music is a real-life *Fantasia* and an unqualified WDW classic. Very popular, very crowded, and a perfect way to end an Epcot day, Illumi-Nations takes place on the World Showcase Lagoon, and the performance coincides with the park closing time. Try to watch from the Mexico or Canada pavilion, so you'll be able to beat most of the crowd to the exits afterward. (If you're staying at the Swan, Dolphin, or Yacht and Beach Clubs and thus leaving via the "back door," try the benches in the America or Italy pavilion.)

Shopping

You'll see things at Epcot that aren't available any-where else in WDW: German wines, Chinese robes, an entire shop devoted to English teas, and a collection of piñatas that would put any Mexican marketplace to shame—all within strolling distance of each other. You don't want to end up carrying those hand-knit Norwe-gian sweaters and Venetian crystal around the park with you, however, so if you make major purchases, ei-ther have them sent to Package PickUp near the front gate, or, if you're staying on-site, have them delivered to your hotel.

AFTERNOON RESTING PLACES AT EPCOT CENTER

- Universe of Energy
- *Circle of Life* or *Food Rocks* in the Land pavilion
- *Honey, I Shrunk the Audience*
- *The Making of Me* in the Wonders of Life pavilion
- The American Adventure
- *Impressions de France*

- Any of the restaurants, since the service is leisurely at lunchtime

BEST RESTROOM LOCATIONS AT EPCOT CENTER

• The restrooms within the Future World pavilions are always crowded, and those around Innoventions aren't much better. But there are places where you can take a relatively quick potty break:

- The Odyssey Restaurant (Baby Services is also located here, so you can take care of everyone's needs with one stop.)
- The restroom behind Kringla Bakeri og Kafe in the Norway pavilion.
- Between the Morocco and France pavilions.
- Near the Group Sales Booth in the Entrance Plaza (near the monorail—a good place to stop as you exit the park).
- Within Future World, the restroom near the Garden Grille Room is your best bet. In fact, many of the sit-down restaurants have their own restrooms, which are less crowded.

THE EPCOT DON'T-MISS LIST

- Spaceship Earth
- Body Wars and Cranium Command in the Wonders of Life pavilion
- Universe of Energy
- World of Motion

- *Honey, I Shrunk the Audience* in the Journey Into Imagination pavilion
- Journey Into Imagination
- The Living Seas pavilion (if you're not touring Sea World later in the week)
- The American Adventure in the America pavilion
- Maelstrom in the Norway pavilion
- IllumiNations
- Innoventions

THE EPCOT WORTH-YOUR-WHILE LIST

- *The Making of Me* in the Wonders of Life pavilion
- Living with the Land in the Land pavilion
- Horizons
- Image Works in the Journey Into Imagination pavilion
- El Rio del Tiempo in the Mexico pavilion
- *Wonders of China* in the China pavilion
- *O Canada!* in the Canada pavilion
- *Food Rocks* in the Land pavilion
- *Impressions de France* in the France pavilion

THE SCARE FACTOR AT EPCOT CENTER

Maelstrom in Norway

This ride sounds terrifying: You encounter a three-headed troll, become caught in a North Seas storm, and narrowly miss going over a waterfall backward. The reality is much more tame than the description. Kids seem especially enchanted by the fact that you ride in Viking ships, and the much-touted "backward plunge over a waterfall" is so subtle that passengers in the front of the boat are not even aware of the impending danger.

Final verdict: Fine for all.

Journey Into Imagination

This attraction, while one of the more child-oriented in Future World, does have a dark segment that explores the world of mystery.

Final verdict: Most kids adore Figment and the peppy theme song, but if one of yours is a bit put off, one parent could always wait with him in Image Works while the rest of the family rides.

Universe of Energy

Again, preschoolers have a range of reactions. The dinosaurs are extremely real-looking, and some of them bend fairly low over your passing theater car, dripping vines from their mouths. Most kids are such dinosaur junkies that they scream only when it's time to get off, but some children are genuinely frightened.

Final verdict: Probably fine for everyone, unless you have a very young child who has trouble distinguishing reality from illusion.

Body Wars in the Wonders of Life

The Disney PR people must love the word *plunge,* for this ride too is described as "plunging through the human immune system as you dodge blood cells and antibodies at breakneck speed in a race against attacking organisms that threaten to destroy your craft and you!" Makes you breathless just to read it!

Final verdict: Body Wars was rated highly among families responding to the survey—although a few people did mention that the visual effects gave them motion sickness, and a few others were put off by the general theme of the ride. ("All that blood," moaned one father.) In general, the ride should be fine for kids over 7, but if you have doubts about whether your child is up to it, use the "baby swap" method with one parent riding first while the other waits with the child. If the first parent feels that the child can handle the ride, the second parent and child can enter just after him. If he feels it was a bit much, the second parent can pass the child through and then ride alone.

Honey, I Shrunk the Audience

This one seems to gross-out more parents than kids. There is the mice-running-up-your-legs effect and the larger-than-life snake, but most kids were very enthusiastic about this show.

Final verdict: Fine for everyone, and one of the more kid-pleasing attractions in all of Epcot. If your child does happen to be shaken by the special effects, have him take off the 3-D glasses and sit in your lap. That way he won't see the images clearly and won't feel the tactile sensations.

6

★★★★★★★★★★★★★★★★★★★★★★

Disney–MGM
Studios
Theme Park

DISNEY–MGM STUDIOS

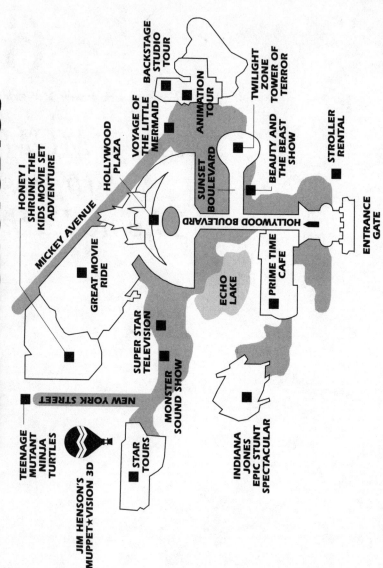

TEENAGE MUTANT NINJA TURTLES

JIM HENSON'S MUPPET★VISION 3D

STAR TOURS

NEW YORK STREET

HONEY I SHRUNK THE KIDS MOVIE SET ADVENTURE

MICKEY AVENUE

HOLLYWOOD PLAZA

GREAT MOVIE RIDE

SUPER STAR TELEVISION

MONSTER SOUND SHOW

INDIANA JONES EPIC STUNT SPECTACULAR

VOYAGE OF THE LITTLE MERMAID

BACKSTAGE STUDIO TOUR

ANIMATION TOUR

SUNSET BOULEVARD

BEAUTY AND THE BEAST SHOW

TWILIGHT ZONE TOWER OF TERROR

STROLLER RENTAL

ECHO LAKE

PRIME TIME CAFE

HOLLYWOOD BOULEVARD

ENTRANCE GATE

GETTING TO THE DISNEY–MGM STUDIOS THEME PARK

Compared to the MK, getting to MGM is a snap.

• Shuttle buses run approximately every 15 minutes from the Ticket and Transportation Center (TTC), Epcot, and all on-site hotels.

• If you're staying off-site and have a car, note that the MGM parking lot is small. If you get there at opening time, you can forgo the parking lot tram and walk to the front gate.

• If you're staying at the Swan, Dolphin, Board-Walk, or Yacht and Beach Clubs, you're a 10-minute water-taxi ride from the MGM gates.

YOUR FIRST HOUR AT MGM

• Once you're through the gate, one parent can handle stroller rental at Oscar's Super Service Station while the other picks up a map/entertainment schedule at Guest Services or Crossroads of the World.

Note: Unlike those at Epcot and the MK, MGM strollers are the lightweight "umbrella" type and are easy to load onto the Backstage Studio Tour tram.

• If your kids are old enough and bold enough for a big-deal ride, go straight to the Twilight Zone Tower of Terror on Sunset Boulevard.

Younger kids? If an early show of the wildly popular Voyage of the Little Mermaid is scheduled, you should head there the minute you enter the gate. Your entertainment schedule will tell you if an 8:30 or 9 A.M. show is planned.

• Pause at the Hollywood Junction Red Car Station, where Sunset Boulevard meets Hollywood Boulevard, to make reservations for either the SciFi Drive-In or the 50's Prime Time Cafe.

Note: These two popular eateries are often closed to reservations within 15 minutes of the park opening. If you're not staying on-site and are thus unable to make your reservations by phone, it is imperative that you make them first thing in the morning at the restaurant reservation booth, where sample menus for all MGM restaurants are on hand.

• Board the Great Movie Ride.

• Board Star Tours.

• If you haven't had breakfast, check out the pastries at Starring Rolls.

MGM TOURING TIPS

• With the exception of Voyage of the Little Mermaid, save theater-style presentations such as SuperStar Television, the Indiana Jones Epic Stunt Spectacular, the Hunchback of Notre Dame Stage Show, and the Monster Sound Show for afternoon or evening. Tour continuous-loading attractions such as the Twilight Zone Tower of Terror, the Great Movie Ride, and Star Tours early in the day.

• MGM is the park where the newer Disney films are showcased, so parades and shows are constantly evolving. The *Aladdin* parade makes way for the *Toy Story* parade, *Pocahontas* leaves the Backlot Theater and *The Hunchback of Notre Dame* moves in, and so on. Consult your entertainment schedule and maps for the latest offerings.

- Save the tours for after lunch or early evening.

- During peak seasons, the Disney people post a gigantic blackboard at the end of Hollywood Boulevard to keep visitors updated on approximate waiting times at various attractions. Consult it whenever you're in doubt about what to do next.

Note: If you're at MGM very early as a result of the "Surprise Mornings" program, the blackboard will also inform you as to which attractions are operative; the whole park doesn't open early for the surprise mornings, but at least six major attractions will be ready to ride.

- Your entertainment schedule not only provides showtimes, but also gives you information on the Celebrity of the Day and what shows are filming. If any Disney Channel shows are in production on the day you visit, Guest Services can tell you how to become a member of the studio audience.

Note: Many of the shows require that audience members be 12 years old, and for some shows, 17.

- MGM is small and easily crisscrossed, so don't feel obligated to tour attractions in any particular geographic sequence. Those 4- and 5-year-olds who would need a stroller in the MK or at Epcot can do without one here.

- If you miss an attraction like the popular Indiana Jones Epic Stunt Spectacular in the afternoon, return in the evening. It's also easier to get tapped for SuperStar Television at one of the less-crowded evening shows.

- Also, after the dinner hour, popular restaurants such as the SciFi Drive-In sometimes will accept walk-ins, especially if you're just dropping by for dessert. As at the other theme parks, the restaurants are still serving food after the park officially closes, so if you

didn't make it into one of the big-deal restaurants earlier in the day, now's your chance.

MGM ATTRACTIONS

Twilight Zone Tower of Terror

The Twilight Zone Tower of Terror combines the spooky
ambience of a decaying, cobwebby 1930s-style Hollywood hotel with sheer thrills. The clever preshow, for
which Disney spliced together clips from the old TV series in order to allow the long-deceased Rod Serling to
narrate the story, invites you to enter an episode of
"The Twilight Zone." The story begins on Halloween
evening, 1939, when five people boarded the hotel elevator: a movie star and starlet, a child actress and her
nanny, and the bellboy. The hotel was struck by lightning, the elevator dropped, and the five passengers
were permanently transported into the Twilight Zone.
The next morning, the indicator on the elevator was
found pointing to the nonexistent 13th floor, and the
hotel has stood abandoned ever since.

After watching the preshow, guests are directed to a
cage "freight" elevator, which ascends—you guessed
it—13 stories. You are seated with a lap-bar, and each
elevator holds about 20 people. On the way up, the elevator stops to reveal a hallway that literally vanishes
before your eyes.

But it's the second stop that will get you: The elevator
moves forward past a series of holographic images, the
doors eventually opening onto a panoramic view of the
park from more than 150 feet in the air. Then you free-
fall; it takes only two seconds to hit the bottom, but it's a
squealer. The fall can be computer-programmed in several different ways, ranging from a teasing bungee-style

drop, in which you descend partially and are then re-lifted to a no-holds-barred plunge. Disney changes the program every two weeks or so to keep even Tower veterans on their toes.

MGM's last few offerings have been geared toward kids, and the Twilight Zone Tower of Terror is a clear effort to draw the interest of the preteens and teens in the family. As with all new attractions, it can be crowded, but the line moves swiftly for this 10-minute ride. If you miss it in the morning, return in the evening for an even more intense experience.

The height requirement is 44 inches, and the Tower is entirely too much for kids under 5.

The Great Movie Ride

Housed in the Chinese Theater at the end of Hollywood Boulevard, the Great Movie Ride debuted as an instant classic. Disney's largest ride-through attraction, it loads steadily and fairly swiftly, but this 25-minute ride draws large crowds and is best toured either early in the morning or in the last hour before the park closes.

Note: Most of the waiting area is inside the Chinese Theater; if you see a line outside, rest assured there are hundreds more tourists waiting inside, and skip the attraction for the time being.

Each tram holds approximately 30 riders, and your tour guide provides an amusing spiel as you glide past soundstage sets from *Casablanca, Alien, The Wizard of Oz,* and other great films. The Audio-Animatronic figures of Gene Kelly, Julie Andrews, and Clint Eastwood are among Disney's best.

Things suddenly turn ugly as your car stalls and the movie scenes come to life. Depending upon which car you've boarded, you're about to be overrun by either a gangster on the lam from James Cagney or a desperado trying to escape John Wayne. Your tour guide may be gunned down or your tram taken hostage, but don't fret too much. In a later scene, drawn from *Indiana Jones and the Temple of Doom,* expect another stunning twist of fortune—just in time to reestablish justice and guarantee a happy ending.

Star Tours

Motion-simulation technology and a slightly jostling cabin combine to produce the real feel of flight in Star Tours, the MGM version of the highly acclaimed Disneyland ride. With the hapless Captain Rex at the helm, your crew is off for what is promised to be a routine mission to the Moon of Endor. But if you think this mission is going to be routine, you don't know diddly about Disney. "Don't worry if this is your first flight," Rex comforts visitors as they board. "It's my first one, too." One wrong turn later and you're ripping through the fabric of space at hyperspeed, headed toward combat with the dreaded Death Star.

George Lucas served as creative consultant, and the ride echoes the charming as well as the terrifying elements of his *Star Wars* series. The chatter of R2D2, C3PO, and assorted droids make even the queues enjoyable. Star Tours is the best of both worlds, with visual effects so convincing you'll clutch your arm rails, but actual rumbles so mild that only the youngest children are eliminated as potential crew members.

Note: As in Body Wars at Epcot, Disney attendants are happy to help families traveling with children under 3 break up their party so that everyone except the baby gets to ride.

Like the Twilight Zone Tower of Terror, this ride takes only 10 minutes from start to finish, so the lines move at an agreeable pace. It's still better to ride in the morning if you can.

SuperStar Television

Want to belly up to the bar at "Cheers"? Ride the range with the Cartwrights? Be discovered by Ed Sullivan or chat with Carson? You get your chance at the highly inventive SuperStar Television, where special effects integrate the actions of audience volunteers with footage from well-known TV shows.

To volunteer your services as an actor, show up at the preshow holding area about 20 minutes before the stated performance time. (Showtimes for Super-Star Television, the Monster Sound Show, and the Indiana Jones Epic Stunt Spectacular vary from day to day, so consult your trusty entertainment schedule.) If your kids would like to join the cast of "Gilligan's Island" or be interviewed by Howard Cosell, there's no secret to getting selected. Work your way to the front of the crowd and shamelessly wave your arms. They aren't looking for shy people here, and kids tapped to perform remembered SuperStar Television as the highlight of their MGM day. If you aren't chosen in one casting section, you can always exit the holding area without seeing the show and try again later.

Once you are selected, you'll be taken backstage for costuming and a brief rehearsal while the rest of the gang files into the 1,000-seat theater. Most volunteers respond ably, and the resulting 30-minute show is usually quite funny. Because of the large seating area, SuperStar Television is a good choice for midafternoon, but if you don't catch it then, try the evening shows, which are never crowded.

The Monster Sound Show

This theater is the smallest at MGM, so check the size of the line before you queue up to watch this "monster" movie featuring Chevy Chase and Martin Short. Audience volunteers add sound effects to the 15-minute film, and when the tape is rolled back the mistakes are screechingly funny. Most kids love this show—and the SoundWorks exhibits as you exit are also a good way to kill some time. (Especially neat are the Phonic Funnies, which let your dub your own voice onto films starring Snow White or Roger Rabbit.) The Monster Sound Show is generally a fine choice for afternoon.

The Magic of Disney Animation Tour

Don't be put off by the name. This 35-minute tour is fast paced, and the preshow featuring Walter Cronkite and Robin Williams is hilarious.

Like the Backstage Studio Tour next door, the Animation Tour is divided into two parts. The walking tour gives you a chance to see Disney animators at work, and the tour winds up with a theater production featuring animated Disney classics.

This is a good choice for afternoon. If you don't mind missing the sight of artists at their desks, the evening tours are also a good choice since they're rarely crowded.

The Indiana Jones Epic Stunt Spectacular

Next to Star Tours and the Twilight Zone Tower of Terror, this is the favorite MGM attraction of teens and preteens. You may think the lines are the most spectacular part of the show, but, because the 2,000-seat theater is so huge, people standing as far back as the 50's Prime Time Cafe are usually seated. Line up about 20 minutes before showtime and be aware that afternoon shows are sometimes a mob scene. If so, try it again during one of the last two seatings of the evening.

As in the other theater presentations, audience volunteers are chosen. (Your odds of being tapped seem to improve if you are sitting near the center front.) Professional stunt people re-create daring scenes from the *Indiana Jones* series, and this 30-minute show is a great chance to learn how those difficult and dangerous stunts end up on film. The finale is spectacular.

The Backstage Studio Tour

The Backstage Studio Tour, which once took nearly two hours, has now been split into segments to make it more palatable to families with young kids. You can take the 25-minute tram ride first, then stop and play in the Honey, I Shrunk the Kids Adventure Zone or take in one of the backlot shows. Then queue up for the second segment, the Special-Effects and Production Tour (see the following listing). It's a much better system.

The tour begins with a tram ride, which scoots you through wardrobe and prop departments and then past huge outdoor sets representing a typical small town and a large city. You'll see the exterior of the home where the Golden Girls "live." The highlight of the tram segment is a stop in Catastrophe Canyon, where you'll be caught in a flash flood, an oil explosion, and an earthquake (prepare to get wet). Later you'll ride behind the Canyon and see how the disasters were created.

After you disembark from your tram, you'll be near the Honey, I Shrunk the Kids Adventure Zone and the Studio Catering Co. snack bar.

Note: Bring your stroller on the tram with you, since you'll disembark far from where you began.

Inside the Magic: The Special-Effects and Production Tour

You can begin the walking segment of the Backstage Studio Tour at leisure, moving ahead to see a naval battle and a storm at sea created in the special-effects water tank, and viewing real soundstages where Disney shows may be in production. Two kids from the audience are chosen to reproduce the infamous flying-bee scene from *Honey, I Shrunk the Kids,* which is a big hit with all the children in the audience, not to mention the lucky pair selected.

Next, you'll watch Bette Midler in a clever four-minute film called *The Lottery,* then walk through the soundstage where the film was made, checking out the props and special-effects equipment up close. Finally, in the postproduction segment of the walking tour, you'll sit back in a theater and enjoy previews of new Disney/Touchstone releases.

The one-hour tour is a big deal, but Disney does a good job of mixing in humor with the more-technical information as well as using big-name stars such as Goldie Hawn and Mel Gibson as "teachers," so most kids hold with the tour better than you might expect.

The Honey, I Shrunk the Kids Adventure Zone

The Adventure Zone is based on the popular Disney movie of the same name. "Miniaturized" guests scramble through a world of giant Legos, nine-foot Cheerios, and spiderwebs three stories high. Kids are generally so entranced by all the tunnels and neat little hiding areas that many a parent has had to go in to retrieve his tots—and then found he didn't want to leave himself.

Children 2 to 5 can enjoy the Junior Adventurers area, with a downsized maze and slide, where they can play in safety away from the rougher antics of the older kids. It is strongly recommended that toddlers stay out of the three-story spiderweb, which requires that you climb all the way through before exiting—a daunting task for little legs. Families with preschoolers must stay alert inside the Adventure Zone—when a child enters a tunnel or climbs to the top of a slide, it's often difficult to judge exactly where she'll emerge. Ergo, the attraction really should be retitled "Honey, I Lost the Kids."

This attraction is very popular with kids 8 and under. The only complaint? It needs to be about four times larger!

Note: You don't have to take the tour to get to the Adventure Zone. Either enter the Animation Courtyard and then take a sharp left down Mickey Avenue, or take a left at the Great Movie Ride and enter the backlot area via the *MuppetVision 3-D* Plaza.

Backlot Show

A themed show runs several times a day in the street behind the Honey, I Shrunk the Kids Adventure Zone. In the past, such luminaries as the Teenage Mutant Ninja Turtles and Ace Ventura have been featured. Disney changes the show to keep it fresh, and a picture-taking and autograph session follows the performance. Consult your entertainment schedule for showtimes.

Voyage of the Little Mermaid

Using puppets, animation, and live actors to retell the beloved story of Ariel and Prince Eric, Voyage of the Little Mermaid has remained one of the hottest shows at MGM. Come early or prepare for an hour-long wait.

The special effects in this show are the best Disney has to offer; during the brilliant storm scene, you'll feel that you're really underwater, and the interplay between the cartoon characters and live actors is ingenious. Toddlers may find certain scenes in the 20-minute show too real for comfort, but everyone else is certain to be dazzled.

MuppetVision 3-D

Look for the hot-air balloon with Kermit's picture, and you'll find the *MuppetVision 3-D* movie. The show combines slapstick with sly wit, and everyone from preschoolers to adults will find something to make them laugh. The 3-D glasses in themselves are a kick, and the 20-minute movie is charming, touching, and loud. Although *MuppetVision 3-D* tested highly among kids ages 2 to 5, some parents reported that kids under 2 were unnerved by the sheer volume of the finale.

The Beauty and the Beast Stage Show

Still red-hot after three years in production, this 30-minute show re-creates musical scenes from the film of the same name. Be at the theater at least 10 minutes before showtime to guarantee a seat, 20 minutes if you expect to be near the stage. It's a good choice for afternoon.

Recognizing the enduring popularity of the production, Disney has finally moved it to a large theater on Sunset Boulevard and provided enough shade to make the afternoon shows pleasant. The new Theatre of the Stars, modeled on the Hollywood Bowl, is the perfect setting for this Broadway-caliber show.

The Pocahontas Stage Show/ The Making of Pocahontas

Because Disney uses MGM to promote its most recent films, the stage shows are always subject to change. As this book goes to press, there is both an outdoor live-action show featuring the cast of *Pocahontas,* and a film showing behind-the-scenes info on the animation process. The stage show is the more engaging of the two, and a good choice for afternoon.

The Hunchback of Notre Dame Stage Show

Who is best qualified to tell the story of Quasimodo? Obviously, it's the gypsies who dwell in the Court of Miracles deep beneath the streets of Paris. By combining magic, music, and lots of audience participation, the gypsies create the sets right before your eyes, using coins, cloth, baskets, rugs, and other objects they've "found" on their travels.

The popularity of such MGM stage shows as Voyage of the Little Mermaid and Beauty and the Beast leaves the Disney producers with a dilemma: How do they keep topping themselves? In the Hunchback of Notre Dame Stage Show, they have opted not to make the special effects bigger, newer, and wilder, but rather to return to age-old magic tricks and illusions. In order to dazzle or confuse their audience, the gypsies do not rely on a pyrotechnic "pow," but rather on transforming one thing into something else. Puppets may change into live performers with the twirl of a cape, Esmerelda may disappear and reappear, and Quasimodo may emerge from his tower amid ringing bells and soaring birds; but the only technology the gypsies use in creating these effects is that which was available in the 15th century.

The Hunchback show plays in the relatively small Backlot Theater. In order to ensure a good seat, you'll need to show up at least 20 minutes early; make it 30 minutes if you want to sit close enough to the stage to participate in the action.

Afternoon Parade

A themed parade—featuring anything from the *Aladdin* gang to the crew from *Toy Story* to whatever film Disney is currently hyping—runs every afternoon. The time and the route are outlined on your map and/or entertainment guide. Stake out curb space 30 minutes in advance during the on-season. Because the parade route is short, the crowds can be 8 to 10 people deep, and no place on the parade route is substantially less crowded than another. Although short, the parades are popular and extremely well done.

Disney Channel Filming

On given days, Disney Channel shows may be in production on the MGM backlots. If so, a sign will be posted at the front gates, telling which show is taping and when, and instructing you to go to Guest Services if you want to be in the studio audience. Many shows require members of the audience be at least 12, others as old as 17.

In the case of the game shows, you may even get tapped to be a contestant, but the odds are statistically against it. Watching a taping is time-consuming and involves a lot of sitting, so visitors on a tight touring schedule or those with kids under 12 are advised to skip the taping sessions.

MEETING THE CHARACTERS AT MGM

MGM is a great place to meet the characters. They appear more frequently than at Epcot or in the MK, there are fewer kids per square foot vying for their attention, and certain favorites—most notably the *Aladdin* characters, the Muppets, Beauty and the Beast, the Little Mermaid, Pocahontas, and the Hunchback—appear only at MGM. Get your camera ready and check out these locations:

- A variety of characters greet visitors as they enter the park, usually around 8:30 or 9 A.M. The same characters return to the entrances around 3 P.M.
- An even larger variety of characters can be found on both Mickey Avenue and Sunset Boulevard from midmorning on. The shift changes about every 30 minutes, so keep checking.
- If "Breakfast with Aladdin" is scheduled at the Soundstage Restaurant, it offers your best shot of getting a picture and autograph with these popular characters.
- The characters are also sometimes found in the afternoon in the Animation Courtyard just outside the Soundstage Restaurant.
- If a parade or ceremony is scheduled for the Celebrity of the Day, the characters will be there in full force. The 3 P.M. parade, although the theme changes, is also a sure bet for seeing characters.

- Periodically the *Star Wars* crew can be found outside the Star Tours ride.
- The Muppets are sometimes "on location" outside *MuppetVision 3-D*.

FULL-SERVICE RESTAURANTS AT MGM

Although, like the rest of WDW, MGM is hardly a bastion of haute cuisine, the food here is fun, with a far greater variety than you'll find in the MK and more punch to the service. Make reservations by phone if you're staying on-site; otherwise, reservations are taken at the booth on Sunset Boulevard each morning for the 50's Prime Time Cafe, the SciFi Drive-In, Mama Melrose's Ristorante Italiano, and the Hollywood Brown Derby. The booth is a real timesaver, because you can make lunch and dinner reservations simultaneously and see sample menus from all of the eateries.

As at Epcot, the food is expensive and the service extremely slow, especially at peak dining hours. If you just want to see the inside of the SciFi Drive-In or the 50's Prime Time Cafe, make your reservation for 3 P.M. or 10 minutes before the park is slated to close and just have dessert. Certain restaurants such as Mama Melrose's often run special deals when kids eat free. As at Epcot, beer and wine are available.

50's Prime Time Cafe

With its kitsch decor and ditsy waitresses dressed like June Cleaver, the cafe is almost an attraction in itself. Meatloaf, macaroni, milkshakes, and other comfort food are served in a fifties-style kitchen while dozens of TVs blare clips from classic sitcoms in the background.

"Hi, kids," says your waitress, pulling up a chair to the Formica-topped table. "You didn't leave your bikes in the driveway, did you? Let me see those hands." Assuming that you pass her clean-fingernails inspection, "Mom" will go on to advise you of your food choices. "I'll bring peas with that. Vegetables are good for you."

The camp is lost on young kids, who nonetheless love the no-frills food and the fact that "Mom" brings around crayons and coloring books, then hangs their artwork with magnets on the front of a refrigerator. But it's baby-boomer parents, who were raised on the sitcoms the restaurant spoofs, who really adore the place. The tacky Tune-In Lounge next door is decorated in exact replicas of the furniture my parents had in their den 40 years ago.

Much of MGM is dedicated to nostalgia, but this is nostalgia on a small and extremely enjoyable scale. You can fill up at lunch or dinner for about $8 per person, and the s'mores, so huge that they cover the pink Fiestaware plate, can be split by the whole family for dessert.

The Hollywood Brown Derby

Terrific Cobb salad as well as veal, pasta, and fresh seafood are served at the Derby, where, not surprisingly, caricatures of movie stars line the walls. Service, however, is extremely slow, making this a bad choice for families with young kids. Lunch for an adult will run about $10, dinner $15. Dining outside is a good option if the kids are rambunctious, but the inside decor is spiffy, too.

The Hollywood & Vine Cafeteria of the Stars

This large, attractive art deco cafeteria offers a wide variety of salads and desserts and an outstanding

rotisserie chicken. The line moves fast and it's nice to
see what you're getting. Lunch or dinner will be about
$8, breakfast a bit less. (Breakfast is a popular meal
here, with fruit plates, eggs and bacon, pancakes, and
all the traditional breakfast foods; it's a good alternative to Starring Rolls if you want more than a pastry to
start the day.) Reservations are not necessary.

The SciFi Drive-In

At least as campy as the 50's Prime Time Cafe, the
SciFi seats diners in vintage cars while incredibly
hokey movie clips run on a giant screen and carhops whiz by on roller skates. Standard drive-in fare
such as milkshakes and popcorn are on the menu, but
more elaborate dinners such as seafood salads and
mesquite chicken are also offered. Kids adore the
setting and give the SciFi high marks. (Even the
food is cutely named: A shortcake dessert is dubbed
"When Berries Collide.") Dark and relatively quiet,
even at high noon, the SciFi is an excellent way to
refresh and regroup after a morning of vigorous touring. Adults should expect to pay about $10 for lunch
or $15 for dinner and, once again, the portions are
enormous.

Mama Melrose's Ristorante Italiano

This restaurant is tucked away near the *MuppetVision
3-D* Plaza and serves "gourmet" brick-oven pizza and a
wide variety of pasta dishes. Expect a rather wacky
New York ambience—sometimes Mama herself turns
up to inspect the premises—and fairly quick service.
The pizzas are a reasonably cheap alternative for lunch;
if everyone wants pasta, expect to pay about $10 a head.
Occasional specials allow kids to eat free.

DECENT FAST-FOOD PLACES AT MGM

Soundstage Restaurant
Decorated like the town of Agrabah from the popular movie *Aladdin,* the Soundstage Restaurant is in the Animation Courtyard and contains a small food court with pizza, salads, soup, and sandwiches. Aladdin, Jasmine, the Genie, and Jafar are often on hand midday to greet diners.

The Backlot Express
Located near Star Tours, the Backlot Express lives up to its name and serves up burgers and chicken within minutes. This large restaurant is a good place to grab a bite during the most crowded hours of the day.

Min and Bill's Dockside Diner
This diner, which is near Echo Lake, serves submarine sandwiches and fruit plates.

The Studio Catering Co.
Most people aren't aware that this snack stand, tucked away in the middle of the Backstage Studio Tour, even exists. So while the masses amble on to the second stage of the tour and the kids explore the nearby Honey, I Shrunk the Kids Adventure Zone, parents can have a drink in peace.

Dinosaur Gertie's
Kids can't resist this big green tyrannosaurus. Gertie's is the place to get ice cream while waiting in line for the Indiana Jones Epic Stunt Spectacular.

Starring Rolls
Your best bet for a fast breakfast, as well as a great spot to pick up cookies, brownies, and pastries before the parade or the closing fireworks.

The Commissary Restaurant

Next to the Great Movie Ride, the Commissary serves salads, stir-fry, and a Mickey Mouse box lunch for kids. The counter service is swift and the food reasonably varied, making the Commissary a good choice for those who just can't face another burger but haven't the time or patience for full-service dining.

Echo Lake Produce or Anaheim Produce

Stop by one of these fruit stands if you're looking for a fast, healthy snack.

THE MGM DON'T-MISS LIST

No   ▪ Star Tours

—   ▪ The Great Movie Ride

—   ▪ The Magic of Disney Animation Tour (35 min)

  ▪ The Indiana Jones Epic Stunt Spectacular

✶   ▪ Voyage of the Little Mermaid

✶   ▪ Beauty and the Beast stage show

✶   ▪ The Hunchback of Notre Dame stage show

✶   ▪ The parade

No   ▪ SuperStar Television

No   ▪ Twilight Zone Tower of Terror

✶   ▪ Honey, I Shrunk the Kids Adventure Zone

✶   ▪ *MuppetVision 3-D*

THE MGM WORTH-YOUR-WHILE LIST

  ▪ The Monster Sound Show

  ▪ The Backstage Studio Tour   2 hrs (split up)

- Inside the Magic: The Special-Effects and Production Tour
- The Pocahontas stage show

THE SCARE FACTOR AT MGM

The Great Movie Ride

The ride begins innocently enough as you drift past re-creations of scenes from classic films. But everyone in my tram, no matter what their age, gave a collective gasp when one movie set "turned real" and our tram driver was killed in a 1930s-style gangland shoot-out. After collecting jewelry from a couple of the riders, the gangster commandeered our tram for the rest of the ride. "Is this supposed to be happening?" wailed one boy who looked about seven, echoing the thoughts, no doubt, of many of the riders. (If your tram manages to elude the gangster, you'll be held up instead by a rootin' tootin' cowboy, who blows up the town bank in an explosion so real that even riders in the back of the tram feel the blast of heat.) Danger lurks throughout the ride in the form of the alien from the movie of the same name, as well as from the green-faced Wicked Witch of the West, who appears in a cloud of quite-convincing mist.

Final verdict: A couple of scenes are startling and in-tense, and this ride will have your family debating "How did they *do* that?" for weeks afterward. Although aspects may scare kids under 4, the fact that the tram driver eventually reappears does underscore the fact that it's all "only pretend."

Catastrophe Canyon

As part of the Backstage Studio Tour, you experience how artificial disasters are created in an outdoor set. Your tram shakes with an earthquake and narrowly misses being swept away by a flood and rockslide.

Final verdict: The tour guide explains how it's all done. Most children find the Canyon the most fun part of the Backstage Studio Tour.

The Monster Sound Show

Despite the somewhat scary-sounding title, this is really a funny film starring Chevy Chase and Martin Short, with volunteers from the audience providing sound effects.

Final verdict: Not scary at all.

Star Tours

The warnings posted at the entryway are a bit paranoid, for most kids love this attraction, especially if they've seen the *Star Wars* movie series.

Final verdict: Fine for kids over 5, unless they are prone to motion sickness. If so, skip this attraction—the flight-simulator technology is capable of persuading your stomach that you're really moving.

Voyage of the Little Mermaid

The storm sequence is very true to the movie that inspired it, with lightning, thunder, and overhead jets of water combining to convince viewers that they are "under the sea." In addition the sea-witch Ursula appears onstage.

Final verdict: Unless your child is young enough to be frightened by noise, or was terrified by the storm scenes in the movie, he or she should be able to handle the show. A significant number of kids in the 2-to-5 age range named this their favorite MGM attraction.

MuppetVision 3-D

This show is funny—but loud. Several parents reported that babies and toddlers were put off by the cannon explosions at the end of the film.

Final verdict: Fine for everyone except sleeping babies and toddlers who might be unnerved by the noise level.

Twilight Zone Tower of Terror

When I toured the Tower of Terror last spring, I noticed any number of 5- and 6-year-olds having a ball. Interestingly, the kids who were frightened by the ride were crying before they even got into the elevator, i.e., it was the atmosphere that got them, not the plunge.

When you do drop, it's faster-than-free-fall—if you hold a penny on your palm, you'll land before the coin does. But the fall lasts less than two seconds, so before you have time to really panic, it's over.

Final verdict: After repeatedly riding with kids of different ages, I've readjusted my thinking on the age recommendation. A hearty 6-year-old can handle this, assuming he passes the 44-inch height requirement.

7

★★★★★★★★★★★★★★★★★★

*The Rest of
the World*

PLEASURE ISLAND

"It's New Year's Eve every night!" is the theme at Disney's Pleasure Island Nightclub Theme Park. This complex of clubs, restaurants, and shops comes alive at 7 P.M. each evening as adults 18 and over pay one admission price for unlimited entry to two dance clubs, two comedy clubs, a country-music bar, a jazz club, and a seventies-style disco. A different band puts on a show each evening, winding down just before midnight when a street party culminates in the New Year's Eve countdown, complete with champagne, fireworks, and confetti.

The $18 admission price gives you unlimited access to all the clubs. If you have a five-day World-Hopper pass, you're entitled to free admission to Pleasure Island for seven straight days from first use. (Even if you don't have the five-day pass, you still shouldn't have to pay full price—there are numerous discount coupons to be found in the freebie magazines at your hotel. These are the only Disney tickets that are regularly discounted.) And if you just want to see the shops and restaurants of Pleasure Island, there is no admission charge until 7 P.M., when the clubs open.)

Although Pleasure Island is clearly geared toward adults, some families do bring their kids. This is a wholesome, Disneyesque nightclub environment—i.e., there's no raunchy material at the comedy club, drunks are discreetly handled, and security is so tight that no one, even the lone woman traveler, is ever hassled. So if for some reason you are reluctant to leave your children at the hotel, Pleasure Island is OK. If your kids are preteens and thus too old for a sitter but too young for a nightclub, a ten-screen movie theater lies right across the bridge from Pleasure Island.

Pleasure Island Touring Tips

• If you choose Pleasure Island for parents' night out, get an in-room sitter for the kids. Most hotel services close down at midnight, and if you stay for the fireworks and street party, you won't be back until after that. With an in-room sitter, the kids can go to bed at their usual hour. (If your hotel doesn't provide in-room sitting, call Fairy Godmothers at (407) 277-3724 before you leave home, or one of the other sitting services listed in Section 8, "Disney After Dark.")

• Visit Pleasure Island after your least demanding touring day. There isn't much walking on the island, but dancing is murder on already puffy feet. Pleasure Island is a good follow-up to a day spent at Typhoon Lagoon or Blizzard Beach; since you won't be visiting a major park, you won't lose a day on your multiday pass.

• You won't be pressured to drink in the clubs, but if you do, you'll soon learn that the alcohol is expensive.

• Even if you don't dance, Pleasure Island is worthwhile. Nearby barstools let you watch the dancers, and the comedy clubs and live bands are very entertaining.

PLEASURE ISLAND TOURING PLAN

• Arrive about 7 P.M. Dine either on the elegant *Empress Lilly* riverboat, which is moored at the Disney Village Marketplace beside Pleasure Island, or at the Portobello Yacht Club, which specializes in upscale Italian cuisine. If you'd like a more casual meal, grab some barbecue at the Fireworks Factory or visit Planet Hollywood, adjacent to Pleasure Island.

• Take in the Comedy Warehouse first. (The dance clubs don't gear up until later.) This 30-minute show, a combination of improvisation and Disney spoofs, is proof positive that comedians don't have to be profane to be funny. And because so much of the material truly is improvised, some guests return to the Comedy Warehouse several times in the course of the evening, seeing an essentially different routine each time.

• Move on to the Neon Armadillo across the street for country-western music with a live band. The free line-dancing classes are a blast, especially after all the participants have had a few "Electric Lemonades."

• For something completely different, try the Adventurers Club, a lavish, eccentric hideaway based on British hunting clubs of the 1930s. You won't be in the bar for long before you realize that some of your fellow patrons are actors . . . and the barstools are sinking and the masks on the walls are moving. Every 30 minutes or so, a seemingly spontaneous comedy routine erupts among the actors; the seance routines are especially memorable. The biggest hoot is the twice-nightly New Members Induction Ceremony, during which hapless bar inductees are encouraged to learn the club salute, club creed, and all-purpose theme song.
Unfortunately, many people just walk in, peruse the bizarre decor of the place, and leave before they have a chance to really get into this particular brand of comedy. Give it time! The Adventurers Club is definitely worth an hour of your evening. There's nothing like this back home—unless you're from the Congo—and the club is a favorite among Orlando locals.

• Next stop by the Jazz Company, which features live music and vocalists and draws an interesting crowd. The Jazz Company has a great selection of wine, many offered by the glass, and so many munchies that if you plan to spend a lot of time here, you may not need to eat supper first. The tables are small, the music relatively subdued, the clientele more mellow—making this the most romantic of the Pleasure Island clubs.

• At 8-Trax, polyester and disco are still king. It's fun to watch the thirtysomethings sitting in their beanbag chairs, valiantly pretending they don't remember the words to old Bee Gees hits. At other times the club spins back even farther in time to late-sixties psychedelia. Sometimes special guests—such as former cast members from "The Brady Bunch"—appear, adding even more camp to the atmosphere.

• Finally, divide your remaining hours between the two dance clubs. The Rock 'n' Roll Beach Club offers a live band and an informal pool-shooting, beer-drinking, resort-style ambience; Mannequins is darker and wilder and features canned music, strobe lighting, and a revolving dance floor.

• Be sure to be back outside for the street party (11 P.M. during the off-season, midnight during summer and holidays) and countdown to New Year's. Flat-out bizarre entertainment can be found all up and down the street. On a recent evening, there were female body builders posing in bikinis, a Velcro wall begging to be leapt against, and a Russian mime troupe.

• Then grab a cappuccino and sit in the cobblestone courtyard at D-Zertz. You may feel like dancing more, or you may decide it's time to head home to the kids.

PLANET HOLLYWOOD

This exciting new restaurant, shaped like a giant blue globe, is located right beside Pleasure Island and near the Disney Village Marketplace. Planet Hollywood is a terrific restaurant for the whole family. Adults will be impressed by the good, reasonably priced food and fast, friendly service. Kids love the decor: Props from a variety of movies pack the three-tier eatery, the bus from the movie *Speed* hovers overhead, and you can entertain yourself indefinitely with the placemats and menus, which are decorated with high-school graduation pictures of stars. Film clips run constantly, and the entire atmosphere is heady and fun.

No reservations are taken, and the place can get packed at mealtime: 90-minute waits are not uncommon at 6 P.M. If you have the kids with you and you can't wait that long, try it at off hours—Planet Hollywood is the perfect spot for an early dinner. Or, since the desserts are among the best in Orlando, stop off for a late-night sweet spree as you're leaving Pleasure Island. (The ebony-and-ivory brownie is beyond compare.)

If you're just in the market for T-shirts and other memorabilia, which are hot souvenirs, they're sold in a separate shop downstairs near the parking lot, so you don't have to enter the restaurant to get your goodies.

DISCOVERY ISLAND

Just a short ride across Bay Lake is thoroughly unmodern, uncrowded Discovery Island, an 11-acre zoological park. There you'll find walking trails, lush natural vegetation, beaches perfect for picnicking, and hundreds of varieties of animal life. Of special interest are the trained birds at Parrots Perch and the Galapagos sea turtles at Tortoise Beach.

Discovery Island launches leave from the MK and Fort Wilderness campground. If you have a five-day pass, which allows you unlimited access to the minor theme parks, you may enjoy taking a break at Discovery Island. In fact, if you're touring in the MK and would like to escape the bustle of the parks for a couple of hours, buy some fast food inside the MK park, then take the launch to Discovery Island for an impromptu picnic. If you don't have a five-day pass, don't spend the time and money ($11 adults, $6 kids 3 to 9) to visit the island; there are undoubtedly similar zoological parks closer to home.

Kids taking the "Wonders of Walt Disney World" seminar "Wildlife Adventure" will spend a very productive afternoon on the island, learning about the conservation of natural plant and animal habitats. For students signed up for the "Wonders" program, no ticket is necessary.

Children ages 8 to 14 can also participate in Kidventure, a less structured class designed to expose youngsters to the nature trails of Fort Wilderness and the zoological and botanical gardens of Discovery Island. This is a real hands-on program—the children learn to identify animal tracks and make track casts. Call (407) 824-3784 for reservations and more information.

RIVER COUNTRY

Billed as an "ol' swimming hole perfect for splashin' and slidin'," River Country has become completely overshadowed by Typhoon Lagoon and Blizzard Beach. But River Country remains a good choice for families with young kids or anyone who doesn't swim very well—the park rarely gets as crowded as Typhoon Lagoon and Blizzard Beach, draws far fewer preteens and teens, and the water level in the center of Bay Cove is only about chest-deep on an 8-year-old.

Bay Cove, the largest section of River Country, features swing ropes, two water slides, and White Water Rapids, an exhilaratingly bumpy inner-tube ride down a winding 230-foot-long creek. The nearby swimming pool offers two small but steep slides which shoot riders into midair; kids smack the water eight feet below with such force that they can barely stagger out of the pool and make it up the stony steps to try it again . . . and again. . . .

Younger kids will prefer the Ol' Wading Pool, a roped-off sandy-bottomed section of Bay Cove with four small slides cut into a wall of boulders, designed specifically for preschoolers; since older kids are kept out of this section, and the slides empty into a mere 18 inches of water, parents can relax on the many lounge chairs scattered along the Ol' Wading Pool beach.

Again, the five-day pass gets you in gratis, but individual tickets are available at $16 for adults, $12 for kids—or buy a $20 (adult) or $14 (child) combo ticket for River Country and Discovery Island. River Country is a fine place to picnic, and there are a couple of fast-food stands on-site.

Whereas Typhoon Lagoon and Blizzard Beach can take up a whole day, a swift-moving 10-year-old can try out every attraction at River Country in two hours flat. For this reason, it's a good water park to drop in to when the theme parks are swamped and sweltering and everyone needs to unwind for a couple of hours.

If you're coming by car or taking a shuttle from the Ticket and Transportation Center (TTC), be aware that the River Country parking lot is quite far from the park itself. You'll catch a shuttle from the parking lot, drive through Fort Wilderness campground, and be let out near the gates. Those coming from Fort Wilderness, or those who have taken the launch from the Magic Kingdom to Fort Wilderness, have only a short stroll to the River Country entrance. Once you're inside, the park is small and easily navigated.

River Country Touring Tips

• Although the oversized swimming pool is heated, making fall and spring swimming a delight, River Country is sometimes closed during December, January, and February. Call (407) 824-4321 for details on hours of operation.

• If you don't have a five-day pass, buy your River Country admission tickets at either your hotel's Guest Services desk or at one of the major theme parks. As the park grows crowded, management sometimes abruptly suspends ticket sales at the gate, but if you already have a ticket in hand, they'll let you in.

• Families not returning to their hotel in midafternoon can use River Country to break up a day in the MK. Stow your bathing suits in one of the lockers beneath the Main Street Railroad Station in the morning; then, when the park heats up and fills up in the afternoon, exit the MK and take the launch marked "Campground and Discovery Island." (The 15-minute boat ride is so pleasant that it almost constitutes an afternoon getaway in itself.) If you're staying off-site, this option is less time-consuming than returning to your hotel pool. After a few hours in the cool water of River Country, you can hop on the launch and be back in the MK within minutes.

• Many families swear that the perfect time for a River Country visit is on a summer night; the park stays open until 8 P.M., but crowds thin about 5 P.M., meaning shorter waits for the slides and a nearly empty pool.

- Horseback riding is located near the River Country parking lot. If you're planning to try the trail rides during your Disney stay, it makes sense to combine horseback riding with an afternoon at River Country. For younger kids, the pony rides and Fort Wilderness petting zoo are located right at the River Country main entrance. The ponies are available from 10 A.M. to 5 P.M., cost $2 to ride, and are incredibly gentle.

- If you think obtaining a rental life vest will better qualify an unsteady swimmer for the slides and tube ride, forget it. The lifeguards have the final say over who is allowed to ride what, and a life vest often tips them off that a child really isn't capable of handling the major slides.

- If you enter River Country early in the morning, head for White Water Rapids first. Because the tube retrieval system is time-consuming, this is the first attraction to draw long lines.

- Remember that you're swimming in a lake, not a pool. The netting does a good job on critter control, but this is not the day to wear your new $90 white swimsuit.

TYPHOON LAGOON

Disney has dubbed its 56-acre Typhoon Lagoon "the world's ultimate water park," and the hyperbole is justified. Where else can you slide through caves, picnic with parrots, float through rain forests, and swim (sort of) with sharks? Typhoon Lagoon was opened in 1989 as the largest water park in the world and was instantly so popular that it was hard to get in to. The opening of the even-bigger Blizzard Beach in 1995 has taken off a bit of the pressure, but it is still difficult to get in to Typhoon Lagoon during peak touring times.

Typhoon Lagoon occasionally becomes so swamped with swimmers that it closes its gates. On four separate days during Easter week 1994, the park became so crowded that no one was admitted after 10 A.M., to the great dismay of families who had donned their suits, swabbed themselves with sunscreen, and prepared for a day in the pools. The moral is: If you're visiting on a holiday or during midsummer, plan to arrive at the water parks at opening time.

For anyone with a five-day pass, Typhoon Lagoon is free for *seven* days following first use. Otherwise, admission is $22 for adults and $18 for children 3 to 9—entirely too much to pay for a morning of splashing around.

Typhoon Lagoon Attractions

- *Humunga Kowabunga:* Two water slides that propel riders down a mountain at 30 mph. No kids under 48 inches are allowed.

  Note: If you're female, a one-piece suit is your best bet. A young Disney employee informed me that the most desired duty in all of Typhoon Lagoon is to stand at the bottom of Humunga Kowabunga, helping riders out of the chute— apparently at least one woman per hour loses her swimsuit top during the descent.

- *Storm Slides:* Three curving slides that deposit riders in the pool below. Kids of any age can ride, but it's suggested they be good swimmers, because, although the pool isn't deep, you do enter the water with enough force to temporarily disorient a nervous swimmer. Most kids 7 to 11 (and some younger) love these zesty little slides, but if

you're unsure if yours are up to it, wait at the edge
of the pool where the slide empties so you can help
them out.

Note: Each of the three slides—the Rudder
Buster, Jib Jammer, and Stern Burner—offers a
slightly different thrill, although none is necessar-
ily wilder than the others.

- *Mayday Falls:* White-water tubing. A Disney employee helps you load into the giant rubber tubes
and gives you a gentle shove. What follows is a
fast, giggly journey that makes you feel like you're
about to lose your tube more than once. No kids
under 48 inches are allowed.

- *Keelhaul Falls:* A corkscrew tube ride that's full of
thrills. Kids under 48 inches are provided with
their own, smaller tube, and lots of kids as young
as 4 reported that they loved this ride.

- *Gangplank Falls:* Four-passenger rafts in white water.
Slower, milder, but much bumpier than Mayday
or Keelhaul, Gangplank is a good choice for families
with kids too young for the other white-water rides.
Gangplank Falls loads slowly however, and the ride is
short, so hit it early in the morning, especially if you
think your kids will want to go down more than once.

Note: If the kids are small, sometimes more than
four people are allowed into a raft.

- *Surfing Lagoon:* Machine-made waves up to six feet
high in a 2.5-acre lagoon. The waves come at 90-
second intervals and are perfectly designed for tubing
and bodysurfing. Every other hour the pool is emp-
tied of tubes, and the wave machine is cranked up to
allow for bodysurfing. A foghorn blast alerts you to
when a big 'un is under way. Although the Surfing
Lagoon lets anyone in, don't take small children too

deep during the hours designated for bodysurfing—
every 90 seconds 400 shrieking teenagers will bear
down upon your head.

- *Whitecap Cove and Blustery Bay:* The Surfing Lagoon has two small, roped-off coves, where smaller
waves lap upon toddlers and shaky swimmers.

- *Castaway Creek:* A meandering 2,000-foot stream
full of inner tubes. Guests simply wade out, find
an empty tube, and plop down. It takes about 30
minutes to encircle the rain forest, and there is a
bit of excitement at one point when riders drift
under a waterfall. But there are numerous exits
along the creek, so anyone who doesn't want to get
splashed can hop out before the falls. In general, a
very fun, relaxing ride, appropriate for any age or
swimming level.

- *Shark Reef:* A saltwater pool where snorkelers
swim "among" exotic marine life, including sharks.
The sharks and fish are behind Plexiglas, of course,
and suiting up to snorkel is time-consuming. Stop
at the Reef only if you have a whole day to spend at
Typhoon Lagoon. The sharks are small and not too
numerous, so anyone expecting the casting call for
Jaws will be disappointed. Most of the fun is in getting to view the brightly colored fish up close, but if
your kids are unsure, the underwater viewing area
will give them a greater feel for what snorkeling is
all about. Take them down to the viewing area first
and let them observe the marine life and other
snorkelers and then make up their own minds.

    Note: The Shark Reef is open only during sum-
mers and holidays.

- *Ketchakiddee Creek:* A water playground sized for
preschoolers, with geysers and bubblers in the

shape of crocodiles and whales, as well as slides and a small white-water raft ride. No one over 48 inches is allowed to ride, which is a pleasant change from most of the park rules, although parents are encouraged to enter the area and help their kids. Lifeguards are everywhere, and lots of chairs are set out nearby for adults.

- *Mt. Mayday Scenic Trail:* This footpath leads almost to the top of Mt. Mayday, where the shipwrecked *Miss Tilly* is impaled, and offers great views of the slides and rides below.

BLIZZARD BEACH

Disney's third and largest water park opened in the spring of 1995. When word got out in the travel industry that Disney was opening another water park, there was great speculation as to the theme. Having already designed the ultimate country swimming hole and the ultimate tropical lagoon, what could the imagineers come up with this time?

A melting ski lodge, of course. Blizzard Beach is built on the tongue-in-cheek premise that a freak snowstorm hit Orlando and a group of enterprising businessmen built Florida's first ski resort. The sun returned in due time, and for a while it looked like all was lost—until someone spied an alligator slipping and sliding down one of the slushy slopes. Blizzard Beach was born. The snow may be gone, but the jumps, moguls, sled runs, and slalom courses remain, resulting in a high-camp, high-thrill ski lodge among the palms.

Blizzard Beach centers around snowcapped Mt. Gushmore. You can get to the top via either ski-lift or a series of stairs, but how you get down is up to you. The bold can descend on the Summit Plummet or Slush Gusher, but there are medium-intensity flumes, inner-tube runs, and family-style white-water rafts as well. The motif extends into every element of the park; there is a chalet-style restaurant, Plexiglas snowmen, and innumerable sight gags such as ski marks running off the side of the mountain. The original skiing alligator has returned as the resort mascot, Ice Gator.

Blizzard Beach was built in response to Typhoon Lagoon's popularity and draws huge crowds. Come early in the morning or prepare for monster waits. A five-day World Hopper pass gets you in free for *seven* days following first use; otherwise, admission is $24 for adults, $18 for children 3 to 9.

Blizzard Beach Attractions

- *Summit Plummet:* The icon of the park, this slide is 120 feet tall, making it the longest flume slide in the world. A clever optical illusion makes it seem that riders are shooting out the side of the mountain into midair; the real ride is very nearly as intense, with a 60-degree drop that feels more like 90. Top speeds on Summit Plummet reach 55 mph, a full 10 mph more than Space Mountain— and you don't even have a seat belt. The height requirement is 48 inches. In short, this flume is not for the faint of heart.

- *Slush Gusher:* Another big slide, but this time with a couple of bumps to slow you down. Still a big-deal thrill, akin in intensity to Humunga Kowabunga at Typhoon Lagoon.

- *Runoff Rapids:* You take a separate set of stairs up the back of Mt. Gushmore to reach these three inner-tube rides. You'll have a choice of tubes that

seat one, two, or three people. (The family tubes
are designed only for the two open slides; if you
want to ride in the dark tunnel slide, you'll have to
brave it alone.) The Rapids are great fun, and each
path provides a slightly different thrill, so many
people try it over and over. But you'll have to carry
your own raft up the seven zillion stairs; visit early
in the morning before your stamina fails.

- *Snow Stormers:* This is a mock-slalom run, which
  you descend on your belly while clutching a foam-
  rubber "sled." The three slides are full of twists
  and runs that splash water back into your face.
  And if you'd like, you can race the sledders in the
  other two tubes to the bottom. Snow Stormers is
  so much fun that, like the Runoff Rapids, hardly
  anyone does it just once.

- *Toboggan Racers:* Eight riders on rubber mats are
  pitted against each other on a straight descent
  down the mountain. The heavier the rider, the
  faster the descent, so the attendant at the top of
  the slide will give kids a head start over adults.
  Not as wild as the Snow Stormers, this ride is a
  good choice for getting kids used to the feeling of
  sliding downhill on a rubber sled. The two rides
  share a mat pick-up station at the bottom of the
  mountain.

- *Teamboat Springs:* The whole family can join forces
  here to tackle white water as a group. The round
  boats, which an attendant will help you board at
  the top, carry four to five people, and the ride downhill is zippy and fun, with lots of splashes and
  sharp curves. This is one of the best-loved rides in
  the park, drawing an enthusiastic thumbs-up from
  preschoolers to grandparents. Since parents and

kids can share a raft, this is another good first ride to test young children's response, before moving on to the Snow Stormers or Runoff Rapids.

- *Ski Patrol Training Camp:* This special section is designed for kids 5 to 9, with medium-intensity slides, a bumpy mogul course, and the Blizzard Beach Ski Patrol Training Camp, where they can walk across barrels, swing from ropes, and test their mountaineering skills. It's a welcome addition for families who have children too old for Tike's Peak but not quite up to the major slides.

- *Tike's Peak:* This is the toddler and preschooler section, with yet smaller slides and flumes, igloo-style forts, and a wading pool that looks like a broken ice-skating rink. There are chairs and picnic areas nearby for parents.

- *Chair Lift:* The chair lift offers transportation to Summit Plummet, Slush Gusher, and Teamboat Springs, and is also a fun ride in itself.

- *Melt Away Bay:* Unlike the huge Surfing Lagoon at Typhoon Lagoon, this swimming area is relatively small and offers mild swells instead of big waves. Fed by "melting snow" waterfalls, the pool area is attractive and surrounded by chairs and shady huts for relaxing.

- *Cross Country Creek:* This lazy creek circles the park. All you have to do is wade in, find an empty tube, and climb aboard. Expect major blasts of cold water as you float through the "ice cave." (There are exits before the cave if this is just a bit too authentic for you.) It takes about 25 minutes to make a full lap, and this is a pleasant experience for any age group.

Typhoon Lagoon and Blizzard Beach Touring Tips

• The water parks draw a rowdy teenage crowd, which means young kids and unsteady swimmers may get dunked and splashed more than they like. If your children are very young, you might be better off at River Country—or staying in the children's sections (Ketchakiddee Creek or Tike's Peak), which are off-limits to older kids.

Kids 10 and up are allowed to visit the water parks without adults. Some families who are staying on-site send their preteens and teens to the water parks via bus while younger kids are napping in the hotel room.

• The water parks are extrapacked on weekends, since they're popular with locals as well as tourists.

• In the summer, evenings are a better bet than afternoons. Call (407) 824-4321 for hours of operation.

• Many visitors arrive with their swimsuits on under their shorts and shirts, which does save time. It's also a good idea to bring your own towels, since rental is $1 per towel and they're small. There are plenty of lockers, which rent for $5 with a refundable deposit. The locker keys come on rubberized bands that slip over your wrist or ankle, so you can easily keep them with you while in the water.

• Don't bother bringing your own snorkels, rafts, or water wings. Only official Disney equipment is allowed in the pools.

You can "rent" life vests for free, although a driver's license or credit card is required as a deposit. Snorkeling equipment can be picked up for no charge at Hammerhead Fred's near the Shark Reef at Typhoon

Lagoon. An instructor runs you through the basics before letting you loose in the saltwater pool.

• Because you're constantly climbing uphill all day, half the time dragging a tube or mat behind you, the water parks are extremely exhausting. If you spend the day at a water park, plan to spend the evening touring passive attractions, such as films or shows—or make this your parents' night out and leave the kids with a sitter.

• The water parks are a good place to picnic, although there are also several places to get fast food.

• If your kids have rubberized beach shoes with non-skid bottoms, be sure to throw them in your beach bag. The sidewalks can be slippery and the pavement can be hot.

• The Lost Kids Station at Typhoon Lagoon is across a bridge and so far from the main water areas that lost children are very unlikely to find their way there on their own. At Blizzard Beach it's at Shoeless Joe's rentals, far from the swimming action. Instruct your children, should they look up and find themselves separated from you, to tell one of the Disney employees. (They all wear distinctive name tags.) The Disney people will escort the children to the Lost Kids Station, and you can meet them there.

Because both of these parks are full of mazes, with many sets of steps and slides, it is easy to get separated from your party. Have standard meeting places and times for older kids.

• There are two schools of thought on Typhoon Lagoon and Blizzard Beach: Should you go once and stay all day, or come several days for just a few hours at a time?

The advantages of going on only one day are that you save commuting time and, by getting there early in the morning, you can hit the major slides and raft rides before the crowds build. Disadvantage? That's a lot of water activity to cram into just one day.

The advantages of going on several days are that the water parks can cool you off and de-stress you after a morning in the theme parks. Most kids, especially those over 7, love the water parks so much that they'll want to come more than once, and if you have a five-day ticket, cost is no problem. Disadvantages? You have to go through the logistical hassles of parking and lockers more than once, and these parks are too large (more than four times the size of River Country) to tromp around every day of your visit. Also, by going every afternoon, you'll be arriving at the most crowded times of the day, when long lines have formed for major attractions. And during the summer, you'll run the risk of arriving after the park has reached peak capacity and been closed to visitors.

Note: If you don't have the five-day pass and are thus having to pay $76 just to get a family of four through the gates, your choice is a simple one—you have to cram it all into one day or go broke.

Possible solutions are to select a day fairly early in your WDW visit and make this your "big" trip to Typhoon Lagoon or Blizzard Beach, the time when you circle the park and try out everything. After that, return on a couple of subsequent days and go to only one attraction. Come back for an hour or two on Tuesday, for example, and spend the whole time in the lagoon itself. On Thursday you can go directly to the slides. If it's summer and crowds are a problem, consider coming in early evening instead of the afternoon.

• Whichever touring method you choose, be sure to visit a water park early in your WDW visit. Several families reported that they saved this experience until late in their trip and then found it was the highlight of the whole vacation for their kids. "If we'd known how great it was, we'd have come every day," lamented one father. "As it turns out, we only went to Blizzard Beach once—on the morning of the day we were due to fly out."

• If you have the five-day pass and it's summer, consider visiting more than one water park—they're very different experiences. Typhoon Lagoon gets the nod in the pool area—the pool there is huge and has those incredible surfing waves. Blizzard Beach has a far superior white-water ride. The slides, tube rides, and kiddie sections are different in theme but similar in thrill level.

• Typhoon Lagoon and Blizzard Beach are often closed for refurbishing during January and February. If you're planning a winter trip, call (407) 824-4321 to make sure at least one of the parks will be open during the week you plan to visit.

THE DISNEY INSTITUTE

Educational may not be the first word that comes to mind when you think of Walt Disney World, but the Disney Institute is aiming to change all that. The Institute was created specifically to give guests the chance to sample programs in animation, cooking, gardening, photography, tennis, and more than 80 other subjects. Guests stay in a secluded, campuslike enclave and spend their days taking classes, enjoying the world-renowned performers who appear each evening, and working out at the spectacular Sports and Fitness Center.

The Disney Institute opened in 1996, in what was once the Disney Village Resort, located near the Disney Village Marketplace and Pleasure Island. The accommodations are either townhouses with full kitchens and sitting rooms, or bungalows with minikitchens. The villas are clustered around a huge lake and the Institute village green. Guests can rent bikes or golf carts or simply walk to classes.

Although the laid-back small-town atmosphere provides much of the Institute's charm, the real draw is the programs. The classes are part of the package—you take as many or as few as you like, with no additional charge. Some classes are designed specifically for kids 10 to 17, but many are created for parents and children to enjoy together. The kids might sign up for a scavenger hunt "field trip" to one of the theme parks, learn comic-strip drawing or sand sculpture . . . then join the adults for a swamp party or class in puppetry or TV production.

The instructors are the best in their fields, some of them Disney imagineers trained to lead guests through creativity exercises, storytelling, or computer animation "the Disney way." One of the comics from Pleasure Island may be your coach for improvisational acting, or an Institute chef may be on hand to show you the secrets of Mexican cuisine. There is an instructor for every 15 students, and many classes are even smaller, ensuring lots of individual attention.

You can either choose a package that emphasizes a specific skill, such as cooking, or opt for one of the "dabbler" packages, which allow you to try a little bit of everything. It's also OK to choose all your courses individually; the reservation system averages 45-minute phone calls, because the counselors are prepared to talk guests through all the available options.

Most guests request a catalog and preselect their courses, but if a program looks unexpectedly interesting once you arrive, the Institute is quite flexible. Counselors are on hand in the lobby to help guests drop or add programs. People often arrive in Orlando and get fired up to try something they'd never do at home—such as acting or rock climbing. The beauty of the Institute is that it encourages you to stretch your preconceived boundaries. Who knows what you're good at if you'll just give it a try?

Youth Central is the hangout place for kids; it has its own kitchen, stereo, big-screen TV, and billiards table. Adults seem to congregate at the whirlpool in the spa area. Although Disney never announces the artist-in-residence in advance, each evening there are several options for entertainment—musical performances, comedians, plays, movies, lectures, and more. The Institute is its own little world, and security is tight, so parents and kids (who are all 10 or up or they wouldn't be in the programs in the first place) can do some things together and split up for others. The system is designed to encourage both family time and new friendships with Institute classmates.

The 38,000 square-foot Sports and Fitness Center is the cornerstone of the campus. You can either take classes or create your own fitness program using the dozens of beyond-state-of-the-art machines. There's also a full-service spa, a basketball court, and adjacent golf and tennis.

There are three-, four-, and seven-night packages available, some of which include dining in the Institute restaurant, Seasons. Seasons is actually four dining rooms in one, the themes corresponding to the seasons of the year, with a different menu every night. One-day admission to a theme park is included in the

package, but beyond this outing, many guests opt to
stay within the Institute. For information or reservations, call 1-800-4-WONDER.

DISNEY VILLAGE MARKETPLACE

For serious shopping—with twice the selection and
half the crowds you'll find in the theme parks—stop by
the Disney Village Marketplace. Mickey's Character
Shop, with stuffed toys, character-theme clothing,
watches, books, and every form of Disney memorabilia
you can imagine, is a good place to start. The Christmas Chalet is another must-see. Team Mickey, featuring sporting equipment and clothes, is full of unusual
souvenirs; a softball "autographed" by all the characters makes a special gift for a young athlete.

Chef Mickey is a popular restaurant and a good
choice for families who'd like to save the time and expense of a character breakfast. Mickey, dressed in a
tall chef's hat and starched white apron, continually
circulates among the tables, stopping for autographs
and pictures. Those seeking more upscale dining can
try the Portobello Yacht Club, which serves Italian cuisine with a nautical flair. Pleasure Island and Planet
Hollywood are a short walk across the bridge from the
marketplace, and a 10-screen theater lies just beyond
another bridge.

The marketplace has a small playground and sand
area to keep younger kids entertained; and if kids 12
and older get restless, they can venture down to the
dock at the Buena Vista Lagoon to rent one of the little
water sprite speedboats. If you're staying off-site, the
marketplace marina is your best option for boat rental.
The cost is $13.50 per half hour, and younger kids can

ride with an adult. The boats appear to be flying, but in reality don't go very fast and are a fun, safe diversion for all ages. (If the whole family would like to get into the act, canopy boats are also available for rent at a rate of $19 per half hour.) The marina area is so engaging that I've spent hours roaming the marketplace, getting a jump on Christmas shopping, only to have my family greet me at the end of my spree with those astounding words, "What? You're finished *already?*"

DISNEY EXTRAS: PARADES, FIREWORKS, DINNER SHOWS, CHARACTER BREAKFASTS, AND HOLIDAY SPECIAL EVENTS

Don't pack your schedule too tightly. Disney works many wonderful extras into the day, and it would be downright criminal to miss them.

Parades

If you love a parade, you've come to the right place. Included in the festivities are the following:

- Afternoon parade in the MK, usually at 3 P.M.
- SpectroMagic, the electrical parade in the MK that runs at both 9 and 11 P.M. during the busy season and on weekends during the off-season.
- Electric Water Pageant, visible from the beaches of the Seven Seas Lagoon from 9 to 10:20 P.M. nightly.
- The MGM parade, which features whichever movie Disney is currently hyping. Usually at 1 P.M., but showtimes vary, so check your entertainment schedule.

- Special parades are sometimes planned at Epcot and MGM. Consult your daily entertainment schedule for times.
- Mind-blowing holiday parades at Easter, Fourth of July, and Christmas.

Note: SpectroMagic has replaced the popular Main Street Electrical Light Parade, which is currently playing at Disneyland Paris. SpectroMagic runs only periodically during the off-season, so call (407) 824-4321 to see which evening during your visit the parade is scheduled and make sure you plan to stay in the MK until closing on that night. If you're going in the summer, when two parades run, remember that the 11 P.M. parade is never as crowded as the 9 P.M. one.

Fireworks

A 5- to 10-minute display is seen in the sky above Cinderella Castle at 10 P.M. nightly during the on-season. Just before the fireworks begin, you'll see one of the Magic Kingdom's niftiest—but least advertised—little extras: Tinkerbell's Flight. A young gymnast, dressed in tights and zestily hacking the air with a magic wand, slides down a wire suspended from the top of Cinderella Castle to a rooftop in Tomorrowland.

Fireworks close the day year-round at Pleasure Island and during the on-season at MGM.

Note: As Robert Smith, a travel consultant with Destination Orlando in Worchester, Massachusetts, points out, the best place to watch the MK fireworks is not in front of Cinderella Castle, as everyone assumes. The fireworks are actually fired from behind the castle, and excellent viewing can be had from the cafe tables in the Fantasyland section. The fireworks are also visible from some locations in the MK resorts; ask if you'll have a view when you book your room.

IllumiNations

This display of fireworks, laser technology, syncopated fountains, and classical music is an unqualified WDW classic. Very popular—and very crowded—IllumiNations takes place on the World Showcase Lagoon, and the performance coincides with the park closing time. See "IllumiNations" in Section 5 for more information.

Dinner Shows

All the dinner shows should be booked before you leave home by calling (407) 939-3463. Reservations are accepted at the time you book your room for on-site guests, 60 days in advance for off-site guests, and are especially crucial for the Hoop-Dee-Doo Musical Revue. The on-site dinner shows are listed as follows.

- *Hoop-Dee-Doo Musical Revue:* The Revue plays three times nightly (5, 7:15, and 9:30 P.M.) in Pioneer Hall at Fort Wilderness campground. You'll dine on ribs and fried chicken while watching a hilariously hokey show, which encourages lots of audience participation. $35 for adults, $25 for kids 12 to 20, and $17 for kids 3 to 11.

- *Polynesian Luau:* You'll enjoy authentic island dancing and not particularly authentic island food at this outdoor show at the Polynesian Village Resort. The two seatings are at 6:45 and 9:30 P.M. Prices are $33 for adults, $25 for kids 12 to 20, and $17 for kids 3 to 11. A better choice for families with young kids is Mickey's Tropical Luau, which features the characters and the Polynesian dancers; it

is presented at 4:30 P.M. Prices are $29 for adults,
$22 for kids 12 to 20, and $13 for kids 3 to 11.

Note: If you're staying off-site and don't want to return to the WDW grounds in the evening, or if you've
waited too late to book a Disney show, be advised that
Orlando is chock-full of engaging family-style dinner
shows that can easily be booked on the afternoon of the
show. See "Off-site Dinner Shows for the Whole Family" in Section 10 for details.

Character Breakfasts

The character breakfasts take at least a couple of hours
and probably should be skipped if you're on a very tight
touring schedule—or are watching the pocketbook
carefully. But families who stayed at WDW for four or
five days gave the breakfasts very high marks, especially if they scheduled them near the end of their stay,
when the kids had had plenty of time to warm up to the
characters. Families who scheduled their character
breakfast on the last day of their visit also noted that it
then doesn't "mess up the day" so badly, since the last
morning of your trip is usually broken up anyway by
the 11 A.M. check-out time at most Orlando hotels.

The food is pedestrian at the character breakfasts,
but who cares? Since it takes a while to meet all the
characters (usually six or seven circulate among the
diners) and eat, either come early or, if you're able to
make a reservation, try to book the first seating of the
day. Prices generally run about $13 for adults, $8 for
children. The more-elaborate Sunday brunches are
also more expensive: about $19 for adults, $11 for kids.

Many of the Disney hotels host continuous-seating
buffets. Most of the time, reservations are not accepted
at the buffets, but during the busiest seasons you can

book in advance. Reservations are accepted and basically required at Breakfast à la Disney; policy fluctuates at the three character breakfasts that take place within the theme parks. To confirm times and prices, and to see if reservations are being accepted in advance during the time you'll be visiting, call (407) 939-3463 before you leave home.

Disney Character Breakfast Buffets

- *The Contemporary Resort:* 7:30 to 11 A.M. at the Contemporary Cafe, featuring the "classic" characters, such as Mickey, Minnie, Pluto, and Goofy.

- *The Polynesian:* 7:30 to 11 A.M. at the Ohana Restaurant. Minnie is your hostess, and the classic characters are featured.

- *The Grand Floridian:* 7:30 to 11 A.M. at 1900 Park Fare. The crew from *Mary Poppins* is featured.

- *The Beach Club:* 7:30 to 11 A.M. at Cape May Cafe. Goofy is your host; expect the classic characters in nautical attire.

- *Wilderness Lodge:* 7:30 to 11 A.M. at Artist Point, featuring the classic characters in western garb.

- *Disney's Old Key West:* 7:30 to 10:15 A.M., Wednesday and Sunday only. This show features Pooh, Tigger, and the gang. Reservations are recommended.

- *Chef Mickey in the Disney Village Marketplace:* Breakfast à la Disney, 7:30, 9, and 10:30 A.M., featuring Mickey and the classic characters. Reservations are recommended.

Character Breakfasts Within the Theme Parks

- *At MGM:* Aladdin's Breakfast Adventure in the Soundstage Restaurant, 8:30 to 10:30 A.M., featuring the *Aladdin* batch, natch. Theme park admission is required.

- *At Epcot:* Breakfast Under the Sea at the Coral Reef Restaurant in the Living Seas pavilion, 8:30 to 10:30 A.M., featuring the characters from *The Little Mermaid*. Sometimes Mickey floats by in the Living Seas tank, all decked out in scuba gear, an event that has been known to cause near-riots among the diners. Theme park admission is required.

- *In the Magic Kingdom:* Once Upon a Time Breakfast at King Stefan's Banquet Hall in Cinderella Castle, 8 to 10 A.M., featuring the characters from *Cinderella*. Theme park admission is required.

If you're staying off-site, the easiest place to take in a character breakfast is at Breakfast à la Disney at Chef Mickey in the Disney Village Marketplace. Many off-site guests also gravitate toward the character breakfasts within the theme parks. Of course, there's also nothing to keep you from driving over and taking in a breakfast at one of the on-site hotels.

Among families surveyed, the theme park breakfasts received the highest marks—mostly because of the cool settings. It's hard to beat the views at Cinderella Castle or the Coral Reef, or the chance to meet Aladdin in his re-created village of Agrabah. Disney originally planned the in-park breakfasts to be seasonal, but they've proven so popular that they're now available year-round. Policy on reservations fluctuates, so call (407) 939-3463 before you leave home to see if you can book a theme park breakfast in advance.

Dinner with the Disney Characters

If your family isn't much for breakfast, you can also see the characters in the evening. 1900 Park Fare in the Grand Floridian runs a buffet from 5 to 9 P.M. at $19 for adults, $10 for kids 3 to 11, with the characters in attendance.

The Liberty Tree Tavern in the MK offers a patriotic dinner with the characters dressed in Revolutionary-era outfits. Make reservations in advance by calling (407) 939-3463.

Staying off-site and willing to settle for "only" Mickey? Your easiest evening option is to visit Chef Mickey, a high-quality restaurant in its own right, located at the Disney Village Marketplace.

Jolly Holidays Packages, Featuring Mickey's Very Merry Christmas Party

Walt Disney World is at its most magical during the holidays. Hours are extended, special parades and shows debut, and a meet-the-characters show and party runs on selected evenings. Tickets for Mickey's Very Merry Christmas Party should be purchased in advance, or are also included in a Jolly Holidays Package, a special all-inclusive holiday deal. Call (407) W-DISNEY for details.

It is quite possible to celebrate Christmas at WDW without getting caught in the crush. The decorations go up just after Thanksgiving, and the special shows, packages, and holiday parties begin soon thereafter. A family visiting in early December can see all the special stuff—except, of course, for the Christmas Day parade—without having to face the harrowing holiday crowds. If school schedules rule out an early-December trip, note that the week before Christmas is slightly less hectic than the week between Christmas and New Year's.

When my family visited last Christmas, we were agog at the hotel decorations. Aladdin's hometown of Agrabah was reconstructed out of gingerbread at Port Orleans; the Yacht and Beach Clubs offered the gingerbread villages of the Little Mermaid and Belle. The on-site hotels hosted fun little parties for their guests, with visits from Santa, stockings for the children, eggnog and cookies, and Victorian carolers giving a homey feel to a hotel holiday. Each hotel has its own themed trees as well—and the sweeping pink poinsettia tree at the Grand Floridian is a classic.

THAT SPORTIN' LIFE: ON WATER

Most on-site hotels have lovely marinas with a variety of watercraft to meet the needs of every age group.

The two major recreational lagoons in WDW are the Seven Seas Lagoon, which is in front of the MK and serves Fort Wilderness and the MK resorts, and the Buena Vista Lagoon at the Disney Village Marketplace. In addition, the Yacht and Beach Clubs share a lagoon with the Swan and the Dolphin; and the Caribbean Beach Resort, Port Orleans, and Dixie Landings all have their own lagoons and watercraft.

Since rates at WDW are raised frequently, it's not a bad idea to confirm prices for boat rentals in advance. In the on-season, reservations are a good idea. Call (407) 824-2621, or press 57 in your on-site hotel room.

Note: You do not have to be a guest of an on-site resort to rent the boats, although the marina will ask for either a resort ID or a WDW ticket, along with a current driver's license for the larger boats. If you're staying off-site and don't want to bother commuting to an on-site hotel, try the Disney Village Marketplace, where water sprites and canopy boats are available.

- *Water Sprites:* Those zippy little speedboats you see darting around the Buena Vista and Seven Seas Lagoons can be rented for $13.50 per half hour. Drivers must be 12 years old, although kids of any age will enjoy riding alongside Mom and Dad. Water sprites can be rented at the marinas of the Polynesian, Contemporary, Grand Floridian, Wilderness Lodge, and Fort Wilderness, or at the Buena Vista Lagoon.

- *Sailboats:* The Polynesian, Contemporary, Grand Floridian, Yacht and Beach Clubs, Caribbean Beach Resort, and Fort Wilderness marinas all provide sailboats, ranging from the two-person Sunfish for $10 per hour to the six-person Capri for $15 per hour. Some styles of boats are easier to manage than others, but the marina employees will be happy to help you select the boat that best suits your skill level.

- *Pontoon Boats:* If your party is larger or less adventurous, head for one of the MK resorts and try touring the Seven Seas Lagoon in a motor-powered pontoon for $35 per hour. Similar canopy boats are available at the Disney Village Marketplace, MK resort marinas, Yacht and Beach Clubs, Disney's Old Key West, Wilderness Lodge, Dixie Landings, and Port Orleans for $18 per half hour or $30 per hour.

- *Pedal Boats:* These small people-powered craft can be rented at either the Seven Seas or Buena Vista Lagoon for $8 per hour. The Yacht and Beach Clubs, Disney's Old Key West, Swan and Dolphin, Port Orleans, Wilderness Lodge, and Fort Wilderness also have pedal boats, with the option of a half hour rental for $5, which is preferable since the legs tire quickly in these vehicles.

• *Canoes and Rowboats:* If you'd like to try fishing in the canals around Fort Wilderness, rent a canoe for either $4 per hour or $9 per day at the Bike Barn. Rowboats rent for $5 per half hour at the Yacht and Beach Clubs marina, Disney's Old Key West, Port Orleans, and Dixie Landings.

• *Water-skiing:* A boat, a driver, and full equipment can be rented at Fort Wilderness, the Polynesian, the Grand Floridian, and the Contemporary marinas. The cost is $82 per hour for up to five people, and reservations can be made 14 days in advance by calling (407) 824-2621.

• *Fishing:* Angling is permitted in the canals—but not the lagoons or lakes—around Fort Wilderness. Rods and reels are for rent at the Bike Barn, and you can either drop a line from shore or take a canoe or pontoon boat deeper into the canals. Guided two-hour expeditions leave three times a day, and up to five people can be accommodated for a $137 fee, which includes the boat, the guide, the equipment, and snacks. Make reservations up to 14 days in advance by calling (407) 824-2621.

If your kids just want to play around with the idea of fishing, you can drop a line for catfish at Ol' Man Island in Dixie Landings. Guests at Dixie Landings and Port Orleans also have their own fishing excursions available; call (407) 934-5409 for details.

• *Swimming:* All the WDW hotels have private pools, but the Contemporary and Dolphin pools are best for serious swimmers, because they have special lanes reserved for laps. The newer hotels—the Swan and Dolphin, the Yacht and Beach Clubs, Port Orleans, and Dixie Landings—boast more elaborately themed pool areas, which almost qualify as mini–water parks.

- *Parasailing:* If you're up—way up—for something different, you can parasail high above the Seven Seas Lagoon. The cost is $45 per person, and riders must be 42 inches in height. Kids can ride in tandem with a parent if they choose, but they'll still have to pay.

Rides leave daily from the Contemporary Resort marina and should be reserved in advance. Call (407) 824-1000, ext. 3586.

THAT SPORTIN' LIFE: ON LAND

- *Tennis:* Several on-site hotels (the Contemporary, the Grand Floridian, the Yacht and Beach Clubs, the Swan, and the Dolphin) have courts that can be reserved 24 hours in advance. Call (407) 824-3578 for details.

The tennis courts at Fort Wilderness and Disney's Old Key West operate on a first-come first-served basis.

There is considerable variation in fees. A court costs $10 an hour at the Contemporary—$12 at the Grand Floridian, Swan, and Dolphin—but tennis is free at the Disney's Old Key West and the Yacht and Beach Clubs. If you'd like private lessons or to participate in a clinic, consider staying at the Contemporary, which has lessons for $40 per hour, $25 per half hour. You can also get a $40 package, which allows the entire family court time for the duration of your stay. The Contemporary also runs clinics, which include videotaped analysis of your play by the club pro. Call (407) 824-3578 for details.

The Grand Floridian, though not the tennis haven that the Contemporary is, also offers lessons at $35 per hour.

• *Golf:* There are now five courses actually on the WDW grounds, with greens fees running about $85 for WDW hotel guests, about $95 for those staying off-site. With such pricey fees, anyone planning to golf a lot should consider the World Adventure or some other package. (Magic Kingdom Club members also get price breaks.) Or play in the early evening, when twilight fees drop to as low as $40.

The five courses are the Palm and Magnolia, two fairly demanding courses located near the MK; the Lake Buena Vista Course, which is near the Disney Institute Villas; and the newest courses, Osprey Ridge and Eagle Pines, which share the Bonnet Lakes Golf Club. Beginners and kids are better off at the nine-hole Oak Trail near the Magnolia, which is a walking course with fees of $24 for adults and $11 for kids under 17. (Two adults can get a reduced rate of $32, and two kids can play for $16.)

To reserve a tee-off time or arrange for participation in a golf clinic, call (407) 824-2270. WDW guests can make tee-off and lesson reservations up to 30 days in advance; those staying off-site can (and should) make reservations seven days in advance.

• *Running:* Jogging trails cut through the grounds of nearly every WDW hotel; consult Guest Services for a map. Fort Wilderness has a 2.3-mile exercise trail complete with posted period stops for chin-ups, sit-ups, and a host of other tortures. The sprawling Caribbean Beach Resort and the Wilderness Lodge, with its invitingly shady trails, are also good choices for runners.

- *Horseback Riding:* Guided trail rides leave the Fort Wilderness grounds five times a day. Surprisingly and disappointingly, children under 9 are forbidden, even though the horses are gentle and the pace is slow. The cost is $17, and reservations can be made up to 14 days in advance. Call (407) 824-2832 before you leave home for reservations and information.

If younger kids really want to saddle up, short pony rides are offered from 10 A.M. to 5 P.M. during the on-season at the petting zoo at Fort Wilderness, for a cost of $2. No reservations are necessary, but if you want to know if the ponies are saddled up on the day of your visit, call (407) 824-2832.

- *Spas:* The Contemporary, Grand Floridian, Swan, Dolphin, Yacht and Beach Clubs, and Disney's Old Key West all have health clubs, and the general cost is $5 per visit or $10 for your entire stay—well worth it when you consider that most of the health clubs have whirlpools and saunas, a nice wrap-up to a day spent walking around the theme parks. Most of the health clubs are for the exclusive use of that particular hotel's guests, but the Contemporary, Swan, and Dolphin facilities are open to all on-site guests.

If working out is really important to you, stay at the Disney Dolphin, whose Body by Jake health club is the most complete, hands-down. The equipment is state-of-the-art, the class schedule is varied, and you can even book a session with a personal trainer. Another option is a stay at the Disney Institute. The health club there is one of the most complete in Florida, with an amazing variety of machines; full tennis, golf, and basketball facilities; and daily classes in everything from boxing to yoga. Limited use of the fitness center facilities is currently available on a daily basis, although this is subject to change when the Institute is full. Call (407) 827-1100 for details.

• *Cycling:* Bikes ($4 an hour or $8 a day) or tandems ($5 an hour) can be rented at the Bike Barn in Fort Wilderness, at the Disney Institute Villas, or at Dixie Landings, Port Orleans, Disney's Old Key West, the Wilderness Lodge, and the Caribbean Beach Resort. If you're driving and staying at one of the really big resorts, most notably the Caribbean Beach Resort or Dixie Landings, consider bringing bikes from home. The sidewalk system is extensive, and cycling is a practical way of getting around.

• *Other:* Still have energy to burn? Get up a volleyball or basketball game at Fort Wilderness. The Yacht and Beach Clubs offer volleyball and croquet. Or play a game of miniature golf *Fantasia*-style at the Board-Walk Resort.

ESPN CENTER

Sports enthusiasts will applaud the opening of the ESPN sports club as part of the BoardWalk complex near Epcot. Set to debut as this book goes to press, the center will contain a broadcast and production facility (meaning athlete celebs will always be on hand) and the ultimate sports bar, featuring—and I'm quoting— "the best ballpark cuisine from around the country." Most fun of all should be the interactive virtual-reality games: You can swap shots with your favorite tennis pro or have all the excitement of playing in the NFL, with none of the bruises.

8

★★★★★★★★★★★★★★★★★★★

*Disney World
After Dark*

DISNEY WORLD AFTER DARK: WITH THE KIDS

Is there life in WDW after 8 P.M.? Sure there is. The crowds thin, the temperature drops, and many attractions are especially dazzling by dark. Orlando is actually a kiddie version of Las Vegas—a town that naps but never sleeps—where miniature-golf courses and McDonald's stay open all night. During peak seasons the major theme parks stay open until midnight, so it's easy to have fun after dark. But, needless to say, the particular kind of fun you'll have depends on whether or not the kids are with you.

Evening Activities for the Whole Family

SpectroMagic in the MK

The latest incarnation of Disney's ever-popular Main Street Electrical Parade, SpectroMagic blends lasers, lights, and fireworks for a dazzling display. Spectro-Magic runs only on selected evenings during the off-season, but every night during the on-season. In the busiest weeks, there are two showings: The 11 P.M. is rarely as crowded as the 9 P.M.

Note: The parade is a don't-miss—if you're visiting during the off-season, plan your schedule to ensure you'll be in the MK on one of the evenings it's slated to run.

The Electrical Water Pageant

If you're staying on-site, the Electrical Water Pageant may actually float by your hotel window, since it is staged on the Seven Seas Lagoon, which connects the Polynesian, Contemporary, Grand Floridian, and Fort Wilderness resorts. Times vary with the season, but generally the Pageant is visible at 9 P.M. from the Polynesian, 9:20 from the Grand Floridian, 9:45 from Fort Wilderness, and 10:05 from the Contemporary. (Call Guest Services at your hotel for exact showtimes.)

If you're not staying on-site, simply ride the monorail to the resort of your choice. The Electrical Water Pageant plays every night, even during the off-season. Although a much shorter and less elaborate show than SpectroMagic, nothing can beat the effect of multicolored lights twinkling on darkened water. Besides, by 9 P.M. most kids would rather sprawl on a beach than camp on a curb.

Movies

If you're staying on-site, check out the offerings in the theater of the Contemporary Resort. Two different Disney classics show each night at 7 and 9 P.M. Movies are also shown at the evening campfire at Fort Wilderness (with Chip and Dale in attendance); and in many Orlando hotels, the Disney Channel is available 24 hours a day.

The 10-screen theater adjacent to Pleasure Island is a good place to park older kids and teens while parents try out the clubs. Call (407) 827-1300 to see what's playing.

Arcades

It's no secret that kids flip for arcades, especially the mammoth Fiesta Fun Center at the Contemporary Resort. Even hard-core pinball junkies are bound to find games they've never seen before.

IllumiNations at Epcot

IllumiNations at Epcot can be viewed from anywhere around the World Showcase Lagoon at closing time. With fireworks, laser lights, stirring music, and choreographed fountains spurting in three-quarter time, IllumiNations is a definite must-see.

Fireworks

A rousing fireworks display can be seen from anywhere in the MK about 10 P.M. during the on-season. The show is short but exciting, and at holiday times a more extensive fireworks extravaganza is presented.

Note: Be there a few minutes earlier to witness Tinkerbell's Flight.

Fireworks also close Pleasure Island each night, and MGM is currently signing off with a more-elaborate-than-usual display called Sorcery in the Sky.

The Rides at Night

Those attractions with the two-hour lines at noon are far more accessible by night, so it's worth revisiting any ride you passed up earlier in the day. In the MK, the Big Thunder Mountain Railroad is much more fun in the dark; Splash Mountain feels like a totally different ride, and Cinderella's Golden Carousel is especially magical at night.

At Epcot it is almost always easy to tour Journey Into Imagination and see *Honey, I Shrunk the Audience* after 7 P.M. (In fact, any Future World attraction is easily boarded during the dinner hour, when everyone heads out to dine in the World Showcase.) At MGM try SuperStar Television or the Indiana Jones Epic Stunt Spectacular; not only are the shows less crowded, but volunteer wannabes stand a better chance of being chosen during the evening shows, especially at SuperStar Television.

Night Swimming

Blizzard Beach, Typhoon Lagoon, and River Country all run extended hours in the summer, and the crowds are far thinner after 5 P.M. It stays hot in Orlando well into a summer evening, and, since you don't have to worry about heat exhaustion or sunburn, many families with young kids actually prefer evening swimming. Hotel pools stay open very late as well, some until after midnight.

DISNEY WORLD AFTER DARK: WITHOUT THE KIDS

Why would any decent parent seek a sitter while on a family vacation? Consider this scenario:

Meaghan's sucking the inside of her mouth. Loudly. Mom keeps making everyone stop while she readjusts the strap of her shoe to accommodate the blister she picked up halfway around the World Showcase Lagoon. You spent $148 to get through the gates of Universal Studios, specifically to ride those highly publicized high-tech rides you've heard so much about, and Devin spends the entire afternoon feeding quarters into the same arcade game that's in the local mall back home. Dad has been singing the first line—and only the first line—of "Zip-A-Dee-Doo-Dah" since Thursday. You've asked to see the kiddie menus from nine different restaurants in nine different Epcot countries, and you end up at the America pavilion fast-food joint because Kristy won't eat anything but a hot dog. It's 108°, this trip is costing $108 an hour, and that infernal sucking sound is getting on the last nerve you have left. In short, you have third-day-itis . . . and it's only the second day of your trip.

Although it may seem un-American or even sacrilegious to suggest building time apart into the middle of a family vacation, the truth is that everyone will have more fun if occasionally you break up the group for a while. Even the most devoted families aren't accustomed to being together 24 hours a day—for every meal, every ride, every potty stop. Every minute.

Some of the hotels in Orlando have responded with programs designed to get the kids involved with other kids so that parents can have some peace and privacy. Kristy can eat her hot dog, Meaghan can give herself hickeys, and Devin can play Cosmic Invaders 77 straight times without parental glares. The adults can dare to order a meal that will take three hours to enjoy and linger over their coffee. Everyone returns refreshed, recharged, and with some happy stories to tell, and you can start the next day actually glad to be together again.

If you decide to schedule at least one parents' night out during your trip, you'll soon learn that Orlando offers an array of child-care options. Several of the on-site hotels have full-fledged kids' clubs, and where else on earth can your child be bedded down by a real-life Mary Poppins? Among the off-site hotels, there is a large range in cost and quality among the programs offered; many of the off-site programs are free of charge to hotel guests (at least during certain hours), which can mean big savings for parents.

The key point is to make your plans before you leave home, either by selecting a hotel that has a kids' club or by arranging for an in-room sitter. If you suddenly get an urge for fine dining at 4 P.M. on a Saturday in July, it will be hard to find a sitter. But if you've checked out your options in advance, it's a breeze.

In-Room Sitters

You'll need to arrange for an in-room sitter if any of the following conditions apply.

- You have a child under the age of 4. Very few of the organized kids' clubs will accept children younger than this, and most require that they be potty-trained.

- You plan to be out after 12 A.M. Most kids' clubs close down at midnight, some as early as 10 P.M. Parents headed for Pleasure Island or Church Street Station, where the action doesn't begin to heat up until 10 P.M., need in-room sitting.

- Your kids are exhausted. If you know in advance that you plan to employ an all-out touring schedule, or your children fall apart after 8 P.M., hire an in-room sitter who can put them in bed at their usual time. Most of the kids' clubs at least try to put preschoolers down in sleeping bags by 9 P.M. (the Hilton actually has beds inside Vacation Station), but this can involve moving them, and possibly waking them, when parents return.

- You have a big family. Even with the add-on per-child rate, you'll come out cheaper with an in-room sitter than trying to book four kids into the Neverland Club.

If you decide you'll need in-room sitting, begin by contacting your hotel. Many hotels are happy to arrange the sitting for you through a licensed and bonded agency (listed on the next page), and this saves a bit of hassle. Guest Services personnel are also apt to give you a good recommendation on which service to try; if guests aren't pleased with a sitter or a service, the hotel is undoubtedly the first to hear about it.

Want to make your own plans? For those staying on-site, KinderCare provides trained sitters for all the Disney hotels, if you call (407) 827-5437 at least eight hours in advance. The rate is $9 per hour, $11 per hour for two kids, and there's a four-hour minimum.

At least six independent agencies dispatch sitters to the off-site hotels, but the following two agencies have received especially high marks from our readers:

Super Sitters   (407) 382-2558

ABC Mothers   (407) 857-7447

These services stay busy during the summer months, so it's not a bad idea to book them before you leave home. Rates are typically $7.50 per hour with a four-hour minimum, and an extra-child charge of $1 an hour per child. A $5 transportation fee is also common, meaning that in-room sitting for two kids for four hours would run $36—not a cheap option, but for many parents it's well worth the cost.

The independent services can be quite inclusive, with service available 24 hours a day, seven days a week. For families willing to pay the extra bucks, sitters will take the kids out to a fast-food place for supper, or even to area attractions. One resourceful divorced father took his two daughters along on a business trip to Orlando, and while he sat in meetings a Super Sitter trotted the girls around the theme parks.

KinderCare Child-Care Center

KinderCare offers a "learning while playing" developmental program for children 1 to 12. The setup is similar to the hundreds of KinderCares nationwide. It's a daytime program: You drop the children off at the facility, which is on the WDW grounds, and pick them up a few hours later. Call (407) 827-5454 for details. The center exists primarily for the use of Disney employees, but visiting children are accepted on a day-by-day basis as space permits. You do not have to be a guest at an on-site hotel to use the service, and the cost is $36 for a 10-hour day, or $8 per hour.

On-Site Kids' Clubs

The following on-site hotels have kids' clubs; all have a (407) area code:

Contemporary	824-1000
Dolphin	934-4241
Grand Floridian	824-2985
Polynesian	824-2170
Wilderness Lodge	824-1083
Yacht and Beach Club	934-8000

The clubs generally run in the evening for kids 4 to 12, and the clubhouses are well stocked with Disney-themed toys—as well as computers, video and arcade games, and large-screen TVs. The cost is $4 per hour, and reservations are required. (Not much advance notice is needed, but you can make reservations by contacting Guest Services at the appropriate hotel; on-site guests get first crack at the available slots, but if the clubs don't fill up, space is available to off-site visitors.) The clubhouses are open from 4:30 P.M. until midnight, and cookies and milk are served at bedtime. Kids must be toilet trained—even Mary Poppins has her limits.

The Polynesian offers a twist—a "dinner theater" for kids 4 to 12 in the Neverland Club, including a full meal and entertainment. Animals and birds are often brought over from Discovery Island, a character drops by, and the evening is wrapped up with ice cream and games. The cost is $8 per child per hour with a minimum three-hour visit. The Neverland Club is open 5 P.M. until midnight, and reservations can be made at (407) 824-2170. Several families surveyed specifically mentioned what a swell evening this was for their kids. One father vividly described how his timid and stranger-shy 4-year-old was so won over by the drop-in visit from Alice in Wonderland that she screamed and clung to the Neverland Club doorframe when her parents returned to pick her up!

Note: Prices, policy, and planned entertainment change quickly at the kids' clubs, so confirm all the information when you make your reservations.

Off-site Kids' Clubs with Fees

Several off-site hotels have their own versions of kids' clubs, with wide-screen TVs, Nintendo games, and wading pools to entertain the children while parents do the town. These programs are well run and flexible—Shamu's Playhouse at the Stouffer, for example, offers a wide range of organized activities and accepts kids as young as 6 months old from 8 A.M. to 11 P.M.

Most of the programs run only at night. Generally, it is not required that you be registered at the hotel in order to take advantage of the program, although this policy can change during busy seasons when the programs are filled. The typical cost is $6 per hour with $3 for each additional child.

Another advantage to these hotels is that they have fine-dining establishments right on the premises: Haifeng and Atlantis at the Stouffer and Arthur's 27 at the Buena Vista Palace are outstanding restaurants with leisurely, adult-paced service. They provide a nice break from the typical theme park dining experience, where you frantically color pictures of Pluto and juggle sugar packets in an effort to keep the kids entertained until the food arrives. All the hotels mentioned here are equipped to either escort the kids to the resort coffee shop for a simple meal or order in room service so the kids can eat while the parents dine out.

At various times the hotels have offered special deals, such as three hours of complimentary child care for parents dining in the hotel's flagship restaurant. This perk seems to come and go, and 24-hour notice is always required, so call to check. Even if you wind up having to pay for the service, this is a good option if you feel a bit nervous about leaving your children back at your hotel with a strange sitter. By dining at a hotel with on-site child care, you have the security of knowing that the kids are in the same building. It also softens the blow for your children of being left behind, since they're going "out," too.

A hotel that provides daytime as well as evening sitting is the Hyatt Regency Grand Cypress. (The Hyatt is known throughout the entertainment industry for the quality of its children's programs.) Daily during the on-season and on weekends year-round, Camp Hyatt offers kids 5 to 12 a wide range of outdoor and craft activities. Kids 3 to 5 are welcome in the Childcare Center, a less-structured program, and the cost for either Camp Hyatt or the Childcare Center is $6 an hour. Since the staff is around from 8 A.M. to 10 P.M. during the on-season, parents can play tennis, take in a round of golf at the resort's outstanding course, or simply relax by the dramatically landscaped pool. If you need child care during dinner hours, both Camp

Hyatt and the Childcare Center are operative on weekend evenings. And the hotel's own Hemingway's, a seafood restaurant located in a grotto on top of the pool waterfall, is a romantic getaway.

But the Hyatt doesn't stop there. Rock Hyatt, oriented toward teens, gives your 15-year-old the opportunity to hang out with her own kind after a stressful day of having to be nice to her younger brothers. Rock Hyatt is free and runs on Friday and Saturday nights year-round.

For more information on the kids' clubs call:

Buena Vista Palace	(407) 827-2727
Hilton at Disney Village	(407) 827-4000
Hyatt Regency Grand Cypress	(407) 239-1234
Stouffer Orlando Resort	(407) 351-5555

Off-site Kids' Clubs Without Fees

Parents who'd like to go out more than once during their vacation, or whose kids just enjoy being around other children, should look for a hotel with a complimentary kids' club. Interestingly, this is not one of those times when you get what you pay for—one might think free child care means a lackluster program, but just the opposite is true. Hotels that are committed enough to families to provide a free kids' club are also committed enough to do the job right. The Sunspree Holiday Inn at Lake Buena Vista, Embassy Suites at Exit 27 off I-4, and the Delta Orlando all have hotel mascots, a program that combines outdoor fun with restful activities, and beeper service to keep you in contact and give you additional peace of mind. And, since most of the activities for the kids are free, you're shaving as much as $35 off the cost of a parents' night out.

These perks are not reflected in the cost of the rooms, either—the Holiday Inn and Delta Orlando start as low as $89 a night; and with villas starting as low as $160, Embassy Suites is a reasonable option for families needing more room.

Note: The programs are free unless food is involved. All the hotels listed will arrange to feed kids between 6 and 9 P.M. if parents wish to dine on their own; the cost for supplying the meals is usually $6 to $8, and the food is always something like pizza or tacos that kids like, generally followed by make-your-own ice-cream sundaes. There may also be a cost if a craft is involved. In some programs, such as at the Delta Orlando or Embassy Suites, kids learn to tie-dye T-shirts or do other fairly involved crafts. If out-of-the-ordinary supplies are required, that cost is passed along to parents. As with the food, however, the hotels try to keep the costs reasonable, usually around $6.

For details call:

Delta Orlando	(407) 351-3340
Embassy Suites	(407) 239-1144
Holiday Inn SunSpree at Lake Buena Vista	(407) 239-4500

DINING WITHOUT THE KIDS

Certain on-site restaurants are more enjoyable without children, so once you've found a sitter, reserve a table for two at one of the following fine establishments.

At Epcot

Chefs de France or Bistro de Paris

Chefs de France features nouvelle cuisine, meaning the sauces are lighter and the preparation simpler than traditional French fare. This is still heady stuff: grouper with lobster sauce, roast duckling with prunes, or salmon-and-tarragon soufflé. The atmosphere is elegant and understated, and the service unrushed. Chefs de France is definitely one of the most expensive eateries at Epcot: Dinner for two runs about $100.

The Bistro de Paris upstairs is just as expensive and just as good. Although the atmosphere is still lovely—high ceilings, brass, and etched glass abound—and the service still attentive, the Bistro represents hearty, casual French dining. Waiters are more than willing to advise you on selections and, as is true at Chefs, it's impossible to go wrong with any of the desserts.

Romance factor: B for Chefs de France, which is "on the street"; A for Bistro de Paris, which is quieter and darker.

Marrakesh

Ready to take a walk on the semiwild side? The music, architecture, and menu in the Moroccan restaurant are truly distinctive, proving beyond a doubt that you aren't in Kansas anymore. You'll be served lamb, couscous, and honeyed chicken by waiters in floor-length robes while belly dancers weave among the tile tables. (The effect of these dancers on husbands is somewhat akin to the effect meeting Mickey has on toddlers: They're stunned while it's happening, but later remember the experience fondly.)

Romance factor: C. The tables are very close together, lots of families bring the kids, and the place can become quite loud.

San Angel Inn Restaurante

The menu here goes far past the tacos and enchiladas most Americans consider Mexican food, and the atmosphere is unparalleled. The restaurant overlooks El Rio del Tiempo, the boat ride that encircles an Aztec pyramid beneath a starry sky. The darkness of the Mexico pavilion, which simulates midnight even at high noon, and the murmur of the rio are hypnotic. Throw in a couple of margaritas and you may never leave.

The *molé poblano* and any of the grilled seafood dishes are consistently good. The friendliness of the service makes the San Angel a good choice even when the children are along.

Romance factor: B

L'Originale Alfredo di Roma Ristorante

The Alfredo in question is the gentleman who created fettucine Alfredo. This is the most popular restaurant in the World Showcase, usually the first to book up despite the fact that it seats 250 people. The restaurant in itself is entertaining: You can watch through a large window as the cooks crank out pasta; the walls are adorned with clever trompe l'oeil murals; and the waiters provide impromptu concerts, ranging from mildly bawdy Italian folk songs to passionate concerti di Verdi.

Most diners, however, have kids along, making the place a little too loud and crowded for romance.

Romance factor: C

The Coral Reef Restaurant

Tucked away under The Living Seas pavilion, this Future World restaurant is also expensive, about $100 for dinner for two. Unfortunately, the Coral Reef is less romantic than the World Showcase restaurants. The room is simply too large to feel cozy and, as at Alfredo's, most families bring their kids, figuring—and rightly so—that little Nathaniel and Erica can stay busy watching the skin-divers while Mom and Dad crack a lobster.

Romance factor: C

Outside Epcot

Victoria and Albert's

For a very special evening, there is one place in the World so elegant and so removed from the classic Disney image that you'll never feel sticky fingers creeping over the top of the booth behind you. Kids are never seen at Victoria and Albert's in the Grand Floridian, where harp music plays, candles flicker, and ties and jackets are required for men.

Where Disney has built a reputation on providing pleasure to the masses, this 50-seat restaurant proves there is also room in WDW for highly individualized service. When Henry Flagler built the railroad that opened Florida to the oil magnates of the late 1800s, Queen Victoria and Prince Albert sat upon the British throne. Now, in one of those "only Disney would go to such trouble" details, all hosts and hostesses in the restaurant call themselves Albert or Victoria.

Your menu will have your name handwritten at the top, waiters describe the selections for the evening, and the chef often circulates among the tables. At the end of a six-course meal, guests are presented with long-stemmed roses, Godiva chocolates, and their menus. This is the most expensive restaurant in WDW, hands down—the prix fixe dinner is $100 per person, $125 with wine—but it's so special that you'll be talking about it years afterward. On the evening we visited, the salad was a floral arrangement in a crouton vase—until Victoria tapped the side of the crouton, releasing the greens into a fan-shaped pattern on the plate; and the coffee service was more elaborate than a Japanese tea ceremony. Call (407) 824-2391 for reservations, or make arrangements through Guest Services.

Note: Victoria and Albert's is the only full-service restaurant in WDW that is not included in the World Adventure or any other package dining plan.

Romance factor: A+

The California Grille

This new restaurant, located atop the Contemporary Resort, has become so popular so fast that Disney is reeling. One clue to the quality: Disney executives lunch here. Not only does the California Grille offer a marvelous variety of cuisine with stylish preparation, but the views from the top of the Contemporary are unparalleled, especially during the Magic Kingdom fireworks. Call (407) 824-1576 for reservations.

Romance factor: A

Outside Walt Disney World

Excellent dining abounds beyond the Disney World gates, and many of the fancier restaurants are in hotels. Dux in the Peabody offers an intimate environment, unusual seafood and game selections, and an outstanding list of California wines, many available by the glass. Arthur's 27, the rooftop restaurant of the Buena Vista Palace, has an award-winning menu and a reputation for consistent quality in both service and food. The huge Hyatt Regency Grand Cypress, a gorgeous destination in itself, is also home to Hemingway's, offering the outstanding cuisine typical of the Hyatts and an atmosphere so lush and tropical it isn't typical of anything at all.

If you venture past the hotels, you'll find there are plenty of places in Orlando that offer good food, reasonable prices, and friendly, unpretentious service. Pebbles, in the Crossroads of Lake Buena Vista, serves up Key West–style food in a casual atmosphere and is a good choice if you're going to nearby Pleasure Island after you eat.

Dining of a campier sort can be found at Church Street Station, a dining and shopping complex in downtown Orlando. Rosie O'Gradys and Lilly Marlene's dish up tasty but casual food, huge specialty drinks, and live music. Late in the evening, Church Street becomes a giant party, with patrons moving from one establishment to the next, sampling the various bar munchies and entertainment offerings.

Planet Hollywood is also a popular place to party—either with or without the kids. And nothing's quite as funky as the Hard Rock Cafe, adjacent to Universal Studios. Both these places rev up late at night, so if you want to get in the true spirit, hire an in-room sitter and eat at 11 P.M.

9

★★★★★★★★★★★★★★★★★★★★

And Another Thing . . .

BARE NECESSITIES: STROLLERS, BABIES, PREGNANCY, SPECIAL NEEDS, AND FIRST-AID

Strollers

• All kids under 3 need a stroller, for napping and waiting in line as well as riding.

• For kids 3 to 6, the general rule is: Strollers are a must at Epcot, nice in the MK, and not really needed at MGM, where the park is smaller and a lot of time is spent in sit-down shows.

• Strollers rent for $6 a day, so if you'll need one every day, consider bringing your own from home. If you have an older child who will need a stroller only at Epcot, however, rental isn't a bad option. If you plan to spend time at more than one park, you don't have to pay twice: Keep your receipt and show it for a new stroller when you arrive at the next park.

• The MK and Epcot strollers are sturdy, drop back to form a completely flat bed, and can hold two kids in a pinch. The MGM strollers are the lightweight, easily collapsible "umbrella" type.

• Tie something like a bandanna or a balloon to your stroller to mark it, thus reducing the probability it'll be swiped while you're inside Peter Pan's Flight. As one mother observed, "Otherwise honest people seem to think nothing about stealing a stroller, but stop when they see they might be taking a personal possession as well."

• Stroller stolen anyway? In the MK, check in at the Trading Post in Frontierland, or Tinkerbell's Toy Shop in Fantasyland. At Epcot you can get a new stroller at the World Traveler Shop between France and the United Kingdom. Return to Oscar's Super Service at MGM. So long as you've kept your receipt, there's no charge for a replacement stroller.

• If at 8 A.M. your 5-year-old swears she doesn't need a stroller, but at noon she collapses in a heap halfway around Epcot's World Showcase, head for the World Traveler Shop between France and the United Kingdom. The World Traveler is also the place to rent a stroller if you're coming from the Swan, Dolphin, BoardWalk, or Yacht and Beach Clubs and thus using the "backdoor" entrance.

• If you have an infant, bring a stroller from home. The rental strollers in the MK and Epcot are too large and too hard for babies who can't sit at all.

• Likewise, if you're staying at one of the more sprawling resorts, such as the Caribbean Beach Resort, Dixie Landings, or Fort Wilderness, bring a stroller from home. It's likely to be quite a trek from your room to the pool or shuttle-bus stop.

Baby Services

Rockers, bottle warmers, high chairs, and changing tables are all found at the Baby Services centers; and diapers, formula, and jars of baby food are for sale. The centers are an absolute haven for families traveling with a very young child. (One mother reported that the attendant on duty was even able to diagnose a suspicious-looking rash on her toddler as a reaction to too much citrus juice, evidently a common Florida malady.

She later took the child to a doctor and learned that the attendant had been right on the money.)

In the MK, Baby Services is beside the Crystal Palace at the end of Main Street. It's inside the Guest Services building at MGM, and near the Odyssey Restaurant at Epcot.

Diapers

Diapers are available at the following locations:

- Baby Services centers
- Stroller-rental shops
- The Emporium on Main Street in the MK
- Celebrity 5 & 10 at MGM

The shops don't waste shelf space on mundane products, so you'll have to ask. Changing tables are available in most ladies' restrooms and now—finally—in some men's. You can always use the Baby Services centers to change infants, and there are potty chairs for toddlers as well.

Breast-feeding

WDW is so casual and family-oriented that you shouldn't feel self-conscious about discreetly nursing in the theaters or restaurants. Some shows, such as the Hall of Presidents in the MK or *Impressions de France* at Epcot, are dark, quiet, and ideal for nursing. Others, like the Country Bear Vacation Hoedown in the MK or the Monster Sound Show at MGM are so loud the baby will probably be too distracted.

If you're too modest for these methods or your baby is easily disturbed, try the rockers in the Baby Services centers.

Pregnant?

I've personally toured WDW twice while pregnant and not only lived to tell the tale, but honestly enjoyed both trips. A few precautions are in order:

• Make regular meal stops. Instead of buying a sandwich from a vendor, get out of the sun and off your feet at a sit-down restaurant.

• If you aren't accustomed to walking five or six miles a day—an average WDW trek—begin getting in shape at home. By taking 30- to 40-minute walks, beginning a couple of months before your trip, you'll be less likely to get sore or poop out once you're at WDW.

• Dehydration is a real danger. Drink lots of fluids and keep a juicebox in your tote bag for emergencies.

• This is definitely an occasion when it's worth the money to stay on-site. Return to your room in midafternoon to cool off, take a nap, or just put your feet up.

• If staying on-site isn't feasible, the Baby Services centers have rockers and are a good place for mothers-to-be to take a break. And the parks are full of benches—sit sown when you can.

• Standing stock-still can be much more tiring than walking, so let your husband stand in line for rides. You and the kids can join him just as he's about to enter the final turn of the line.

• Once you're inside the holding area for theater-style attractions, such as the Country Bear Vacation Hoedown or Universe of Energy, find a bench and sit down. If the benches are taken, sit on the floor near the wall and don't stand up when the Disney attendant gets on the loudspeaker and asks everyone to move into the theater; all the people in the holding area will be admitted into the theater, so it's pointless to get up now and all mob the turnstiles at once. Let everyone else go ahead and then amble through. (This is a good strategy for anyone who is utterly exhausted, pregnant or not.)

• Most important of all, use this book to check out restroom locations in advance (see the "Best Restroom Locations" listings in Sections 4 and 5).

Special Needs

• Wheelchairs can be rented at any stroller-rental stand, and most attractions are accessible by wheelchair. (Epcot has a few of those 3-wheel motorized wheelchairs for rent, which can be very convenient considering the miles you'll cover in a typical Epcot day.) Attendants will be happy to help guests with special needs board and disembark from rides.

Once they're in the theme parks and ready to ride the attractions, guests in wheelchairs are boarded through their own gates and are often able to avoid waiting in lines altogether.

If someone in your party is in a wheelchair, be sure to request a copy of the *Guidebook for Disabled Guests,* either when you order your tickets in advance or at the wheelchair-rental booth. It's a specific guide to how each ride should be boarded.

• A tip from frequent visitors: If you're traveling with someone in a wheelchair, it's emphatically worth the money to stay on-site. Disney does an excellent job of offering disabled guests a number of transportation options. The ferry and monorail are wheelchair-accessible, but, if needed, you can request a van with a motorized platform. The resorts offer rooms with specially equipped bathrooms and extralarge doors; and life jackets for the handicapped are available at resort pools and water parks. The Polynesian gets high marks from readers with special needs, but for those seeking a less-expensive option, the All-Star Resorts have several rooms especially designed to meet the needs of the handicapped for $79 a night.

• Portable tape players and cassettes for sight-impaired guests are available, as are TDDs for the hearing-impaired. Check with City Hall in the MK, Earth Station at Epcot, and Guest Services at MGM.

Deaf guests have a special phone line to call for park information: (407) 827-5141.

• All on-site hotels are equipped to refrigerate insulin.

• Finally, not a tip but a word of reassurance: If you're traveling with someone who has a chronic health problem or disability, rest assured that WDW is one of the most stress-free vacations you could have planned. Because WDW is frequently visited by children sponsored by the "Make a Wish" Foundation and other programs like it, the personnel at WDW are accustomed to dealing with a wide variety of challenges and have proven themselves able to accommodate visitors who are quite seriously ill. The key is to make everyone at both your hotel and within the theme parks aware of your presence and the possibility you'll need special assistance. Then relax. These people will help you in every way they can.

First-Aid

Next to the MK's Crystal Palace is the first-aid clinic, staffed by two nurses. Epcot has a first-aid clinic located beside the Odyssey Restaurant; MGM's is in the Guest Services center. Although most patients suffer from such maladies as sunburn, motion sickness, and minor scrapes, the clinics are also equipped to handle major emergencies and, when necessary, ambulance service to an area hospital.

It's worth remembering that any medical problem that could occur at home could also occur in the midst of a vacation. I've received letters from people who have broken bones, fainted from the heat, and come down with chicken pox while in Orlando. Their general advice to others is: Seek medical help the minute you even suspect their may be a problem. Waiting only makes the solution more painful and more expensive.

Should you suffer a medical emergency, take comfort in the fact that the Disney people have received ringing endorsements for their response in times of crisis. One mother who developed an eye infection from a scratched cornea reported that the nurse at the Epcot first-aid clinic, immediately recognizing the severity of the problem, arranged for her transport to Sand Lake Hospital so she could see an ophthalmologist. "We only had a long weekend," she writes, "and I would have felt horrible if the kids spent it in a hospital waiting room. But as it was, the nurse handled everything, and my husband and children were able to remain in the park while I was treated. My husband kept phoning the nurse for updates, and I met up with them back at Epcot a couple of hours later, looking like Long John Silver."

Another mother wrote: "When our 8-year-old son developed a (repeat) ear infection in the middle of the

Magic Kingdom, we went to the first-aid clinic. There a sweet nurse gently examined him, contacted his doctor back in Ohio to get his regular prescription, and gave him Tylenol for his immediate relief. By the time we arrived back at our rooms at Port Orleans, the prescription was there, and by the next morning Nicky was back on his feet and ready to go."

A woman who suffered a miscarriage while staying at an on-site hotel also offers the highest praise to the staff there, both for their swift medical response and their emotional support.

General First-aid Tips

• If someone begins to feel ill or suffers a boo-boo in the parks, head straight for the first-aid clinic. If they can't fix it, they'll find someone who can.

• Likewise, all on-site hotels and most off-site hotels have physicians on call 24 hours a day. Contact Guest Services or call (407) 396-1195 between 8 A.M. and 10 P.M. for in-room health care. Turner Drugs in Orlando, (407) 828-8125, will deliver to any on-site hotel room (and many off-site ones) 24 hours a day. There's a $5 charge for delivery, with a surcharge between 10 P.M. and 8 A.M.

• For minor health problems, visit the Medi-Clinic at the intersection of I-4 and Route 192, or the Lake Buena Vista Clinic, which will pick you up at your hotel room between 8 A.M. and 8 P.M. For more serious illnesses or injuries, head for the emergency room at Sand Lake Hospital.

• No matter where you're staying, of course, in a true emergency, you should dial 9-1-1.

HOW TO GET UP-TO-DATE INFORMATION

If you need information before you leave home:

• Write:

Walt Disney World Guest Information
P.O. 10040
Lake Buena Vista, FL 32830-0040

• Subscribe to *Disney Magazine;* eight quarterly issues (a two-year subscription) is $16.95. Write:

Disney Magazine
P.O. Box 37263
Boone, IA 50037-2263

If you need information once you check into your hotel:

• Both on-site and off-site hotels provide a wealth of material upon check-in. Study the brochures and maps your first evening.

• On-site hotels provide continuous information about park operating hours, special events, and touring tips on channel 5. Channel 10 offers an especially helpful program about dinner theaters, evening parades, and special shows, called "Disney Nights."
Resorts in the Disney Village Hotel Plaza have similar services on channel 7, and some of the large off-site hotels have their own entertainment information channels, which keep you up-to-date not only on Disney but on all Orlando-area attractions.

• Magic Kingdom radio is 1030 AM. Epcot is 810 AM. Tune in as you drive into the parks.

• Guest Services in both on-site and off-site hotels is equipped to answer most questions.

• If you still have questions, call (407) 824-4321. A real live person will tell you what time Epcot closes on May 7, the price of Minnie's Revue for a 10-year-old, and how tall you have to be to ride Splash Mountain.

If you need information once you're in the parks:

• Check with Guest Services, which is located near the main gate of all three major theme parks.

• At Epcot there are terminals for the WorldKey Information System (which operate like those located inside the Earth Station under Spaceship Earth) in the Germany pavilion and on the bridges that connect Future World to the World Showcase. You'll have access to a Disney employee within seconds.

• Flag down the nearest person wearing a Disney tag. The "cast members" at the theme parks are remarkably helpful and well informed.

SAVING TIME

• Prepare as much as you can before you leave home. You should purchase theme park tickets, reserve rental cars, and book shows or special dinners long before you pull out of your own driveway. Every call you make now is a line you won't have to stand in later.

• Visit the most popular attractions before 11 A.M. or after 5 P.M.

• Eat lunch either at 11 A.M. or after 2 P.M. This system will have you eating while everyone else is in line for the rides, and riding while everyone else is eating.

• It also saves time—and money—to make lunch your big meal of the day. Most families opt to eat a large breakfast and large dinner and snack at lunch; go against the crowds by eating your big meal in early afternoon, when the parks are too hot and crowded for effective touring anyway.

• Split up. Mom can make the dinner reservations while Dad rents the strollers. Mom can take the 9-year-old to Space Mountain while Dad and the 4-year-old try out the Delta Dreamflight. Security in WDW is very tight, so preteens and teens can tour on their own, meeting up with the rest of the family periodically.

• Be aware that once you cross the Florida state line, there is an inverse relationship between time and money. You have to be willing to spend one in order to save the other. One family proudly listed such cost-saving measures as staying 30 miles outside of Orlando and cooking every meal themselves. They concluded by stating that it took them six days to tour the three major parks, something most families can manage comfortably in four days. Considering the high cost of admissions, it's doubtful that they saved very much money at all and they certainly wasted time.

• If you have three days or less to tour, it is imperative that you go during the off-season. You can see in three days in November what would take six days to see in July.

• Don't feel you have to do it all. If you study this guide and your maps before you go, you'll realize that not every attraction will be equally attractive to your family. The World won't come to an end if you skip a few pavilions.

• The full-service restaurants within the theme parks can be very slow. If you're on a tight touring schedule, stick to fast food or sidewalk vendors and order a pizza at night when you get back to your hotel room.

• If you're staying on-site, make all your dining reservations by phone.

SAVING MONEY

Saving money at WDW is somewhat of an oxymoron, but there are certainly ways to minimize the damage.

• Purchase a Magic Kingdom Club Gold Card. A two-year membership qualifies you for savings of up to 30% at Disney hotels during certain seasons of the year, discounts on theme park tickets, meals, souvenir purchases, and a host of other benefits.

• If the cost of flying the whole family down and then renting a car is prohibitive, consider renting a van in your hometown and driving to Orlando.

• Eat as many meals as possible outside of the parks. If you have a suite, fixing simple meals there is clearly your most economical option. Many Orlando hotels offer free breakfasts to guests, and there are numerous fast-food and family chain restaurants along International Drive and the I-4 exits.

• If you'd like to try some of the nicer Epcot restaurants, book them at lunch when prices are considerably lower than dinner. Many Epcot eateries also offer an Early Value Meal from 4:30 to 6:30 P.M. Recently at Chefs de France, I had an appetizer, entrée, dessert, and beverage for $15, a huge savings in a restaurant where a three-course meal would typically be $35.

And remember that restaurant portions are huge, even with kiddie meals. Consider letting two family members share an entrée.

• Children's value meals run about $2.50 at the fast-food places and $4 at the sit-down restaurants. Kids sometimes eat free at certain establishments, such as Mama Melrose's at MGM and Marrakesh at Epcot. The signs announcing the restaurants offering this deal are well posted.

• Except for maybe an autograph book and a T-shirt, hold off souvenir purchases until the last day. By then the kids will really know what they want, and you won't waste money on impulse buys.

• Purchase film, blank videotapes, diapers, and sunscreen at home before you come. These things are all available in the parks, but you'll pay dearly for the convenience.

• The All-Star Resorts, Caribbean Beach Resort, Port Orleans, Dixie Landings, and Fort Wilderness campground provide the most economical on-site lodging. Off-site, there are several Comfort Inns and Days Inns along I-4 and International Drive, most offering shuttle service to the parks.

• If you're driving to Orlando and not arriving until afternoon or evening, don't reserve your on-site room until the second day of your visit. It's silly to pay for a whole day of Grand Floridian amenities if you'll be checking in at 10 P.M. Instead, stop your first night at a budget motel, rise early and check out the next morning, and then go straight to your on-site hotel. They'll let you unload your bags, pick up your tickets and resort ID, and go on to the theme parks.

• If you move from park to park in your car, save your parking receipt so you'll have to pay the $6 only once. Likewise, be sure to save stroller receipts.

• If you plan to try any of the minor parks, such as Typhoon Lagoon, Blizzard Beach, or Pleasure Island, buy the five-day pass. Without it, you'll pay separately for each minor park, which can add up very fast. Some families reported that they went to one of the water parks every day during their WDW stay—a treat that is easy with a five-day pass but totally unfeasible otherwise.

• Call the Orlando Visitors Bureau at 1-800-255-5786 before you leave home and request a Magic Card, which entitles you to savings on restaurants, area attractions, and many off-site hotels. The Bureau will also send you a Vacation Planner booklet, with lots of discounts for off-site hotels, restaurants, and dinner shows. If you belong to the Entertainment Club, stay at one of the hotels listed in the back, which offer 50% price breaks to members.

• The dinner shows are expensive, costing a family of four about $120, and even a character breakfast can set you back $40 or more. If your budget is tight, skip these extras and concentrate on ways to meet the characters inside the parks.

One cost-saving option is to visit the Diamond Horseshoe Jamboree in lieu of the Hoop-Dee-Doo Musical Revue at Fort Wilderness. The shows are a lot alike, but the Hoop-Dee-Doo will cost $124 for a family of four, and the Diamond Horseshoe Jamboree is free.

• The employees of many of the companies that have exhibits inside of WDW, such as General Electric and Exxon, are entitled to discounts and benefits similar to those of Magic Kingdom Club cardholders. (Employees of the federal government also qualify for these price breaks.) Most companies don't publicize this benefit, but if your employer does sponsor an exhibit inside WDW, contact the personnel office well before you leave home and see if any discounts are offered on park admissions or on-site lodging.

• Disney park admission prices have skyrocketed, with four substantial raises in the past three years. Buy your tickets when you make your hotel reservations, and you'll be protected in case Disney decides it's time for another "adjustment."

MEETING THE DISNEY CHARACTERS

Meeting the characters is a major objective for some families, and a nice diversion for all. If your children are young, prepare them for the fact that the characters are much, much larger than they appear on TV and are often overwhelming in person. I recently visited WDW with a 20-month-old whose happy babble of "my Mickey, my Mickey" turned into a wary "no Mickey, no Mickey" the minute she entered the MK gate and saw that the mouse in question was a good six feet tall. Kaitlyn's reaction is not atypical; many kids panic when they first see the characters, and pushing them forward only makes matters worse. The characters are trained to be sensitive and sensible (in some cases more so than the parents) and will always wait for the child to approach them. Schedule a character breakfast on the last morning of your visit; by then cautious youngsters have usually warmed up.

Many kids enjoy getting character autographs, and an autograph book can become a much-cherished souvenir upon your return home. You also might want to prepare the kids for the fact that the characters don't talk. As many as 30 young people in Mickey suits might be dispensed around WDW on a busy day, and they can't all be gifted with that familiar squeaky voice. So the characters communicate, and pretty effectively, through body language.

Also be aware that because of the construction of their costumes, the characters can't always see what's beneath them too clearly. Donald and Daisy, for example, have a hard time looking over their bills, and small children standing close by may be ignored. If this appears to be happening, lift your child to the eye level of the character.

It's easier to see the characters at MGM than in the MK. The newer characters, i.e., those from *Toy Story, Pocahontas, Aladdin, Beauty and the Beast, The Lion King,* and *The Little Mermaid*—appear exclusively at MGM, and the character-to-kid ratio is vastly better there than in the MK. If your kids insist on spending every day in the MK, the chance to see Ariel or Nala at MGM may just lure them from the MK rides.

Want to actually meet the characters? To get close enough for autographs and pictures? If so, try the following locales:

- Mickey's Starland in the MK. (Be sure to line up to see Mickey in his dressing room after the show. The other characters can be found outside, milling around the area near the railroad.)

- The Main Street hub in the MK, just after the park opens.

- Sunset Boulevard and Mickey Avenue at MGM. These areas of the park are rarely crowded—except with characters!

- The Animation Courtyard and Soundstage Restaurant, where the Aladdin characters appear throughout the day.
- The character breakfasts and buffet dinners.
- The Odyssey Restaurant at Epcot, for several afternoon appearances, or the Electric Umbrella, also at Epcot, for breakfast. If you're trying to save money, a stop at one of these fast-food places is a good alternative to a character breakfast or dinner.

If you're visiting on a busy day, there may well be an extra meet-and-greet session planned. If so, it will be listed on your entertainment schedule and the blackboards that keep you posted on wait times for rides.

If you want to simply *see* the characters, check out the afternoon parade in the MK, as well as SpectroMagic. The MK also runs at least two shows daily during the on-season, which feature either the characters or the stars of the Disney Channel shows; times are listed on your entertainment schedule. The Lion King Show is a huge hit with young fans, many of whom know the words by heart.

Although the theme changes fairly often, MGM features an afternoon parade daily, as well as scheduled appearances by the Muppets, the stars of Disney's latest family film, and other luminaries. Performance times are listed on your entertainment schedule.

ON A DIET?

Vacation dieting is always tough, and fast food abounds in WDW, which makes it even more difficult. But Executive Chef Edwin Wronski and his staff are making an effort to meet the American Heart Association's recommendations for healthy eating by reducing the amount of oil used when frying, and substituting yogurt for cream in sauces and salads. Increasingly, fresh fruit (instead of mayonnaise-laden salads) is served, vegetables are steamed, and meats are broiled.

Restaurants that serve meals meeting the low-fat standards set by the American Heart Association are indicated on your map with a red heart. Chefs at many restaurants—most notably the Nine Dragons at the China pavilion at Epcot—are quite willing to adapt recipes, serving sauces on the side and leaving out forbidden ingredients.

Fruit stands can be found on Main Street and in Liberty Square in the MK, near Echo Lake and on Sunset Boulevard at MGM, and between the China and Germany pavilions at Epcot. They make it easier for families on the move to select grapes or watermelon instead of chips or ice cream and also provide juice instead of the omnipresent theme park soft drink.

Picky Eaters

- Try the cafeterias: the Crystal Palace in the MK, Hollywood and Vine at MGM, and Le Cellier in the Canada pavilion at Epcot. The food court in the Land pavilion at Epcot also offers lots of options.

- Several of the on-site hotels run buffets in the interest of moving people in and out fast, but they're also a draw for families who can't agree on what to eat.

- Nearly all of the theme park restaurants offer such standards as peanut butter and jelly, albeit at $3 a sandwich. If a kiddie menu isn't posted at the door, ask the host if you can see one before you're seated in the restaurant.

- Kiddie meals, based on the McDonald's Happy Meal concept, are turning up all around the theme parks and hotel restaurants for about $3. You get either a burger, hotdog, chicken nuggets, or a sandwich in a cartoon-covered box, along with fries, a drink, and a prize.

BEST BREAKFASTS IN WALT DISNEY WORLD

Wasn't it Archimedes who said, "Give me a good breakfast and I can move the world"? The following meals will at least set you up for an active morning of touring:

- Bagels and cream cheese at the Sunshine Season food court in the Land pavilion at Epcot.

- Heart-shaped waffles with powdered sugar at Kringla Bakeri og Kafe in the Norway pavilion at Epcot.

- Pastries are available throughout WDW but are especially good at the Boulangerie Patisserie in the France pavilion at Epcot, Starring Rolls at MGM, and the Main Street Bakery in the MK.

- Lady and the Tramp character waffles at Tony's Town Square Cafe on Main Street in the MK.

- And the absolute best is banana-stuffed French toast at Cinnamon's Coral Isle Cafe at the Polynesian Resort. Worth a special trip!

If for you the best breakfast is a fast breakfast, be aware that all of the on-site hotels have a food court or coffee shop that opens extremely early. On those mornings when the kids are moving slowly, one parent can always go for juice, cereal, and muffins and bring the tray back to the room. (At the All-Star Resorts, they even send around a mobile pastry-and-juice cart.) If you're staying off-site, hit one of the drive-thrus on your way into the park.

It's worth considering the character breakfasts if you have children under 9. (For details on locations, times, and prices, see "Disney Extras: Parades, Fireworks, Dinner Shows, Character Breakfasts, and Holiday Special Events" in Section 7.)

Sunday brunch buffets are big business in Orlando—one reason why the theme parks tend to be blissfully uncrowded on Sunday mornings. The off-site hotels are fiercely competitive when it comes to their Sunday buffets, each trying to outdo the others in terms of selection and the size of the spread. If you're in the mood for something special and rather elegant, the Hyatt Regency Grand Cypress is widely considered to have the biggest and best buffet of them all.

THINGS YOUR DON'T WANT TO THINK ABOUT

Rain

Go anyway. Short of an all-out hurricane, Disney attractions are open as usual, and crowds will be thin. If you get caught in one of those afternoon cloudbursts so common in Florida summers, rain ponchos are available for about $5 in most of the larger shops. Although hardly high fashion, they're better (and safer) than trying to maneuver an umbrella though crowds while pushing a stroller.

Lost Kids

Obviously, your best bet is not to get separated in the first place. Savvy families have standard meeting spots.

Note: Everyone designates Cinderella Castle or Spaceship Earth, one reason why those places are always mobbed. Plan to catch up with your crowd at a more out-of-the-way locale, such as the flower stall on Main Street or the gardens beside the Canada pavilion.

If you do get separated and your kids are too young to understand the idea of a meeting place, act fast. Lost-kid logs are kept at the Baby Services centers at the major parks; more important, Disney employees are well briefed about what to do if they encounter a lost child, so the odds are good that if your child has been wandering around alone for more than a couple of minutes, he or she has been intercepted by a Disney employee and is on the way to Baby Services. In real emergencies—if the child is very young or is handicapped, or if you're afraid he's been nabbed—All Points Bulletins are put out among employees. So if you lose a child, don't spend a half hour wandering around. Contact the nearest Disney employee and let the system take it from there.

Note: The one glitch in the system is that sometimes lost kids are so interested in what's going on around them that they don't look lost, and thus no Disney employee intercepts them. It's worth taking a couple of minutes to explain to young children that if they get separated from Mom and Dad they should tell someone wearing a Disney name tag. The Disney employee can call the child's name in to Baby Services and, assuming you've contacted Baby Services to report the child as missing, the attendant there can tell you where the child is.

Closed Attractions

Because Walt Disney World is open 365 days a year, there is no down-time for refurbishing and repairing rides. Thus at any given time, as many as four attractions throughout WDW may be closed for repairs. If an attraction your family eagerly anticipated is closed, it can be heartbreaking. Call (407) 824-4321 before you leave home and ask which attractions are scheduled to be shut down for maintenance during your visit. That way if Space Mountain or Star Tours is closed, at least you'll know before you get to the gate. There's still a slight chance that a ride will be malfunctioning and temporarily closed when you visit, but the Disney people are so vigilant about repairs that this happens only very rarely.

Auto Breakdowns

If you return to the parking lot at the end of the day to find your battery dead or your tire flat, walk to the nearest tram stop. WDW roads are patrolled continuously by security personnel who can call for help.

The Disney Car Care Center (824-4813) is located near the toll plaza at the MK entrance. Although prices are high, the Car Care Center does provide towing and minor repairs in an emergency. If the car can't be swiftly repaired, don't despair—the day isn't lost. WDW personnel will chauffeur you to any of the theme parks or back to your hotel.

By far the most common problem is forgetting where you parked. Be sure to write down your row number as you leave your car in the morning. Although Pluto 47 seems easy to remember now, you may not be able to retrieve that info 12 brain-numbing hours later.

Running Out of Money

The Sun Bank, which has branches all around Walt Disney World, gives cash advances on MasterCard and Visa, provides refunds for lost American Express or

Bank of America traveler's checks, and exchanges foreign currency for dollars.

Crime

Florida has received some very bad press over the past several years because of crimes against tourists. It's worth noting that the vast majority of these attacks have taken place in the Miami area, several hours south of Orlando, and that Orlando itself remains a relatively safe haven for tourists.

Nonetheless, use common sense, especially in trying to avoid the most common crime: theft. Make use of the lockers so that you won't have to carry valuables or new purchases around the parks, take cameras and camcorders onto the rides with you, and be extracautious at the water parks, where you may be tempted to leave your wallet on your lounge chair while riding the waves. It's far better to either wear a waterproof fannypack in the water or rent a locker, returning to it whenever you need money. The locker keys are on elasticized cords that fit around your wrist, so there's no hassle in hanging on to them.

Two much more serious crimes were highly publicized a few years ago: a break-in and rape at an on-site hotel and a kidnapping from within one of the major parks. The kidnapping turned out to be part of a custody battle and not a random crime, but reports like this remind us that there's always a chance we'll encounter violence while vacationing. Don't let paranoia ruin your trip—statistically, Orlando remains a safe haven for visitors—but do keep your wits about you, making sure that hotel doors are bolted, rental cars are locked, and that you stick to major roads while exploring. Most important, be sure your kids know what to do if they get separated from you.

BEST SOUVENIRS

Looking for a slightly unusual souvenir? Consider these:

- Boldly colored T-shirts featuring the flags of Epcot countries, available at Disney Traders, near the mouth of the World Showcase Lagoon.

- Autograph books, which can be purchased nearly anywhere on the first day of your trip. The signatures of the more obscure characters such as Eeyore or the Queen of Hearts are especially valuable.

- Characters in vehicles, purchased at the small trinket shops near the stroller-rental stands. Mickey rides a moveable crane, Minnie a pink roadster, Donald a locomotive, and so on; these figures are the perfect size for a toddler's chubby fist. At $3 each, they're one of the few souvenir bargains to be found at WDW.

- Anything featuring Figment, the googly eyed purple star of Journey Into Imagination. Available throughout Future World at Epcot.

- Disney watches, with an outstanding selection to be found at Uptown Jewelers on Main Street in the MK. Check out the Goofy watch—it runs backward.

- A piñata from the Mexico pavillion at Epcot.

- Character Christmas ornaments, found in abundance at Mickey's Christmas Carol in Fantasyland, It's a Wonderful Life at MGM, and the Christmas Chalet at the Disney Village Marketplace.

- Planet Hollywood T-shirts, available in a separate shop downstairs from the restaurant.

• Endor Vendors, adjacent to the Star Tours ride at MGM, offers a slick selection of silver-and-black jackets.

• Also at MGM, old movie posters and other campy memorabilia are sold at Sid Cahuenga's One-of-a-Kind.

• Character cookie cutters or presses that stamp Mickey's visage onto toast and pancakes are at Yankee Trader in Liberty Square in the MK. A Disney-themed breakfast on your first Saturday home is a nice way to fight those posttrip blues.

• There's a cool Hollywood Tower Hotel gift shop complete with bathrobes, towels, ashtrays, and "I survived" T-shirts as you exit the Twilight Zone Tower of Terror.

• Get character-theme athletic gear at Team Mickey in the Disney Village Marketplace. You'll find some items here that you won't see anywhere else, such as Mickey golf balls, softballs, and basketballs, and Little Mermaid ballet tights.

• And, of course, mouse ears are sort of retro-chic. Get your name stitched on at the Mad Hatter in Fantasyland.

FAVORITE TEEN AND PRETEEN ATTRACTIONS AT WDW

The following attractions received the highest approval rating from the WDW visitors we surveyed, ages 11 to 16.

In the Magic Kingdom

- Space Mountain
- Splash Mountain

- Alien Encounter
- Big Thunder Mountain Railroad
- The Mad Tea Party

At Epcot

- *Honey, I Shrunk the Audience*
- Body Wars
- IllumiNations
- The American Adventure
- Innoventions

At MGM

- The Twilight Zone Tower of Terror
- Star Tours
- Indiana Jones Epic Stunt Spectacular
- The Monster Sound Show

In the Rest of the World

- Blizzard Beach
- Typhoon Lagoon
- Water Sprites
- Planet Hollywood

SNAPSHOTS YOU JUST CAN'T LIVE WITHOUT

You can rent 35mm cameras at any of the Kodak Camera Centers for a nominal fee. Film and two-hour photo developing are widely available throughout WDW.

Needless to say, the prices of both are higher than at home, but it's good to know you can get more film fast if you go into a photo frenzy.

Note: The employees at the Camera Centers are generally knowledgeable about photography and are a good source of advice if you've borrowed a big-deal camera from Aunt Lizzie and can't figure out how to advance the film.

For those postcard-perfect shots, Kodak has well-marked Photo Spot locations throughout all the major theme parks. But if, like most parents, what you really want to focus on is your own kids, try the following locations.

In the Magic Kingdom

- Dumbo, just before takeoff. Once he rises it's just too hard to get a good angle on the riders.
- With Cinderella, in the downstairs waiting area of King Stefan's Banquet Hall.
- Among the interactive exhibits and cardboard stills in Mickey's Starland.
- With Mickey, of course, in his Starland tent.

At Epcot Center

- In front of the entrance fountains, or the neat anti-gravity fountains at Journey Into Imagination.
- Leaning against the railings inside the Land pavilion, with hot-air balloons in the background.

At MGM

- Halfway through the Backstage Studio Tour, there's a break for bathrooms, snacks, and pictures à la *Who Framed Roger Rabbit*. The kids can even pose beneath the steamroller that nearly did in the Toontown gang.

- Also part of the Backstage Studio Tour: the Honey, I Shrunk the Kids Adventure Zone. Lots of fun shots here, but most families seem to like the camp of posing inside a nine-foot-high canister of Kodak film.

- With your waitress-mom at the 50's Prime Time Cafe or in your SciFi Drive-In car.

- With the gossip columnist, budding starlets, autograph hounds, or other "streetmosphere" players on Hollywood Boulevard.

- In front of Dinosaur Gertie's.

- On the lawn of the Golden Girls' house, in the middle of Residential Street, on the Backstage Studio Tour.

- Measuring your footprints against those of the real-life stars in the concrete courtyard of the Great Movie Ride.

It's also fun to buy one of those waterproof disposable cameras and go wild at Blizzard Beach and Typhoon Lagoon.

CAMCORDER TAPING TIPS

Camcorders can be a hassle to carry on the rides, but it's way too risky to leave them in strollers while you're inside the attractions. Consider taking your camcorder with you on only one day, preferably the last day of the trip when you're revisiting favorite attractions—that way you'll leave with a "WDW Greatest Hits" tape.

• If you do plan to take your camcorder with you frequently, make use of the lockers located near the main gates of all three parks. Lockers can be especially helpful if you'll be riding Space Mountain and Big Thunder Mountain Railroad, where you'll risk jarring the machine, or Splash Mountain, where there's a very good chance it'll get wet.

• Don't pan and zoom too much, because sudden camera moves disorient the viewer. If you're filming the kids, say, on the teacups, use the wide-angle setting and keep the camera stationary. Attempting to track them in close-ups as they spin past is too tough for anyone but a pro.

• Camcorders can be rented at the Kodak Camera Center on Main Street in the MK or at the Camera Center near Spaceship Earth at Epcot. Rental is $25 a day, and a refundable deposit of $300 is required. (The deposit is generally taken on a credit card, and the imprint is destroyed when you return the camera undamaged.)

• If you rent or borrow a camera, familiarize yourself with the machine before you begin to actually take pictures. Novices tend to use rapid, jerky movements.

• If you're making vocal commentary, such as "We're in Frontierland now, looking toward Big Thunder Mountain Railroad," be sure to speak loudly. The background noise of the parks will muffle your words.

• Don't point into the sun. This can permanently damage the camera.

• Camcorder filming is allowed inside attractions— even many of those in which flash photography is prohibited.

• Film events such as parades, character shows, and theater-style attractions—for example, the Country Bear Vacation Hoedown or the Indiana Jones Epic Stunt Spectacular. These are especially fun to watch once you're home.

• Remember to ask each time you board the monorail if the driver's cab is vacant. Sooner of later you'll get the chance to ride up front, and one bonus is the chance to film panoramic views of the parks as you enter.

TIPS FOR EXTRACROWDED TIMES

If your schedule is such that you simply have to go Easter week or in midsummer, the following tips will make the trip more manageable.

• Stay on-site. You'll have the advantage of the Surprise Mornings, and you won't have to hassle with the traffic jams that paralyze Orlando during the on-season. It's also very helpful to be able to make dining reservations in advance.

• Allow an extra day—or two. First of all, you won't be able to see as much in a single day as you would if you were going at a less-crowded time. Second, you'll tire more easily when the crowds are thick and need longer rest periods to recuperate. Many families schedule an entire day off from touring in the middle of their week, and this is really helpful when you're going in the busy season.

• You *must* be at the parks when they open. By 10 A.M. you'll be facing hour-long waits at many rides, and the parks may even close to arriving guests.

• Read the sections on each park and choose the two or three things you most want to see. Focus on them and be aware that when you're touring at a crowded time, you probably won't get to "see it all." Just make sure that what you do see is the best.

TIPS FOR BIG FAMILIES

If you're seeing WDW with a really big brood, the following tips—all offered by family reunion veterans—might make things run more smoothly.

• Staying on-site makes splitting up much easier, because you can rely on the WDW transportation system instead of the family car. This is especially vital if you have a wide variation in the age, stamina, or risk-tolerance of family members.

• Best on-site lodging options for large families include the trailers at Fort Wilderness, Disney's Old Key West, the Disney Institute Villas, and the new Board-Walk Resort.

• Rent a pager through Guest Services at your hotel or one of the major theme parks. Because big groups tend to scatter, a pager can be invaluable for getting everyone reassembled when it's time to eat or head for home. Lacking this, you can also leave messages for each other at Guest Services.

• Have everyone wear the same color T-shirt or hat each day. A tour guide passed along this tip, which makes it much easier to spot "your people" in a sea of faces.

• If the adults plan to head out for a night, an in-room sitter is generally less expensive than drop-off child care when more than three kids are involved.

10

★★★★★★★★★★★★★★★★★★★★

*Life Beyond
Disney:
Universal
Studios,
Sea World,
and Other
Orlando
Attractions*

UNIVERSAL STUDIOS

Should You Visit MGM or Universal Studios?

Proving once again that imitation is the sincerest form of flattery, Universal and Disney-MGM opened studio theme parks a scant 18 months apart. Both parks offer mind-blowing technology, and there is a real split of opinion among the families surveyed as to which is better. In general, families with children under 11 preferred MGM; a quick scan of several attractions MGM has added since opening—*MuppetVision 3-D,* Voyage of the Little Mermaid, the Beauty and the Beast stage show, the Honey, I Shrunk the Kids Adventure Zone, and the Hunchback of Notre Dame stage show—shows that Disney is making a concerted effort to gear MGM more toward younger kids. Universal, in contrast, is best known for high-thrill adventures such as Kongfrontation, Jaws, and Back to the Future, which scare the socks off of preschoolers but delight preteens and teens.

With a $37 adult admission fee and a cost of $30 for kids 3 to 9, Universal is as expensive as MGM, but many area hotels offer slightly discounted tickets, and anyone flying down on USAir, the official airline of Universal Studios, gets a price break as well. Families surveyed also noticed that Universal seems less crowded than MGM. It is generally conceded at Disney that MGM was too small the day it opened, and although management has tried to control the crowds by keeping MGM open later at night than originally planned, the park can still become claustrophobic. Universal is larger, and major attractions are spread out geographically, so—with the exception of the area around the main entrance—few sections of the park ever become unbearably crowded.

Universal does a good job of controlling crowd flow by breaking many presentations into stages. At Alfred Hitchcock, for example, a group of visitors is admitted into the first theater while the previous group is in theater two, and the group that entered before them is in the third phase of the show. That means that although the total presentation time is 40 minutes, a group is let into the first theater to begin the cycle every 15 minutes, dramatically reducing waiting time. Universal also stages several shows—the Animal Actors Stage Show and the Wild West Stunt Show, for example—in theaters so enormous that large groups can be seated at once, ensuring that even on the most crowded days anyone arriving at the theater 10 minutes before showtime can see the show.

In regard to how well the parks manage their own technology, the nod has to go to MGM. Universal has been plagued with attraction breakdowns since the week it opened, and in the early days many visitors requested refunds after highly publicized rides either malfunctioned or were closed for hours at a time. (The Jaws ride was shut down completely due to the frequency of malfunctions, but reopened, at last, in 1994.) Although Universal has made great strides since these early months, glitches are still fairly common, so be forewarned that some attractions may be shut down for an hour or two on the day you visit. On one day when my family toured, Murder She Wrote, E.T. Adventure, and Earthquake were all closed at different times during the course of an eight-hour period. It makes you appreciate the smooth competence of Disney more than ever.

Nonetheless, Universal packs some major punches, and Back to the Future, E.T. Adventure, Kongfrontation,

Jaws, The Funtastic World of Hanna-Barbera, and Earthquake match or surpass anything offered at WDW. So is Universal or MGM better? Since at this time each park is small enough to be comfortably toured in a day, there's no reason not to see both and draw your own conclusions.

YOUR FIRST HOUR AT UNIVERSAL STUDIOS

• Parking is easy if you arrive 20 minutes before the main gate opens. (Call either 363-8230 or 363-8000 the day before you plan to visit to confirm hours of operation.) After getting your tickets, you'll wait in a small holding area for about 10 minutes. Hanna-Barbera characters such as Woody Woodpecker and the Flintstones often circulate among the crowd to pose for pictures and give autographs.

• Generally, guests are allowed through the main turnstiles about 10 minutes before the official opening time. If a Nickelodeon Studios show is filming on the day you're visiting, this will be indicated on a sign outside the main turnstile, along with directions on how to get tickets.
Note: Watching a taping is time-consuming and may take as long as two hours. If your kids are young and will be skipping many of Universal's scary attractions anyway, you'll have the time. But if your children are older and you'll be trying to cram all the big rides into your day, you won't have time to view a taping.

• After entering the main turnstile, early-arriving visitors are allowed partway down Plaza of the Stars and Rodeo Drive, the two major streets at Universal Studios. If you want to see Back to the Future, Jaws, or E.T. Adventure first, go down Rodeo Drive as far as you're allowed. If you'd rather see The Funtastic World of Hanna-Barbera, Kongfrontation, or Earthquake first, go down Plaza of the Stars until you're stopped by the ropes. Families who haven't had breakfast may have time for a pastry and gourmet coffee at the Beverly Hills Boulangerie before the ropes drop.

• Once the ropes drop, go directly to The Funtastic World of Hanna-Barbera. Because of its proximity to the main gate, this attraction draws large lines from 10 A.M. on and must be visited early.

• After you've saved Elroy, try to convince the kids not to linger too long in the interactive play area behind the Hanna-Barbera ride. You can always come back again in midafternoon, but now you need to move on to the other big-name attractions as quickly as possible.

• If your kids are old enough, ride Kongfrontation, Jaws, and Back to the Future in rapid succession. (At this time of day, you shouldn't encounter any waits longer than 15 minutes.) If your kids aren't up to the high-intensity rides, head toward E.T. Adventure, then the water ride in Fievel's Playground.

• If you have tickets for a Nickelodeon taping, it's probably time to head back toward the Nick Studios gate. If you're not planning to watch a taping, you're undoubtedly worn down from the impact of the rides you've taken in and are ready for a break. Visit a theater-style attraction such as Ghostbusters, the Horror Makeup Show, the Wild West Stunt Show, Murder She Wrote, or the Animal Actors Stage Show next.

UNIVERSAL STUDIOS TOURING TIPS

• The same basic plan you used in the Disney theme parks will also apply here. You need to visit major attractions—Kongfrontation, Back to the Future, E.T. Adventure, Jaws, Earthquake, and The Funtastic World of Hanna-Barbera—either early in the morning or in the evening. Take in the tours and theater-style attractions in the afternoon.

If you miss one of the major continuous-loading attractions in the morning, hold off on it until two hours before the park closes. Midday waits of up to 90 minutes are common at such popular attractions as Kongfrontation, but the crowds do ease off a bit during the dinner hour, and by the time the crowd has moved to the lake to watch the Dynamite Nights Stunt Spectacular, the lines at major attractions have become much shorter.

• A bulletin board located across from Mel's Drive-In keeps you posted on upcoming showtimes and the approximate waiting times for continuous-loading attractions. Because Universal is big and spread out, crowd movement is uneven, so the board is definitely worth perusing on a crowded afternoon—you may find there's a 40-minute wait at Kongfrontation but a mere five-minute wait at Earthquake.

• If you plan to see Universal in one day, it's unlikely you'll have time for a midafternoon break, such as returning to your hotel or visiting a water park. But the numerous theater-style attractions at Universal offer plenty of chances to rest up, and small kids can nap.

• If the kids burn out from too much riding or sitting, Universal offers a pleasant alternative to arcades—although, needless to say, the park has those too—in the form of the carnival midway in the Amity Beach section of the park. This section, modeled after the New England seacoast village that was beset by the great white star of *Jaws,* is rarely crowded. The kids can throw balls in a bushel basket or try their luck at hoops while munching candy apples and popcorn. Playing the midway is like stepping back into a different era and is a nice mental break from all the pizzazz of the rides.

Fievel's Playground offers the same sort of escape for kids under 8. As in the Honey, I Shrunk the Kids Adventure Zone at MGM, however, the playground can become unbearably crowded, especially around the popular water ride, which can draw lines so long that a 40-minute wait is not uncommon in midafternoon.

• The theaters that feature the Horror Makeup Show, Alfred Hitchcock, Ghostbusters, and Murder She Wrote are high capacity, so even if the lines in midafternoon look discouraging, odds are you'll still be seated. Consult the entertainment schedule that you receive with your ticket, or check the sign at the attraction entrance for showtimes, and then put one parent in line about 20 minutes before the show is due to start. The other can take the kids for a drink or bathroom break. If you all opt to wait in line together, be aware that Universal has placed trash cans all through the queue areas of the high-capacity attractions in acknowledgment of the fact that visitors on a tight touring schedule may well be eating or drinking in line.

Likewise, the outdoor theaters for the Animal Actors Stage Show, Beetlejuice's Graveyard Revue, and the Wild West Stunt Show are huge. So long as you're through the gate 10 minutes before showtime, you'll get a seat.

• It is not necessary to take the Production Tour to orient yourself to the layout of the park, as some people assume. Universal is laid out in sections that correspond to the movie locales of the major rides—Earthquake, for example, is located in the San Francisco section of the park, whereas Kongfrontation and Ghostbusters are naturally enough found in the New York section. A quick lap around the park will alert you to the locations of the major attractions and—if you opt to take it at all—the tram ride can be safely saved for afternoon when you'll welcome the chance to sit.

• If you plan to see the Dynamite Nights Stunt Spectacular on the lake (which shows at the park closing time), be there at least 20 minutes before showtime. Unlike IllumiNations or the fireworks that close the Disney parks, the stunt show is a boat race and subsequent explosion that takes place at water level, so unless you're actually standing lakeside, you won't see much.

• Headed toward Back to the Future or another intense attraction? Universal employees are prepared to help families traveling with a baby or toddler do a "baby swap" so that everyone can ride.
Note: If there is some question about how well a child will handle a ride, let one parent ride first, then return with the verdict. If the first parent feels it's OK, the second parent can immediately board with the child. If the parent feels the ride's too intense, the second parent can pass the child through and ride alone.

Universal employs height restrictions on only one ride, Back to the Future, and even then kids need be only 40 inches to ride. (But just because any kid big enough to sit up is allowed on Jaws or Kongfrontation, that doesn't mean it's a good idea to take them; consult the ride descriptions later in this section for information on the special effects.) Other attractions, such as E.T. Adventure and The Funtastic World of Hanna-Barbera, provide separate stationary seating for kids under 40 inches, thus allowing families to go through the attraction as a group.

• Presently, Universal is running a promotion whereby day visitors can reenter the park after 3 P.M. on another day at no extra charge. The revisit has to be within seven days of the original visit, and you pick up this second-day ticket at a designated desk near the exit. If you're running short of time, would really like to watch a Nick Studios taping, or the kids are pooping out, take Universal up on their offer and come back another afternoon.

• Try to see the new stuff early in the morning. This will be especially true for Terminator II, set to open as we go to press.

UNIVERSAL STUDIOS ATTRACTIONS

Back to the Future

Flight-simulation technology makes a quantum leap forward—or is it backward?—in Back to the Future, which has drawn rave reviews since opening in the spring of 1991. After being briefed by Doc Brown (played by Christopher Lloyd of the movie series) in a preshow video that bad-boy Biff has sabotaged his time-travel experiments, you'll be loaded into six-passenger

Deloreans. What follows is a high-speed chase back through the prehistoric era. The cars bounce around, but it's the flight-simulation techniques that are the real scream-rippers, far more intense than those provide by Disney's Star Tours or Body Wars. (Passengers who can bear to glance away from the screen will notice that as many as 12 Deloreans, arranged in tiers, take the trip simultaneously, making Back to the Future a sort of ultimate drive-in movie.)

At one point in your trip through the prehistoric era, you're even swallowed by a dinosaur, making the ride much too much for most kids under 7, although technically anyone over 40 inches is allowed to board. If your child does want to try it, brief him or her that the majority of the effects can be erased simply by closing your eyes—and that's not a bad tip to keep in mind yourself if you're prone to queasiness. For those with strong stomachs, however, the ride is pure pleasure— still one of the hottest things in Orlando after nearly six years in operation, which is high praise in a town that takes its fun seriously.

Earthquake

After a preshow hosted by Charlton Heston, visitors travel through two separate theaters, where they learn how special effects and stunts were done in the *Earthquake* movie. (The special effects and intricate models of San Francisco are somewhat of a revelation to most kids, since few have seen the original movie, which was made more than 20 years ago.) In the second preshow, audience volunteers are drafted to play quake victims, which is great fun for the kids who are chosen. Sitting front and center in the theater ups your chances of being picked.

Note: Several Universal attractions, most notably Earthquake, Alfred Hitchcock, and Murder She Wrote, require visitors to move from theater to theater in the course of the presentation. It helps the lines outside the attraction to move steadily, but is tough on families lugging a sleeping child. If your youngster dozes off during one of the preshows of the theater-style attractions, it is easier to hold her than attempt to put her down, since you'll undoubtedly be moving on within a few minutes.

After the preshows, you'll be loaded onto your subway for the ride segment itself. Earthquake is a very short ride and less intense than you may have been led to believe from the advertisements. Most kids will hold up through the rumbles, fires, floods, and train wrecks just fine and, as one mother wrote, "Its fun to feel it really happen instead of watching it on a screen." And it's even more fascinating to watch the water recede, the concrete mend itself, and the fires implode when the ride is over!

Kongfrontation

You'll go head-to-head with one of the fiercest monsters in movie history in the justifiably popular Kongfrontation. The long "underground" queue area, meant to emulate the subways of New York, sets the mood with TV cameras overhead reporting to you that the ape is loose and on a rampage. You'll eventually be loaded onto trams (which carry about 30 riders) and lifted above the fiery streets of a city under siege. Riders will twice confront King Kong up close, coming near enough to inspect his four-foot fangs and feel the hot blast of banana breath in their faces. This is one real-looking ape, and the ride is simply too intense for toddlers. Some parents of kids as old as 8 reported that the combination of the darkness, the bursts of flames, and, of course, the mega-ape had their kids clutching their arms and ducking their heads.

Older kids love the ride, however, and rate it extremely high—especially the impressive finale where Kong grabs your tram car and "drops" you back onto the street. (The actual fall is only about 10 feet; this attraction relies heavily on its atmospheric effects to scare its riders.) As your wounded tram limps to a halt, you'll learn that your close brush with disaster has made the evening news. A video camera inside your car filmed your reaction to the drop, and the tape is replayed on a TV camera above your head, adding a novel closing to a powerfully fun ride.

Note: The Universal people are no dummies; every major attraction empties through a gift shop selling memorabilia from the movie or TV show the attraction is based on. You can pick up Jetsons T-shirts after riding The Funtastic World of Hanna-Barbera, Slimer toys after seeing Ghostbusters, and an ashtray from the Bates Motel as you exit Alfred Hitchcock. But Safari Outfitters, adjacent to Kongfrontation, is one of the best gift shops in all of Universal Studios. You can pose clutched in the fist of King Kong himself for a family souvenir shot; the pictures are developed immediately and at $5 per pose it's a fun and reasonably priced memento.

The Funtastic World of Hanna-Barbera

This attraction features a high-speed cartoon flight-simulation chase and is very popular with kids of every age group.

The premise of the ride is established in the brief preshow, when you learn that Dick Dastardly has kidnapped Elroy Jetson and that it is up to you, along with Yogi Bear and Boo Boo, to rescue him. You'll go into another room to be loaded into cars that contain six to eight passengers. Because the cars will be lurching about a bit during the movie, children under 40 inches tall, pregnant women, anyone with back or neck problems, or those who are just plain gutless are ushered to stationary seats at the front of the theater.

The flight-simulation effects can convince even the most skeptical adults that they're really flying, and most kids squeal with delight as they meet up with other well-known Hanna-Barbera characters, such as the Flintstones and Scooby Doo. Needless to say, Elroy is safely back with his family by the end of the ride. After Yogi brings you in for a rather rough landing, you go on to the interactive area, where you can make a choir of birds sing by stepping on a huge piano and color your own cartoon via computer.

Note: Like Alfred Hitchcock and the other attractions along the Plaza of the Stars, huge lines form by 10 A.M. as late-arriving visitors walk through the front gate and simply queue up to the first attractions they see. Visit The Funtastic World of Hanna-Barbera first thing in the morning, both to avoid the crowds and to use the ride as a gauge for how well your kids will handle the more intense flight-simulation ride, Back to the Future.

E.T. Adventure

This charming ride is as technologically impressive and atmospherically seductive as anything at MGM, but, because there's nothing scary about it, the entire family can enjoy it as a group.

The attraction begins with a brief preshow featuring Steven Spielberg and E.T., after which you file through a holding area and—somewhat mysteriously at the time—are required to give your name in exchange for a small plastic "interplanetary passport." Then you move to the queue area which winds through the deep dark woods and which is so evocative that it even smells and sounds like a forest. (Universal in general does a bang-up job of setting the moods in the queue areas; Kongfrontation has many visitors in a lather of nerves before they even board the ride, and E.T. is designed to make you feel small and childlike.)

After handing your "passport" to the attendant, children under 40 inches tall or anyone elderly, heavy, pregnant, or otherwise unsteady are loaded into flying gondolas. Others get to ride bicycles, and the lead bike in each group has E.T. in the front basket. You rise up and fly over the forest in an effective simulation of the escape scene in the *E.T.* movie. After narrowly missing being captured by the police, you manage to return E.T. to his home planet, a magical place populated by dozens of cuddly aliens.

The ride closes on a stunning note, for as you sail past E.T. for the final time, he bids you farewell by name. When you give your name to the attendant before you enter the queue area, your name is computer-coded onto the plastic passport. As you give up the passport and mount your bicycle, the cards are fed into a computer. The ride thus "knows" who is riding in which batch of bicycles, which enables E.T. to say, "Good-bye Jordan, Good-bye Leigh, Good-bye Kim . . ." as your family flies past.

Or, maybe it's just magic.

Note: Unfortunately, this "personal good-bye" system is the most frequently malfunctioning part of the ride, so I wouldn't mention it to the kids at all. That way, if it works, everyone is extra-delighted, and if it doesn't, the ride is still an upbeat experience.

Ghostbusters

The popular Ghostbusters attraction begins with a very funny preshow in which the audience is pressured into buying a Ghostbusters franchise, and a gaggle of hapless volunteers are drafted to demonstrate the equipment.

You'll witness a variety of special effects in this show—which is far more sloppy than scary. In the first part, Slimer, Gozer, and the Terror Dogs appear to be winning, but after the Ghostbusters get into the act, the bad guys are history. The climax of the show is when the Marshmallow Man is blown away in an ecto-plasmic energy blast. Any kid familiar with the movie and cartoon series shouldn't be overly frightened by the ghouls; the volume, however, is loud enough to frighten babies, toddlers, and some preschoolers.

Alfred Hitchcock: The Art of Making Movies

You'll pick up 3-D glasses in the holding area, but only part of the film that follows requires them. This rapid-fire montage of classic scenes from Alfred Hitchcock thrillers will go right over the heads of most kids, who aren't familiar enough with the movies to tense up when they see that *Psycho* shower curtain. The brief 3-D effect, however, is a thrilling adaptation from a scene in *The Birds;* and you don't have to be a Hitchcock buff to get chills down your spine as those ravens appear to be coming right off the screen toward you.

After the movie, you'll be directed into a separate theater, where audience volunteers will illustrate how the infamous shower scene in *Psycho* was shot. This part may be too scary for younger children; if one of the kids would like to see the 3-D movie but skip *Psycho,* inform the attendant, who will let you walk straight through the second theater and into the inter- active area, where you can play with the props until the rest of your party joins you.

The interactive area is interesting, giving guests a chance to try out action special effects. And if you miss the Bates Motel Gift Shop on your way out, Mother will be very upset.

Jaws

As the people of Amity Beach learned, that darn shark just won't stay away.

Although closed down for more than two years due to malfunctions, Jaws is now back on-line in a big out- door set. The shark rises from the water several times quite suddenly, the unseen boat before you "gets it" in a gruesome way, and there are also grenade launches, explosions, and a fuel spill. There's tremendous splash- ing—especially on the left side of the boat—and most of the boat captains throw themselves totally into the experience by shrieking, shouting, and firing guns on cue. It all adds up to one action-packed boat ride.

Kids 7 to 11 gave Jaws a strong thumbs-up, and the ride was popular with many kids under 7. The fact that you're outdoors in the daylight, however, dilutes the in- tensity; the really brave should wait until evening—the "Shark in the Dark" effects are much scarier.

Note: Interestingly enough, Universal invested $50 million on the ride, which is more than six times what Steven Spielberg spent on the original 1975 movie.

The Gory, Gruesome, and Grotesque Horror Makeup Show

This show was formerly titled the Phantom of the Opera Makeup Show, but Universal evidently figured that while not every visiting kid knew who the Phantom was, they all knew what gory and gruesome meant. A witty pair of young actors illustrate certain makeup effects onstage, but you'll also see clips from *The Exorcist, The Fly,* and an astounding man-to-beast transformation scene from the little-known *An American Werewolf in London.* Although the movie clips and general gore level is too high for preschoolers, most kids over 7 can stomach the show which is, in the final analysis, an informative illustration of how special effects have become more and more believable over the years.

The Animal Actors Stage Show

If your children are strung out from a combination of 90° heat, 3-D birds, and man-eating dinosaurs, the Animal Actors Stage Show will offer a welcome change of pace. The show features apes, birds, and Benji-clone dogs, and takes place in a large open-air arena. Kids in both the 4 to 7 and the 7 to 11 age groups rated the animals very highly. This attraction is fun to videotape and watch again later at home.

Murder She Wrote Mystery Theater

This amusing show, which allows the audience to select the outcome of an episode of the well-known TV series, has been overlooked and somewhat underrated by the crowds, which rush past it on their way to the theme rides. Fans of the TV series will find the attraction especially engaging—they even get to choose a dinner date for their beloved Angela Lansbury—but the presentation is so wittily presented and encourages so much audience participation that almost everyone ends up having fun.

As at most of the theater-style Universal attractions, you move from theater to theater as you edit the show, add sound effects, and ultimately select the outcome of the episode. Although kids under 7 won't get most of the jokes, kids 7 to 11 will enjoy the attraction more than you'd guess, especially if they're chosen to come up onstage and help with the sound effects, a possibility that becomes more likely if you sit near the front of the theater.

The Wild West Stunt Show

Funny, fast moving, and full of surprises, this show ranks at the top of the list with kids 7 to 11 and rates highly with kids under 7 as well. The shoot-'em-ups, fistfights, and explosions are played strictly for laughs, and sometimes the comedy tends to overshadow how dangerous these stunts really are. A good choice for the whole family, and, like the Animal Actors Stage Show, it's fairly easy to get into even in the crowded afternoon.

Fievel's Playground

Fievel's Playground is a cleverly designed play area filled with western-style props, including a harmonica that plays notes as kids slide down it, a giant talking

Tiger the cat, canteens to squirt, cowboy hats to bounce in, spiderwebs to climb, and a separate ball pit and slide area for toddlers.

The centerpiece of the playground is a 200-foot water ride in which kids and parents are loaded into "sardine cans built for two" and swept through a sewer. The ride is zippier than it looks, will get you soaking wet, and is so addictive that most kids clamor to get back on again immediately. The water ride is very popular and loads slowly, so by afternoon the lines are prohibitive; if you come in the morning, it is possible to ride several times with minimal waits, but by afternoon one ride is all you can reasonably expect.

Note: Fievel's Playground often opens an hour or two after the general park. If you ride the big-deal rides and then show up at the playground at the opening time indicated on your entertainment schedule, you'll be able to try the water ride without much of a wait.

Fievel's Playground is great fun, and most kids could happily stay for an hour or two. The only drawbacks are that, like the Honey, I Shrunk the Kids Adventure Zone at MGM, it needs to be much, much larger; and Universal unwisely lets preteens and teens in. Their rowdy play makes the area downright unsafe for younger kids, especially in the afternoon when the playground is crowded. How about a few reverse height restrictions, guys?

A Day in the Park With Barney

Designed to appeal to Universal's youngest guests, A Day in the Park With Barney is actually an enclosed, parklike setting with pop-art colored flowers and trees. Barney appears several times a day in a song-and-dance show, and there is also an interactive indoor play area designed for toddlers. This play area is far cooler and calmer than Fievel's next door, and the nearby shop and food stand are never crowded.

Universal has located all the stuff for very young children close together—hang an immediate right on Rodeo Drive after you enter the park and follow the signs to E.T. Adventure. The Animal Actors Stage Show, A Day in the Park With Barney, E.T. Adventure, and Fievel's Playground are all located within close proximity to one another, so a family with kids under 7 can set up base here for the afternoon.

Rocky and Bullwinkle Live

This seasonal stage show features not only Rocky and his "enormoose" friend Bullwinkle, but also Boris and Natasha (who have headed for Hollywood, since jobs are getting hard to find in the spy business), Dudley Do-Right, and Snidely Whiplash. The distinctive style of humor created by the late Jay Ward is in truth so sophisticated that many of the jokes will go right past the kids. The production is enjoyable on several levels, however, and the kids will giggle at the pure silliness of the situations while the adults smirk at the satire and in-jokes. The characters hang around after the show for autographs and pictures, and Rocky and Bullwinkle both arrive and depart via a bright blue prop plane, which rolls through the streets of the park, stirring up a bit of excitement.

Rocky and Bullwinkle Live runs only during summer and on major holidays. The show takes place outdoors and is completely exposed to the sun, so afternoon performances can be sweltering. Come to the first show of the day or wait until evening.

Beetlejuice's Graveyard Revue

A rock 'n' roll dance show starring Dracula, the Wolfman, Phantom of the Opera, and Frankenstein and his Bride, the Revue is very popular with the 7 to 11 age group and teens—although the show so is goofy and upbeat that younger kids certainly won't be frightened by the ghouls.

This is a high-tech show featuring pulsating lights, fog machines, synchronized dancing, and wry renditions of rock classics. (My personal favorite is the Bride of Frankenstein's version of "You Make Me Feel Like a Natural Woman.") Since the theater is huge and this 15-minute show plays frequently throughout the day, getting in isn't too tough—work it into your schedule whenever it happens to suit you.

Lucy: A Tribute

Fans of "I Love Lucy" should take a few minutes to walk through this exhibit, which houses memorabilia from the famous TV show, including scale models of the Tropicana and the Ricardos' apartment, clothes and jewelry worn on the show, personal pictures and letters from Lucy and Desi's home life, and the numerous Emmys that Lucille Ball won over the years. The "California Here We Come Game" is a treat for hard-core trivia buffs. By answering questions about episodes of "I Love Lucy," game participants get to travel with the Mertzes and Ricardos on their first trip to California. They lost me somewhere in the desert, but perhaps you'll do better.

The Production Tour

Since the preshow film has been scrapped, all that's really left of the Production Tour is a tram ride through the streets of the theme park, with your tour guide pointing out painfully obvious facts, such as, "We're on the streets of San Francisco now." Although many visitors flock to the tour immediately upon entering the park, thinking it will orient them to the location of major attractions, it provides scant practical information. And, unlike the MGM Backstage Studio Tour, the ride spends very little time behind the scenes. All in all, the Production Tour is skippable, especially for families with young kids.

The Nickelodeon Tour

After being labeled somewhat of a drag by reviewers and families, this tour has been revamped and is now much more fun. Even if you opt to skip the filming of a Nick show, your kids will enjoy the 45-minute walk-through tour. You'll see the sets of shows they'll immediately recognize, perhaps get a glimpse of a show in production, then move on to the popular Game Lab, where audience volunteers play games and one lucky kid is slopped and glopped in the best Nickelodeon tradition. Kids 7 to 11 rated the tour very highly, as did younger kids who were familiar with Super Sloppy Double Dare and the other Nick game shows.

Note: Even if you don't plan to take in the tour or a filming, drop by the Nick Studios entrance and check out the Green Slime Geyser, which periodically erupts and spews into the air an unearthly colored substance about the consistency of pudding. The bathrooms in the Nickelodeon section have green slime soap in the soap dispensers. For some preschoolers, this is the highlight of the trip.

Screen Test Adventure Studio

The Screen Test Adventure Studio is part attraction, part souvenir stand, and it takes the technology found at MGM's SuperStar Television one step further. Through the use of costumes, mock-up sets, and film splicing, you and your family can fly with William Shatner, Leonard Nimoy, and the rest of the *Star Trek* crew and take home a video reminder of your acting debut. (You can also film yourselves visiting major attractions at Universal Studios—in other words, reacting to shouted directions with a blank screen behind you. The backgrounds of Kongfrontation and Earthquake will be added later. But on the day I observed, few families selected this option; almost everyone suited up in polyester and headed for the bridge of the Starship *Enterprise*.)

The cost of the experience is $30, with a $6.50 charge for additional videotapes. Up to six members of a family can assume roles and enter into the fun, and the resulting tape does make an unusually clever—if somewhat expensive—reminder of your visit to Universal Studios.

Coming Soon: Terminator II in 3-D

He said he'd be back, and now he is. As we go to press, Universal is debuting its latest action show, based on the popular film series *The Terminator*. Billed as "a total sensory experience" blending stunts with 3-D special effects, Terminator II is bound to be popular. As with new attractions, come early or expect a big wait.

SHOWS AT UNIVERSAL STUDIOS

Showtimes are listed on the entertainment schedule that comes with your ticket; take in at least a couple. Kids especially enjoy The Blues Brothers and Ghostbusters.

Note: The Ghostbusters street show, which runs only in the summer, is an entirely different presentation from the one inside the Ghostbusters building.

If you're trying to do the whole park in a day, it's a good idea to plan your meals around the musical shows, such as eating your noontime burger at Mel's Drive-In while the Hollywood Hi-Tones croon ballads from the '50s, or taking in a bit of Irish folksinging at Finnegan's Bar and Grill along with your evening meal of shepherd's pie and ale. It's like a free dinner show!

The most well-known of the Universal Studios shows is the Dynamite Nights Stunt Spectacular, which is staged at closing time every evening. The show is Universal's answer to the popular Indiana Jones Epic Stunt Spectacular at MGM and involves a high-speed boat chase that ends in a fiery explosion. Be aware that you must stake out your position early. One of the best vantage spots is on the small pavilion in front of the Animal Actors Stage Show—if you don't mind getting splashed, that is.

BEST FOOD BETS AT UNIVERSAL STUDIOS

The fastest fast food is simply a hotdog from one of the many vendors scattered throughout the park, but you'll be missing much of the fun if you eat on the run for all three meals. Universal has many appealing dining choices and, in general, the food is far tastier and cheaper than that within the Disney theme parks. There's not only a good selection, but they keep the lines moving, even during lunchtime on busy summer days.

In addition, since most families have a one-day ticket and are trying to cram all of Universal into 12 straight hours of touring, few break up the day by actually leaving the park. That means you'll need to rest up in the afternoon or risk having the kids—and maybe the parents—collapse in tears of exhaustion at 6 P.M. A late lunch or early dinner is advised, since it will get you off the streets during the hottest and most crowded times of the day, and give everyone a chance to rest and regroup before heading on to those attractions you missed earlier. Some of the restaurants listed accept reservations at the door, which is a good idea if you'll be dining at peak hours.

The Hard Rock Cafe

What's there to say? The Hard Rock Cafes, found in major cities all over the world, are justifiably famous for their funky atmosphere, raucously friendly service, and tasty, unassuming food. The one in Orlando is the largest of all, with a correspondingly large collection of pop memorabilia; even the guitar-shaped building is fascinating. (Note the pink Cadillac crashing into the front of the facade.) Hard Rock T-shirts and sweatshirts are highly valued souvenirs, especially among status-conscious teenagers and preteens, and it would be a shame to visit Universal and not take in the Hard Rock Cafe.

The problem is when to go. The Hard Rock Cafe does not take reservations, and large crowds are the norm from midafternoon on. If you have young kids along, the best bet is to eat an early lunch around 11 A.M., when the Cafe isn't so crowded that you can't get up and look around. Another crowd-busting option is an early dinner around 4:30 or 5 P.M.

Others swear that the Hard Rock gets better as the day wears on, and it's impossible to truly get into the spirit of the place before dark. If adults in your party would like to linger over drinks and listen to the music, this is a good option for a parents' night out.

Note: You can enter the Hard Rock Cafe from Universal Studios or from a separate parking lot, so you do not have to have a Universal Studios ticket to enter the restaurant. It is, in fact, popular with Orlando locals, which is one reason why it is always hard to get in.

If you just want to buy a Hard Rock T-shirt or sweatshirt, you can purchase merchandise downstairs without entering the restaurant.

Finnegan's Bar and Grill

Friendly, informal, and with the added bonus of live music during peak dining hours, Finnegan's is a great place to rest up and pig out. It's dark inside, too, even on the most blistering summer afternoons, and kids can stretch out and nap in the booths.

Lombard's Landing

If you crave a fancier meal, such as prime rib or fresh pompano, Lombard's Landing is a beautiful restaurant in the Fisherman's Wharf section of San Francisco. The service is leisurely and the atmosphere a bit more elegant than most of the park restaurants, so opt for Lombard's only if your kids can be counted on to behave reasonably well (or sleep) through a 90-minute meal. Lombard's Landing becomes quite crowded at dinner, so a late lunch or midafternoon meal is a better bet. Reservations are advised.

Cafe la Bamba
A good choice for Mexican, with margaritas and live music on the patio during lunch and dinner.

Studio Stars
Big eaters in the party? Studio Stars runs lunch and dinner buffets (adults $10, children $5), which are a good choice if you want more than a burger but you still want to get your food quickly. Reservations are advised.

Mel's Drive-In
Unquestionably the place to go for fast food, Mel's offers home-style burgers and fries, served up with '50s music and a bevy of carhops on roller skates. The drive-in is based on the one in the film *American Graffiti,* and even kids far too young to remember the movie, much less the decade being spoofed, will fall for the table-based jukebox and vintage cars parked outside. If you plan ahead and arrive about 15 minutes before show-time, you can claim one of the outside tables and catch a performance by the Hollywood Hi-Tones, an excellent a capella group, while you eat.

Louie's
A nice spot for a fast Italian dinner, especially if you're headed for the nearby Dynamite Nights Stunt Spectac-ular, Louie's offers spaghetti for kids at a reasonable $3 and a choice of hearty pasta favorites for adults.

And if you just want a snack, try one of the following.

Schwab's Pharmacy

We can't promise you'll be discovered here as Lana Turner allegedly was, but the milkshakes are made the old-fashioned way and served up in pedestal glasses.

San Francisco Pastry Co.

If you need a break after riding Earthquake or Back to the Future, stop off for a brownie, a kiwi tart, or a fantastic flan. (The Key West flan with lime is the best!)

Chez Alcatraz

Sweets aren't your thing? You can always sit by the dock of the bay here in the San Francisco district and enjoy a crab or shrimp salad. Just don't leave your food if you go back for a napkin—those seagulls circling overhead mean business.

SNAPSHOTS YOU JUST CAN'T LIVE WITHOUT

Universal offers a wealth of great photo opportunities, surpassing the Disney parks in the sheer variety of campy locales for an unusual family shot. Your kids would look great in any of the following poses.

- Perched on the hood of one of the brightly colored vintage cars permanently parked outside Mel's Drive-In.
- With their heads inside the mouth of the great white shark strung up in the Amity Beach section.
- Vamping and camping it up with Mae West, Charlie Chaplin, the Blues Brothers, or any of the other Hollywood stars who roam Rodeo Drive.

- In front of the Bates Motel, located near the Hard Rock Cafe.

- In front of the globe and fountains outside the main turnstile.

- In front of the green slime machine beside the Nickelodeon Studios entrance.

- For $5 you can pose on a bike with E.T., beneath the mouth of a T-Rex, or in the grip of King Kong. Just stop by Safari Outfitters as you exit Kongfrontation, the Jurassic Park booth, or E.T.'s Photo Spot.

- Kodak sponsors Trick Photography Photo Spots scattered throughout the park, although the most elaborate can be found in the "boneyard" of props in front of the Production Tour. By placing your camera in the indicated spot and arranging your family in front of specially scaled props, you can turn the kids into the crew of a NASA space shuttle or photograph them in front of the Hollywood Hills.

FAVORITE TEEN AND PRETEEN ATTRACTIONS AT UNIVERSAL STUDIOS

Most visitors 11 to 17 rated Universal as "grosser and wilder" than MGM, and in this age group that's a compliment. Attractions especially popular with teens and preteens include the following:

- Kongfrontation
- Back to the Future
- Jaws
- Alfred Hitchcock: The Art of Making Movies
- The Gory, Gruesome, and Grotesque Horror Makeup Show

- Terminator II in 3-D
- Dynamite Nights Stunt Spectacular
- Beetlejuice's Graveyard Revue

And, not surprisingly, this age group considered a visit to the Hard Rock Cafe an essential wrap-up to a perfect day at Universal Studios.

UNIVERSAL STUDIOS DON'T-MISS LIST

- The Funtastic World of Hanna Barbera
- Kongfrontation
- E.T. Adventure
- Back to the Future
- Jaws
- The Animal Actors Stage Show—if your kids are under 10
- The Wild West Stunt Show
- Fievel's Playground—if your kids are under 10
- Terminator II in 3-D

UNIVERSAL STUDIOS WORTH-YOUR-WHILE LIST

- Ghostbusters
- Earthquake
- Alfred Hitchcock: The Art of Making Movies
- Murder She Wrote Mystery Theater
- The Gory, Gruesome, and Grotesque Horror Makeup Show
- Dynamite Nights Stunt Spectacular

- The Nick Tour—if your kids are under 10
- Rocky and Bullwinkle Live
- A Nickelodeon show—if one of your child's favorites is in production on the day you visit
- A Day in the Park With Barney—if you have preschoolers along

YOUR LAST HOUR AT UNIVERSAL STUDIOS

• If you want to see the Dynamite Nights Stunt Spectacular, find a spot around the lagoon at least 20 minutes before showtime. Benches are everywhere, so after you stake out a good spot, one member of your party can go back for snacks so you can enjoy a picnic while waiting for the show.

• If you don't care to see the lagoon show, you'll find that it draws so many people to one spot that it's now much easier to get into rides such as Kongfrontation or Jaws, which may have been swamped all day. The Jaws ride is much more atmospheric at night (when it is dubbed the "Shark in the Dark"), so if you're brave enough, make it your last stop.

• As you work your way toward the exit, many characters such as the Ghostbusters, the Blues Brothers, and the Hanna-Barbera cartoon gang will be circulating among the crowds. If you haven't gotten pictures or autographs earlier, here's your chance.

• Some of the shops and restaurants stay open 20 to 30 minutes past the official park closing time. If the exits seem glutted, stop for a drink or check out the shops until the crowd disperses.

• If the second-day tickets that allow you to reenter for free after 3 P.M. are offered, stop by and pick them up as you exit the park.

• Forget about slipping into the Hard Rock Cafe for a nightcap as you leave. Eleven thousand other people have the same good idea.

THE SCARE FACTOR AT UNIVERSAL STUDIOS

The shows and tours are family-oriented and fine for everyone, but some of the big-name attractions are entirely too frightening for preschoolers.

Universal imposes very few height restrictions and thus gives parents little guidance. Kids under 40 inches are banned from Back to the Future and are required to use special seating on E.T. Adventure and The Funtastic World of Hanna-Barbara, but beyond these minimal restrictions, parents are the ones who decide who rides what.

Any child old enough to sit on his own can ride Jaws, Earthquake, and Kongfrontation. Universal seems to set the rules based on how physically wild the ride is—and none of the rides listed bounces you around too much. But they're psychologically scary, and a visit to Kongfrontation or Alfred Hitchcock may lead to more bad dreams than even the wildest of roller coasters. Although individual reactions obviously vary from child to child—my own 4-year-old son adores Kongfrontation—read the ride descriptions and consult the following list to help you decide.

Fine for anyone:

- The Funtastic World of Hanna-Barbera—especially if you choose the stationary seats
- E.T. Adventure
- Animal Actors Stage Show
- Murder She Wrote Mystery Theater
- Earthquake
- Ghostbusters—unless the child is afraid of loud noises or the dark
- Lucy: A Tribute
- Rocky and Bullwinkle Live
- Beetlejuice's Graveyard Revue—unless the child is afraid of loud noises
- Fievel's Playground, including the water ride
- A Day in the Park with Barney.

Wait until your kids are at least 7 to try:

- Kongfrontation
- Back to the Future
- Jaws
- Alfred Hitchcock: The Art of Making Movies
- The Gory, Gruesome, and Grotesque Horror Makeup Show

SEA WORLD

Opened in 1973, the same year as the Magic Kingdom, Sea World is best known as the home of Shamu and the killer whales. But other exhibits are equally fascinating, such as the Penguin Encounter, where you can observe the tuxedoed charmers both above and below the ice floe—and witness their startling transformation from awkward walkers to sleek swimmers.

Note: Check your entertainment schedule for feeding time, when the trainers slip about on the iceberg with buckets of fish and the penguins waddle determinedly behind them. The birds ingest the fish in one amazing gulp, and you can stand on the top observation level and watch for as long as you like.

If your kids are too cool to like cute, try the Terrors of the Deep exhibit, where you'll encounter sharks, moray eels, and barracudas at close quarters. The Discovery Cove show featuring leaping dolphins and white beluga whales is especially popular with kids, as is the hilarious sea-lions show. The water-skiing show, updated frequently to keep the themes fresh, is always amusing. The Shamu show, of course, is an enduring classic.

Note: Be sure to pose the kids for a snapshot atop the Shamu statue as you enter the stadium.

All of the shows take place in enormous open-air theaters, so touring Sea World is as simple as consulting your entertainment schedule (which is also your map) for showtimes and being at the theater about 10 minutes early.

Sea World's newest offering is Wild Arctic, an exhibit dedicated to polar bears. You can opt to ascend to the top of the exhibit to view the bears either by walking or via a motion-simulation helicopter "ride." (Kids must be 42 inches tall to take the motion-simulation ride.) Lines at Wild Arctic are long just after the nearby Shamu show lets out; if you visit while one of the Shamu shows is in progress, you'll get through much more quickly.

Sea World has recently opened an exhibit dedicated to one of Florida's own endangered species, the manatee, as well as a section called Key West at Sea World, which features sea turtles, dolphins, stingrays, and other species indigenous to the Florida Keys. Another area simulates the natural environment of the California sea lions. Like the Penguin Encounter, these continuous-viewing exhibits do not have specific showtimes and can be visited at your leisure as you circle the park.

The Budweiser Clydesdales are also part of the Sea World family, and most children are thrilled at the chance to meet these huge but gentle creatures. At certain times of day, noted on your entertainment schedule, one of the horses is taken into a paddock and children are allowed to get close enough to have a picture taken. The nearby Anheuser-Busch Hospitality Center is a quiet, cool oasis; there are free beer samples for adults, and the deli inside is never as crowded as the other Sea World restaurants.

Sea World is a low-stress experience, much less frenetic than the other Orlando parks. It can easily be seen in six or seven hours and is laid out so that the crowds pretty much flow from one scheduled show to the other. If you follow the recommended show schedule, you'll minimize backtracking. The park is so beautifully landscaped that you often can't see one stadium from the other, and the sense of space is a welcome change after a week spent in the Magic Kingdom or MGM. But the openness also means that children up to age 5 will benefit from a stroller; fortunately, the dolphin-shaped rental strollers are so cute that most kids climb in without a fuss.

If you're feeling guilty about taking the kids out of school, Sea World offers educational tours (*Quick:* Can

you tell the difference between a sea lion and a seal?).
"Animal Lover's Adventure," a 90-minute tour appropriate for any age, is available daily. It takes visitors into
the habitats of several different Sea World animals and
explores what they eat, how their group dynamics work,
and how they care for their young. "Animal Training
Discoveries" is available several times a week and lasts
for only 45 minutes, but due to the subject matter is a
better choice for kids 10 and up. This tour focuses primarily on one animal, which varies from day to day, and
allows you to meet the trainer and ask questions.

The tours are reasonably priced (adults $6, children
$5), and reservations are not necessary. Either buy
your tour ticket when you purchase your general-
admission ticket, or, if you get the urge to join a tour
after a few hours in the park, return to Guest Services
near the main entrance.

Note: If more than one tour is scheduled, don't take
the first one of the day; let the kids explore the theme
park for a while and see a few shows during the empty
morning hours, then return for the tour in the afternoon as the park becomes more crowded.

For families who want a more in-depth program, request a Camp Sea World brochure in advance. Sea
World offers a variety of educational programs lasting
from one day to one week—and even sleep-overs in the
park for kids in grades two to six. The sleep-overs,
which take place within the animal habitats, give kids
the unique opportunity to bed down within view of
penguins, sharks, and moray eels. Advance reservations for all Camp Sea World programs are a must.
Call (407) 363-2380 for more information.

Small children at Sea World welcome the numerous
chances to get close to the beasties. My 4-year-old son
loved feeding the harmless-looking but actually quite

vicious seals and the vicious-looking but actually quite harmless stingrays. For $3 you can get three small fish and toss them to the seals, sea lions, or dolphins. The dolphins and stingrays are in shallow tanks so that children can reach over and touch them as they glide by. Running a hand along the flank of a dolphin or flinging a fish into the whiskered mouth of a furiously barking sea lion is a real kick for a young child, and the experience will probably stay with her long after the shows and tours have faded from memory.

Another kick for kids is Shamu's Happy Harbor, a play area that puts those at MGM and Universal to shame. Shamu's Harbor is not only happy but huge, with an elaborate web of climbing nets, a ship heavy-laden with water-firing muskets, a splashy climb-through area, a variety of ball pits to sink into, and padded pyramids to climb. After a few hours spent in shows and exhibits, stop by and let the kids just play for a while. There's a shaded seating area below the climbing pits so that parents can relax. A separate play area for smaller kids ensures they don't become tangled up in the webs, get whacked by an older kid on a tire swing, or, worst of all, become confused in the mazes and exit far from where Mom and Dad are waiting. Since several of the play areas involve water, some parents let kids wear their bathing suits under their shorts. It provides a nice in-park break on a summer day full of touring. There's a midway and arcade next door, so older kids can hang out while the younger ones play.

A note about the shows, especially the Shamu show: If you opt to sit in "splash zone"—the first four rows of the stadium—Shamu's good-bye wave will leave you not just splashed, but drenched straight through to your underwear. Kids enjoy the surprising blast of saltwater, but if you're touring off-season and it's chilly, it may be wiser to sit farther back and laugh at the unwary tourists seated down by the tank.

Sea World admission is $38 for adults, $32 for kids 3 to 11, but numerous discount coupons can be found floating around Orlando, and sometimes specials drop the price as low as $21 for adults. The park opens at 9 A.M., is virtually empty until 11 A.M., and can be comfortably toured in a single day. Have your hand stamped as you leave, spend the afternoon relaxing at your hotel or at one of the water parks, and return for the evening show, the fireworks, and—if you purchased tickets earlier in the day—the popular nightly Polynesian luau. Call (407) 351-3600 for more information.

GATORLAND ZOO

The—*ahem*—unique ambience of Gatorland Zoo is established by the fact that you enter through a giant blue concrete gator mouth. Although most of the alligators within are rendered passive by the Florida sun, things do perk up four times a day at the Gator Jumparoo. The gators leap as high as five feet out of the water to retrieve whole chickens from the hands of the trainers. One young cynic surveyed pointed out that the animals jump highest at the first show of the day, aka "breakfast." The Gator Wrestlin' Show and Snakes of Florida are also big hits with kids.

This funky little place, which also has a small zoo and a train ride, can be easily toured in two or three hours. Children might like a souvenir shot of them holding either an alligator or a boa constrictor. And while Sea World certainly doesn't serve dolphin, Gatorland suffers no qualms about biting the hand that feeds it. You can pick up a few cans of Gator Chowder at the gift shop, surely a unique thank-you for those neighbors back home who are watering the plants while you're away. Gatorland Zoo admission is $12 for adults, $9 for kids 3 to 11. Call 1-800-393-JAWS or (407) 855-5496.

WET 'N WILD

The atmosphere doesn't stack up to the Huck Finn feel of River Country or the tropical splendor of Typhoon Lagoon, but for families staying off-site, Wet 'n Wild is a great place to cool off without getting back into the mouse race.

This was the original water theme park in Orlando and in terms of sheer thrills, the preteen crowd surveyed claim it's still the best. The six-story plunge of Der Stuka, the twisting tubes of the Mach 5, or a spiraling descent through The Black Hole are not for the faint of heart. Wet 'n Wild's wildest attraction, the Bomb Bay, sends riders on a six-second free-fall down a 76-foot slide and is, like the other big-deal attractions, strictly off-limits to children under 48 inches. These rides are enough to knock the breath out of even a strong swimmer; some kids who make the height requirements still aren't up to the intensity of the attractions, so if you have doubts steer your 8-year-old toward the smaller slides and flumes.

Small children and others who are chicken of the sea can slide along in a Bubba Tub or float down the Lazy River in a big rubber tube. Wet 'n Wild also includes a $1.5 million children's water playground, billed as a "safe, fun environment for kids 1 to 10." Preschoolers and unsteady swimmers have their own wave pool, a miniature raging rapids, and fiberglass flumes designed for riders under 48 inches tall. It's the perfect addition for families whose children range in ages and who need a place that can be both Wet 'n Wild and Wet 'n Mild.

Admission is $23 for adults, $18 for kids 3 to 9, but your best bet is to arrive in late afternoon or early evening, when prices are cut in half. Discounts take effect at 3 P.M. during the off-season and at 5 P.M. in summer, when the park stays open until 11 P.M. Crowds become far more manageable as the sun goes down, and summer evenings offer live entertainment, poolside karaoke, and the laid-back party atmosphere of a beach club. Wet 'n Wild is located on International Drive, which is exit 30A off I-4. Call (407) 351-1800 for details.

THE MYSTERY FUN HOUSE

A good place for rainy days, the Mystery Fun House is full of mazes, sloping floors, and optical illusions and includes a *Jurassic Park*–themed miniature golf course and arcade. Admission for all ages is $8. Starbase Omega next door charges $7 a head regardless of age and features an alien planet with a space-gravity surface, targets, and a laser tag game that's a great hit with teenagers who'd like the chance to interact with other humanoids. Numerous discount coupons are available (some lowering the price as much as 50%) as well as a combination ticket allowing holders access to both the Fun House and Starbase Omega. Call (407) 351-3355 for details.

For an even wilder thrill, check out Rickey's Rockets in the parking lot, which offers a type of bungee jumping in reverse for $20. Riders are shot up into the air slingshot-style on bungee cord. Worth watching, even if you're not up to the ride.

FUN 'N WHEELS

Go carts and bumper boats (and a few standard kiddie rides) can be found at Fun 'n Wheels, located just off International Drive. The rides are on a pay-as-you-go basis (the cars cost about $4 per person, the bumper boats about $3) and the park stays open until 11 p.m. Call (407) 351-5651 for details.

Still Looking for Something to Do?

In addition to Orlando attractions, there's Cypress Gardens to the south, Cape Canaveral to the east, and Busch Gardens to the west, all within a 90-minute drive.

OFF-SITE DINNER SHOWS FOR THE WHOLE FAMILY

Disney isn't the only company in Orlando offering family dinner theaters. The dinner theaters that follow differ greatly in theme, with some more suitable for children than others, but each offers a four- or five-course meal, unlimited beer and wine, and a live show. Prices run about $34 for adults, $21 for kids 3 to 11, but discount coupons (some cutting the price of an adult dinner as much as $10) can be found all around Orlando at Guest Services booths, family-style restaurants, and those freebie magazines aimed at vacationers. There is generally one seating nightly in the off-season, two during the on-season, so you'll need to call for exact showtimes and to make reservations. The halls hold between 400 and 1,000 people; come prepared to buddy up to that couple from Michigan.

Of the dinner theater options listed here, Wild Bill's and Medieval Times are the best for young children—they can enter into the raucous action with no fear of disturbing anyone. Older kids will be able to better appreciate the music and humor of Capone's or the challenge of the Sleuth's Mystery Dinner Show.

Arabian Nights
Arabian Nights features more than 60 horses, including White Lipizzans and a "mystical unicorn." The highlight of the evening is a high-speed chariot race re-created from the movie *Ben Hur*. The main course is prime rib. Call 1-800-553-6116 or (407) 396-1787.

Wild Bill's Fort Liberty
A favorite of younger kids, this Wild West show offers knife throwers, rain dancers, lasso twirlers, and the comical soldiers from E Troop. (If you remember the old "F Troop" TV show, you get the general picture.) Barbecue, fried chicken, and corn on the cob are served up chuck-wagon style. Call 1-800-883-8181 or (407) 351-5151.

Medieval Times
Dueling swordsmen and jousting knights on horseback perform in a huge pit while guests dine on roast chicken and ribs. Several of the gentlemen surveyed gave a must-see rating to the serving wenches' costumes. Medieval Times was the favorite dinner theater of kids in the 7 to 11 age group, largely because the arena is divided into competing teams bearing different colors, and the performers do a wonderful job of urging spectators to cheer for "their" knight. Call 1-800-229-8300 or (407) 239-0214.

King Henry's Feast

The portly monarch is searching for his seventh wife—portraits of her six unlucky predecessors hang in the entry hall—as magicians, jugglers, and minstrels offer a kinder, gentler version of Medieval Times. Chicken and ribs are on hand for the revelers. Call 1-800-883-8181 or (407) 351-5151.

Capone's

Expect Italian food and mobsters aplenty in this cheerful version of a Chicago prohibition-era speakeasy. Capone's offers massive portions of pasta and musical comedy in the best *Guys and Dolls* tradition. Call (407) 397-2378.

Sleuth's Mystery Dinner Show

And now for something completely different. . . . As you munch hors d'oeuvres and mingle with suspicious characters in an English drawing room, be sure to keep your wits about you. A crime is about to unfold, and it is up to you to collect the clues, interrogate the suspects, and formulate a theory. The family who comes up with the most accurate solution wins a prize. The meal is very civilized as well—prime rib or Cornish game hen with herb dressing. Call (407) 363-1985.

Index